Noël Coward

COLLECTED PLAYS: SEVEN

QUADRILLE, 'PEACE IN OUR TIME', TO-NIGHT AT 8.30
(WE WERE DANCING, SHADOW PLAY, FAMILY ALBUM,
STAR CHAMBER)

Quadrille: 'Miss Fontanne plays the madcap Marchioness with the crackle and sheen of a five-pound note. Her eyes mock marvellously, her voice cuts like a knife into a wedding cake, and the scene in Act Three, on the eve of her elopement with Mr. Lunt, is as delicious as crushed ice.' *Evening Standard*, 1952

'The idea of *"Peace in Our Time"*,' Coward wrote, 'was conceived in Paris shortly after the Liberation ... I began to suspect that the physical effect of four years intermittent bombing is far less damaging to the intrinsic character of a nation than the spiritual effect of four years enemy occupation. This in time led me to wonder what might have happened to London and England if, in 1940, the Germans had successfully invaded and occupied us, which they so very nearly did.'

The volume also contains four plays from the *To-night at 8.30* sequence: *We Were Dancing* 'provides a marvellously compact illustration of the way the English public school spirit prevails even in moments of strenuous passion' (*The Times*, 1971). Coward in 1954 wrote: *'Shadow Play* is a musical fantasy ... which gave Gertie and me a chance to sing as romantically as we could, dance in the moonlight and, we hoped, convince the audience that we were very fascinating indeed. It always went extremely well so I must presume that we succeeded'; and *'Family Album* is a sly satire on Victorian hypocrisy, adorned with an unobtrusive but agreeable musical score. It was stylized both in its décor and its performance, was a joy to play and provided the whole talented company with good parts.' *Star Chamber*, closely based on Coward's experiences trying to co-ordinate his Actors' Orphanage charity committee, was only once performed and is published here for the first time.

in the same series
(*introduced by Sheridan Morley*)

Coward

Collected Plays: One
(Hay Fever, The Vortex, Fallen Angels, Easy Virtue)

Collected Plays: Two
(Private Lives, Bitter-Sweet, The Marquise, Post-Mortem)

Collected Plays: Three
(Design for Living, Cavalcade, Conversation Piece,
and Hands Across the Sea, Still Life, Fumed Oak
from To-night at 8.30)

Collected Plays: Four
(Blithe Spirit, Present Laughter, This Happy Breed,
and Ways and Means, The Astonished Heart, 'Red Peppers'
from To-night at 8.30)

Collected Plays: Five
(Relative Values, Look After Lulu!
Waiting in the Wings, Suite in Three Keys)

Collected Plays: Six
(Semi-Monde, Point Valaine, South Sea Bubble,
Nude With Violin)

also by Noël Coward

Collected Revue Sketches and Parodies

The Complete Lyrics of Noël Coward

Collected Verse

Collected Short Stories

Pomp and Circumstance
A Novel

Autobiography

also available

Coward the Playwright
by John Lahr

Noël Coward

COLLECTED PLAYS

SEVEN

QUADRILLE

'PEACE IN OUR TIME'

and

We Were Dancing
Shadow Play
Family Album
Star Chamber

from

TO-NIGHT AT 8.30

Introduced by Sheridan Morley

Methuen

METHUEN WORLD CLASSICS

Published by Methuen 2003

3 5 7 9 10 8 6 4 2

This collection first published in Great Britain in 1999
by Methuen Publishing Ltd
215 Vauxhall Bridge Road, London SW1V 1EJ

Quadrille was first published in 1952 by
Heinemann and republished in 1958 in Play Parade Vol. 5

'Peace in Our Time' was first published in 1947 by
Heinemann and republished in 1958 in Play Parade Vol. 5

To-night at 8.30 was first published in 1936 by Heinemann
and republished in 1954 in Play Parade Vol. 4

Star Chamber was first published in 1999 in this edition

Copyright in all the plays is by the Estate of the late Noël Coward
Introduction copyright © 1999 by Sheridan Morley
Chronology copyright © 1987, 1999 by Jacqui Russell

The right of the authors to be identified as the authors of this work has been asserted
by them in accordance with the Copyright, Designs and Patents Act, 1988

ISBN 0 413 73400 5

Methuen Publishing Limited Reg. No. 3543167

A CIP catalogue record for this book
is available from the British Library

Typeset by Deltatype Ltd, Birkenhead, Merseyside
Printed and bound in Great Britain by
Cox & Wyman Ltd, Reading, Berkshire

CAUTION

These plays are fully protected by copyright throughout the world. Application
for performance, etc., should be made *by professionals* to Alan Brodie
Representation Ltd, 211 Piccadilly, London W1J 9HF, and *by amateurs* to Samuel
French Ltd, 52 Fitzroy Street, London W1P 6JR. No performance may be given
unless a licence has been obtained. *Star Chamber* was not included in the regular
run of *To-night at 8.30* and publication does not constitute an indication that
performance rights are available.

This paperback is sold subject to the condition that it shall not, by way of trade
or otherwise, be lent, resold, hired out or otherwise circulated without the
publisher's prior consent in any form of binding or cover other than that in
which it is published and without a similar condition including this condition
being imposed on the subsequent purchaser.

CONTENTS

INTRODUCTION

This, the seventh volume in this series of Coward's plays, contains another wide range of his playwriting: of the two full-length plays, *Quadrille* is a glittering Victorian comedy of marital misapprehension, and *'Peace in Our Time'* a fascinating what-if study of how England might have behaved under German occupation in World War Two. The four short plays are the last selection from the ten that made up *To-night at 8.30*. *We Were Dancing* is the opening play of the first group, and is the first Coward play to be set in Samolo, the mythical island he was also to use in a full-length comedy, an operetta and his only novel. *Shadow Play* is a darker musical one-acter about a couple on the verge of divorce, while *Family Album* is a slight, sly satire on Victorian family hypocrisy. The last play, *Star Chamber*, was a standby satirising the fund-raising committee of a charitable home for actors, one not unlike the committee Noël himself had recently chaired for the Actors' Orphanage.

Quadrille was written in 1951/2 and was staged at the Phoenix in London from September 1952 for almost a year. Once again it was written for Noël's beloved friends Alfred Lunt and Lynn Fontanne, with whom he had thus far scored one great hit (*Design For Living*, 1932) and one major flop (*Point Valaine*, 1934). It fell somewhere between the two, as Noël later wrote:

> *Quadrille*, which I wrote specifically for Lynn and Alfred, is a romantic Victorian comedy which the critics detested and the public liked enough to fill the Phoenix Theatre for a year. It has, to my biased mind, a great deal to recommend it. To enlarge on the Lunts' performance of it would be redundant ... In addition to their ineffable contribution, the décor and the dresses were designed with exquisite colour and taste by Cecil Beaton. In addition even to these matchless attributes it has in it some evocative and well-written scenes, notably the 'Railway' speech in Act 3 Scene 3.

For the *Observer*, Kenneth Tynan was as usual less convinced: 'Everything is said twice over, and what was meant for a gracious sparkle ends up as a condescending wink ... charm and technique on stage, however loving, are not proof against overwriting, and under the weight of these lines the plot collapses and we are left only with negative virtues ... the play is not snobbish, it is not vulgar, but it is also not the pure, fantastic Coward at whose invention we used to chuckle long after the curtain had dropped.'

Rehearsals were, as always when Coward and the Lunts worked together, fraught with nerves and, on this occasion, not helped by the fact that a week before they were due to open Noël had been racing at Folkestone, bought an evening paper and been stupified to read 'Gertrude Lawrence dead'. His oldest friend and working partner for more than forty years was just 54, and it was cancer. Racked by grief, crying so hard he could barely see to write, Noël contributed a *Times* obituary in which he said 'no one I have ever known, however talented, however gifted, contributed quite what she contributed to my work'.

It was of course entirely true, but did not make the Lunts feel any happier about the new play of his they were about to perform. Nevertheless, with names like theirs and Beaton's and Coward's on the poster, *Quadrille* ran a respectable 330 performances under Robert Helpmann's direction and the Lunts then took it on to Broadway in 1955, where once again it was coolly received by critics but much loved by admirers of what was then known as 'all that Luntery'. It is not a play that has ever enjoyed a major revival at home or abroad, though it was seen in a French translation in Paris late in the 1950s.

'*Peace in Our Time*' is a work of considerably more fascination, certainly historically if not always dramatically. At the outset of World War Two, Noël had maintained a flat in Paris while working for the British secret service and setting up Radio Fécamp. Shortly before France fell, he had been sent by Churchill to Washington on a similar propaganda mission, and thus only returned to Paris in 1946 to find his elegant apartment vandalised by its Nazi occupiers before they fled. Worse still, he found that a number of his pre-war French friends and fellow artists, among them Arletty and Chevalier and Guitry, were all now up on varying charges of collaboration, and Noël began to wonder what it would have been like in 1940 if London, rather than Paris, had been invaded by the Germans. Who would have collaborated, and who would have remained loyal to the Crown?

From this slender query there grew, late in 1946, a play called 'Peace in Our Time' which, set in the bar of a London pub, traces events in Britain under a German occupation, between the winter of 1940 and the eve of liberation in 1945, through the lives and attitudes of the publican's family, the staff and regular customers. As Noël himself explained:

> The idea of 'Peace in Our Time' was conceived in Paris shortly after the Liberation ... the city itself seemed to be unchanging, physically at least untouched by the horrors of enemy occupation. It didn't take me long however to realise that, behind the façade, a great deal had changed; the sense of immediate relief had faded, and there was an atmosphere of subtle disintegration, lassitude and above all suspicion ... There was an epidemic of malicious denunciation, some of it justified, a great deal of it not ... This led me to wonder what would have happened to London and England if, in 1940, the Germans had successfully invaded and occupied us, which they so very nearly did ... I decided to place the entire action in the bar-parlour of a London pub, that being the most easily manageable meeting-ground for various types of Londoners.

Like This Happy Breed, which of all Coward's other plays this one most resembles, 'Peace in Our Time' displays an absolute belief in the unconquerable common sense, patriotism and ultimate imperturbability of the British middle class; one of its characters even quotes at some length from the 'This England' speech of Shakespeare's Richard II. The play has, again, seldom been revived since its first staging in the summer of 1947, though when it did turn up in a major regional touring revival of the early 1990s it meant, once again, a radical critical reappraisal of the Coward image.

'Peace in Our Time' is an attempt to telescope character-impressions of Britain under five years of increasingly harsh enemy occupation into two acts and eight scenes. Again, as in *This Happy Breed*, there is an episodic mix of melodrama, sentiment and occasional comic relief here, but the result is heavier and ultimately perhaps less satisfactory, and the press did not take kindly to Noël's speculations, especially as one of them was that a columnist on a left-wing political weekly would be among the first to collaborate.

The play, 'directed by Alan Webb under the author's supervision', opened in Brighton in July 1947 and then, after some drastic rewriting on the road, reached the Lyric Theatre on Shaftesbury Avenue. Though Harold Hobson for the *Sunday Times* led a small band of determined admirers, Beverly Baxter for the *Evening Standard* was sure enough of a flop to head his review 'Crisis for Coward'.

A large cast headed by Elspeth March and Bernard Lee also included such future stars (many of them Noël's personal discoveries) as Alan Badel, Kenneth More and Dora Bryan, and on this occasion the actors emerged with considerably more credit than the playwright: 'It was,' wrote Alan Dent, 'like watching 36 very competent swimmers paddling about in six inches of water.' Other reactions in the press were of pained surprise; Coward was simply not expected to come up with this kind of 'problem play', and his style seemed to them oddly ill-suited to its content.

It transferred briefly from the Lyric to the Aldwych before closing after 160 performances, and its interest, like that of the anti-war *Post-Mortem*, is in the light it throws on the 'other' Coward, a writer of serious dramas still so little noticed that, even while 'Peace in Our Time' was running, Harold Clurman was able to write for the *New York Times* that 'all Noël Coward's plays reveal a state of mind in which contempt and indifference to the world have been accepted as a sort of artistocratic privilege'.

It would be difficult to find a play expressing less 'contempt and indifference to the world' than 'Peace in Our Time', though Graham Greene (perhaps suspecting he may have been targeted as one of the 'left-wing journalists') also now put the boot in: 'Mr Coward was separated from ordinary life by his early theatrical success, and one suspects that when he does overhear the common speech he finds himself overwhelmed by the pathos of its very cheapness and inadequacy. But it is that sense of inadequacy that he fails to convey, and with it he loses the pathos.'

In the *Daily Telegraph*, however, W. A. Darlington took the view that 'This play cannot possibly fail. It is too moving, too exciting, too deft—and too timely. We need to be reminded, just now, that we are people of spirit.'

For Noël, who had once been on a Nazi blacklist in the event of a real invasion of Britain, the play raised many important issues of courage and cowardice under occupation; to John Lahr however, 'Coward's political play never had the élan, the detachment, the playfulness or the impact of his songs, which corrupted the public with pleasure; the war made Coward aware of laughter and song as political weapons, but both are lacking in the plays.'

The working title of '*Peace in Our Time*' was the more descriptive *Might Have Been*, and Philip Hoare reckons that this was

a sombre fantasy filled with character types: cockney stalwarts, tarty women, intellectual homosexuals, all supposedly denizens of the Shy Gazelle public house despite their air of having just checked out of the Savoy. Only the circumstances are drastically different; Churchill has been executed, the royal family are prisoners at Windsor, and the Isle of Wight is a concentration camp. The phlegmatic patriots of the pub are a stalwart lot ... with the added spice of sensationalism. An escaping prisoner of war is branded on his forehead; the publican's daughter is tortured to death. Polemical and politicised, '*Peace in Our Time*' ends with hand-to-hand fighting in Sloane Street as the reinvasion of Britain is triumphant. One wonders whether Coward would have liked a reinvasion of his own, in the new socialist Britain.

Crucially, for a man of exquisite timing, he had misjudged his moment. The British public did not want to be reminded of years of deprivation and war; the depressing picture of a defeated people undergoing shortages and domination was all too close to the truth, since Britain was still suffering from austerity and rationing. His audiences expected the escapism of his late war films, *Brief Encounter* and *Blithe Spirit* ... he had not delivered the goods.

A note in Noël's diary, when he first thought of the play, reads 'Think this is really a honey of an idea and it has fallen into place with such remarkable speed that I feel I must do it almost immediately. Oh dear, I do hope it stays as good to me as it seems now.'

Some months later, when it was clear that *'Peace in Our Time'* was not to be the success he dreamed of, he added 'If that play turns out to be a flop, I shall be forced to the reluctant and pompous conclusion that England does not deserve my work. It is a good play, written with care and heart and guts, and it is beautifully acted and directed ... I have a sick-at-heart feeling about England anyway. We are so idiotic and apathetic, and it is nothing to do with the "after the war" feeling, because we were the same at Munich and before that ... I shall have to manage my life carefully in the next few years; I shall have to plan many partings and reunions with not too much time in between.'

And so to the final set of four plays in the epic sequence of ten that made up *To-night at 8.30* in 1936. We need briefly to remind ourselves of the circumstances, though these will be found in more detail in my Introductions to the two earlier volumes of *Coward Plays* in which the rest of the *To-night at 8.30* titles appear.

Six years after their triumph with *Private Lives*, Noël and Gertie (Gertrude Lawrence) had elected to renew their partnership at the Phoenix Theatre, only now, given the deep boredom both experienced in performing the same script night after night, Noël had decided to write them a sequence of nine plays which would be performed with the same cast as three sets of three, alternating matinees and evenings.

It was a vastly ambitious scheme, and in the event Noël wrote ten plays, the last of which appears here for the first time in print (*Star Chamber*), added when it was felt that the jokes about death and wills in *Victorian Family Album* might have been rendered somewhat tasteless by the death of King George V during the run. In the event, *Star Chamber* was only played once at a Saturday matinee, at which everyone seems to have decided it really didn't work on stage, despite being closely based on Noël's experiences trying to co-ordinate a committee of thespians in aid of his Actors' Orphanage charity.

Of the other three plays here, *We Were Dancing* was described originally by Noël as 'a light episode, little more than a curtain-raiser. It was never intended to be anything more than this and, unlike its author, it fulfilled its promise admirably.'

Many of the plays in *To-night at 8.30* were subsequently filmed, most famously of course the *Still Life* that became *Brief Encounter*, but even Noël himself was amazed when, in 1942, MGM announced their intention to film the infinitely more slender *We Were Dancing* as a vehicle for Norma Shearer and Melvyn Douglas. Inevitably, given that the original ran a mere forty-five minutes, the film bore almost no resemblance to the play beyond its title, and there is no indication in his *Diaries* that Noël ever even saw the film.

We Were Dancing therefore remains notable mainly for its first introduction of the mythical island of Samolo, which was so frequently to figure in Noël's later writing, from the novel *Pomp and Circumstance*, through the musical *Pacific 1860*, to the comedy *South Sea Bubble*.

Shadow Play, by contrast, was a romantic musical fantasy set in a cinematic flashback convention, very courageous for the stage of 1936. In it, Noël and Gertie, the only ever theatrical answer to Fred Astaire and Ginger Rogers, danced and sang in the moonlight and generally exuded overpowering charm through a rather fragile account of a marriage being retrieved from the brink of collapse by some early memories.

'A pleasant theatrical device,' wrote Noël of this one, 'which gave Gertie and me a chance to sing as romantically as we could, dance in the moonlight and, we hoped, convince the audience that we were very fascinating indeed. It always went extremely well, so I must presume that we succeeded.'

Shadow Play is intriguing now as a kind of dark, almost cynical sequel to *Private Lives*: six years later, Elyot and Amanda seem to have gone as wrong with remarriage as we kind of always knew or feared they would, and here they are, again in the moonlight listening to the potency of cheap music, but perhaps for the last time.

Family Album, sometimes known as *Victorian Family Album*, was the period piece of the sequence, as Noël said, 'a sly satire on Victorian hypocrisy, adorned with an unobtrusive but agreeable musical score. It was stylised both in its décor and its performance, was a joy to play, and provided the whole talented company with good parts.'

The company for *To-night at 8.30*, which ran for Noël's usual three-month season in London and the same in New York, included such varied talents as those of his current lover, Alan Webb, another subsequent director Anthony Pelissier, as well as Edward Underdown and Coward's ever-faithful Joyce Carey. Reviews were ecstatic on both sides of the Atlantic, and no one was to know, not even Noël and Gertie themselves, that (apart from one very brief California revival just after the war), this was to be the last time that the most famous theatrical partnership of the mid-century was to appear on stage together. 'Mr Coward,' summarised Ivor Brown for the *Observer*, 'who used to write very slight, long plays has now composed very full brief ones.' The actor Sir Seymour Hicks was so impressed by this ten-fold achievement that, on the last night of the London run in 1936, he solemnly presented Noël with one of his most treasured possessions, a sword which had once belonged to Edmund Kean.

Sheridan Morley
1998

CHRONOLOGY

1899 16 December, Noël Pierce Coward born in Teddington, Middlesex, eldest surviving son of Arthur Coward, piano salesman and Violet (*née* Veitch). A 'brazen, odious little prodigy', his early circumstances were of refined suburban poverty.

1907 First public appearances in school and community concerts.

1908 Family moved to Battersea and took in lodgers.

1911 First professional appearance as Prince Mussel in *The Goldfish*, produced by Lila Field at the Little Theatre, and revived in same year at Crystal Palace and Royal Court Theatre. Cannard the page-boy, in *The Great Name* at the Prince of Wales Theatre, and William in *Where the Rainbow Ends* with Charles Hawtrey's Company at the Savoy Theatre.

1912 Directed *The Daisy Chain* and stage-managed *The Prince's Bride* at Savoy in series of matinees featuring the work of the children of the *Rainbow* cast. Mushroom in *An Autumn Idyll*, ballet, Savoy.

1913 An angel (Gertrude Lawrence was another) in Basil Dean's production of *Hannele*. Slightly in *Peter Pan*, Duke of York's.

1914 Toured in *Peter Pan*. Collaborated with fellow performer Esmé Wynne on songs, sketches, and short stories – 'beastly little whimsies'.

1915 Admitted to sanatorium for tuberculosis.

1916 Five-month tour as Charley in *Charley's Aunt*. Walk-on in *The Best of Luck*, Drury Lane. Wrote first full-length song, 'Forbidden Fruit'. Basil Pycroft in *The Light Blues*, produced by Robert Courtneidge, with daughter Cicely also in cast, Shaftesbury. Short spell as dancer at Elysée Restaurant (subsequently the Café de Paris). Jack Morrison in *The Happy Family*, Prince of Wales.

1917 'Boy pushing barrow' in D.W. Griffith's film *Hearts of the World*. Co-author with Esmé Wynne of one-acter *Ida Collaborates*, Theatre Royal, Aldershot. Ripley Guildford in *The Saving Grace*, with Charles Hawtrey, 'who ... taught me many points of comedy acting', Garrick. Family moved to Pimlico and re-opened boarding house.

1918   Called up for army. Medical discharge after nine months. Wrote unpublished novels *Cats and Dogs* (loosely based on Shaw's *You Never Can Tell*) and the unfinished *Cherry Pan* ('dealing in a whimsical vein with the adventures of a daughter of Pan'), and lyrics for Darewski and Joel, including 'When You Come Home on Leave' and 'Peter Pan'. Also composed 'Tamarisk Town'. Sold short stories to magazines. Wrote plays *The Rat Trap*, *The Last Trick* (unproduced) and *The Impossible Wife* (unproduced). Courtenay Borner in *Scandal*, Strand. *Woman and Whiskey* (co-author Esmé Wynne) produced at Wimbledon Theatre.

1919   Ralph in *The Knight of the Burning Pestle*, Birmingham. Repertory, played with 'a stubborn Mayfair distinction' demonstrating a 'total lack of understanding of the play'. Collaborated on *Crissa*, an opera, with Esmé Wynne and Max Darewski (unproduced). Wrote *I'll Leave It to You*.

1920   Bobbie Dermott in *I'll Leave It to You*, New Theatre. Wrote play *Barriers Down* (unproduced). *I'll Leave It to You* published, London.

1921   On holiday in Alassio, met Gladys Calthrop for the first time. Clay Collins in American farce *Polly with a Past*: during the run 'songs, sketches, and plays were bursting out of me'. Wrote *The Young Idea*, *Sirocco*, and *The Better Half*. First visit to New York, and sold parts of *A Withered Nosegay* to *Vanity Fair* and short-story adaptation of *I'll Leave It to You* to *Metropolitan*. House-guest of Laurette Taylor and Hartley Manners, whose family rows inspired the Bliss household in *Hay Fever*.

1922   *Bottles and Bones* (sketch) produced in benefit for Newspaper Press Fund, Drury Lane. *The Better Half* produced in 'grand guignol' season, Little Theatre. Started work on songs and sketches for *London Calling!* Adapted Louise Verneuil's *Pour avoir Adrienne* (unproduced). Wrote *The Queen Was in the Parlour* and *Mild Oats*.

1923   Sholto Brent in *The Young Idea*, Savoy. Juvenile lead in *London Calling!* Wrote *Weatherwise*, *Fallen Angels*, and *The Vortex*.

1924   Wrote *Hay Fever* (which Marie Tempest at first refused to do, feeling it was 'too light and plotless and generally lacking in action') and *Easy Virtue*. Nicky Lancaster in *The Vortex*, produced at Everyman by Norman MacDermot.

1925   Established as a social and theatrical celebrity. Wrote *On With the Dance* with London opening in spring followed by *Fallen*

Angels and *Hay Fever*. *Hay Fever* and *Easy Virtue* produced, New York. Wrote silent screen titles for Gainsborough Films.

1926   Toured USA in *The Vortex*. Wrote *This Was a Man*, refused a licence by Lord Chamberlain but produced in New York (1926), Berlin (1927), and Paris (1928). *Easy Virtue, The Queen Was in the Parlour*, and *The Rat Trap* produced, London. Played Lewis Dodd in *The Constant Nymph*, directed by Basil Dean. Wrote *Semi-Monde* and *The Marquise*. Bought Goldenhurst Farm, Kent, as country home. Sailed for Hong Kong on holiday but trip broken in Honolulu by nervous breakdown.

1927   *The Marquise* opened in London while Coward was still in Hawaii, and *The Marquise* and *Fallen Angels* produced, New York. Finished writing *Home Chat*. *Sirocco* revised after discussions with Basil Dean and produced, London.

1928   Clark Storey in Behrman's *The Second Man*, directed by Dean. Gainsborough Films productions of *The Queen Was in the Parlour*, *The Vortex* (starring Ivor Novello), and *Easy Virtue* (directed by Alfred Hitchcock) released – but only the latter, freely adapted, a success. *This Year of Grace!* produced, London, and with Coward directing and in cast, New York. Made first recording, featuring numbers from this show. Wrote *Concerto* for Gainsborough Films, intended for Ivor Novello, but never produced. Started writing *Bitter-Sweet*.

1929   Played in *This Year of Grace!* (USA) until spring. Directed *Bitter-Sweet*, London and New York. Set off on travelling holiday in Far East.

1930   On travels wrote *Private Lives* (1929) and song 'Mad Dogs and Englishmen', the latter on the road from Hanoi to Saigon. In Singapore joined the Quaints, company of strolling English players, as Stanhope for three performances of *Journey's End*. On voyage home wrote *Post-Mortem*, which was 'similar to my performance as Stanhope: confused, under-rehearsed and hysterical'. Directed and played Elyot Chase in *Private Lives*, London, and Fred in *Some Other Private Lives*. Started writing *Cavalcade* and unfinished novel *Julian Kane*.

1931   Elyot Chase in New York production of *Private Lives*. Directed *Cavalcade*, London. Film of *Private Lives* produced by MGM. Set off on trip to South America.

1932   On travels wrote *Design for Living* (hearing that Alfred Lunt and Lynn Fontanne finally free to work with him) and material for new revue including songs 'Mad about the Boy', 'Children of the Ritz' and 'The Party's Over Now'. Produced in London as

Words and Music, with book, music, and lyrics exclusively by Coward and directed by him. The short-lived Noël Coward Company, independent company which enjoyed his support, toured UK with *Private Lives*, *Hay Fever*, *Fallen Angels*, and *The Vortex*.

1933 Directed *Design for Living*, New York, and played Leo. Films of *Cavalcade*, *To-night Is Ours* (remake of *The Queen Was in the Parlour*), and *Bitter-Sweet* released. Directed London revival of *Hay Fever*. Wrote *Conversation Piece* as vehicle for Yvonne Printemps, and hit song 'Mrs Worthington'.

1934 Directed *Conversation Piece* in London and played Paul. Cut links with C. B. Cochran and formed own management in partnership with John C. Wilson. Appointed President of the Actors' Orphanage, in which he invested great personal commitment until resignation in 1956. Directed Kaufman and Ferber's *Theatre Royal*, Lyric, and Behrman's *Biography*, Globe. Film of *Design for Living* released, London. *Conversation Piece* opened, New York. Started writing autobiography, *Present Indicative*. Wrote *Point Valaine*.

1935 Directed *Point Valaine*, New York. Played lead in film *The Scoundrel* (Astoria Studios, New York). Wrote *To-night at 8.30*.

1936 Directed and played in *To-night at 8.30*, London and New York. Directed *Mademoiselle* by Jacques Deval, Wyndham's.

1937 Played in *To-night at 8.30*, New York, until second breakdown in health in March. Directed (and subsequently disowned) Gerald Savory's *George and Margaret*, New York. Wrote *Operette*, with hit song 'The Stately Homes of England'. *Present Indicative* published, London and New York.

1938 Directed *Operette*, London. *Words and Music* revised for American production as *Set to Music*. Appointed adviser to newly formed Royal Naval Film Corporation.

1939 Directed New York production of *Set to Music*. Visited Soviet Union and Scandinavia. Wrote *Present Laughter* and *This Happy Breed*: rehearsals stopped by declaration of war. Wrote for revue *All Clear*, London. Appointed to head Bureau of Propaganda in Paris, to liaise with French Ministry of Information, headed by Jean Giraudoux and André Maurois. This posting prompted speculative attacks in the press, prevented by wartime secrecy from getting a clear statement of the exact nature of his work (in fact unexceptional and routine). Troop concert in Arras with Maurice Chevalier. *To Step Aside* (short story collection) published.

1940   Increasingly 'oppressed and irritated by the Paris routine'. Visits USA to report on American isolationism and attitudes to war in Europe. Return to Paris prevented by German invasion. Returned to USA to do propaganda work for Ministry of Information. Propaganda tour of Australia and New Zealand, and fund-raising for war charities. Wrote play *Time Remembered* (unproduced).

1941   Mounting press attacks in England because of time spent allegedly avoiding danger and discomfort of Home Front. Wrote *Blithe Spirit*, produced in London (with Coward directing) and New York. MGM film of *Bitter-Sweet* (which Coward found 'vulgar' and 'lacking in taste') released, London. Wrote screenplay for *In Which We Serve*, based on the sinking of HMS *Kelly*. Wrote songs including 'London Pride', 'Could You Please Oblige Us with a Bren Gun?', and 'Imagine the Duchess's Feelings'.

1942   Produced and co-directed (with David Lean) *In Which We Serve*, and appeared as Captain Kinross (Coward considered the film 'an accurate and sincere tribute to the Royal Navy'). Played in countrywide tour of *Blithe Spirit*, *Present Laughter*, and *This Happy Breed*, and gave hospital and factory concerts. MGM film of *We Were Dancing* released.

1943   Played Garry Essendine in London production of *Present Laughter* and Frank Gibbons in *This Happy Breed*. Produced *This Happy Breed* for Two Cities Films. Wrote 'Don't Let's Be Beastly to the Germans', first sung on BBC Radio (then banned on grounds of lines 'that Geobbels might twist'). Four-month tour of Middle East to entertain troops.

1944   February–September, toured South Africa, Burma, India, and Ceylon. Troop concerts in France and 'Stage Door Canteen Concert' in London. Screenplay of *Still Life*, as *Brief Encounter*. *Middle East Diary*, an account of his 1943 tour, published, London and New York – where a reference to 'mournful little boys from Brooklyn' inspired formation of a lobby for the 'Prevention of Noël Coward Re-entering America'.

1945   *Sigh No More*, with hit song 'Matelot', completed and produced, London. Started work on *Pacific 1860*. Film of *Brief Encounter* released.

1946   Started writing 'Peace in Our Time'. Directed *Pacific 1860*, London.

1947   Gary Essendine in London revival of *Present Laughter*. Supervised production of 'Peace in Our Time'. *Point Valaine* produced,

London. Directed American revival of *To-night at 8.30*. Wrote *Long Island Sound* (unproduced).

1948 Replaced Graham Payn briefly in American tour of *To-night at 8.30*, his last stage appearance with Gertrude Lawrence. Wrote screenplay for Gainsborough film of *The Astonished Heart*. Max Aramont in *Joyeux Chagrins* (French production of *Present Laughter*). Built house at Blue Harbour, Jamaica.

1949 Christian Faber in film of *The Astonished Heart*. Wrote *Ace of Clubs* and *Home and Colonial* (produced as *Island Fling* in USA and *South Sea Bubble* in UK).

1950 Directed *Ace of Clubs*, London. Wrote *Star Quality* (short stories) and *Relative Values*.

1951 Deaths of Ivor Novello and C. B. Cochran. Paintings included in charity exhibition in London. Wrote *Quadrille*. One-night concert at Theatre Royal, Brighton, followed by season at Café de Paris, London, and beginning of new career as leading cabaret entertainer. Directed *Relative Values*, London, which restored his reputation as a playwright after run of post-war flops. *Island Fling* produced, USA.

1952 Charity cabaret with Mary Martin at Café de Paris for Actors' Orphanage. June cabaret season at Café de Paris. Directed *Quadrille*, London. 'Red Peppers', *Fumed Oak*, and *Ways and Means* (from *To-night at 8.30*) filmed as *Meet Me To-night*. September, death of Gertrude Lawrence: 'no one I have ever known, however brilliant ... has contributed quite what she contributed to my work'.

1953 Completed second volume of autobiography, *Future Indefinite*. King Magnus in Shaw's *The Apple Cart*. Cabaret at Café de Paris, again 'a triumphant success'. Wrote *After the Ball*.

1954 *After the Ball* produced, UK. July, mother died. September, cabaret season at Café de Paris. November, Royal Command Performance, London Palladium. Wrote *Nude With Violin*.

1955 June, opened in cabaret for season at Desert Inn, Las Vegas, and enjoyed 'one of the most sensational successes of my career'. Played Hesketh-Baggott in film of *Around the World in Eighty Days*, for which he wrote own dialogue. October, directed and appeared with Mary Martin in TV spectacular *Together with Music* for CBS, New York. Revised *South Sea Bubble*.

1956 Charles Condomine in television production of *Blithe Spirit*, for CBS, Hollywood. For tax reasons took up Bermuda residency. Resigned from presidency of the Actors' Orphanage. *South Sea*

Bubble produced, London. Directed and played part of Frank Gibbons in television production of *This Happy Breed* for CBS, New York. Co-directed *Nude With Violin* with John Gielgud (Eire and UK), opening to press attacks on Coward's decision to live abroad. Wrote play *Volcano* (unproduced).

1957 Directed and played Sebastien in *Nude With Violin*, New York. *Nude With Violin* published, London.

1958 Played Gary Essendine in *Present Laughter* alternating with *Nude With Violin* on US West Coast tour. Wrote ballet *London Morning* for London Festival Ballet. Wrote *Look After Lulu!*

1959 *Look After Lulu!* produced, New York, and by English Stage Company at Royal Court, London. Film roles of Hawthorne in *Our Man in Havana* and ex-King of Anatolia in *Surprise Package*. *London Morning* produced by London Festival Ballet. Sold home in Bermuda and took up Swiss residency. Wrote *Waiting in the Wings*.

1960 *Waiting in the Wings* produced, Eire and UK. *Pomp and Circumstance* (novel) published, London and New York.

1961 Alec Harvey in television production of *Brief Encounter* for NBC, USA. Directed American production of *Sail Away*. *Waiting in the Wings* published, New York.

1962 Wrote music and lyrics for *The Girl Who Came to Supper* (adaptation of Rattigan's *The Sleeping Prince*, previously filmed as *The Prince and the Showgirl*). *Sail Away* produced, UK.

1963 *The Girl Who Came to Supper* produced, USA. Revival of *Private Lives* at Hampstead signals renewal of interest in his work.

1964 'Supervised' production of *High Spirits*, musical adaptation of *Blithe Spirit*, Savoy. Introduced Granada TV's 'A Choice of Coward' series, which included *Present Laughter*, *Blithe Spirit*, *The Vortex*, and *Design for Living*. Directed *Hay Fever* for National Theatre, first living playwright to direct his own work there. *Pretty Polly Barlow* (short story collection) published.

1965 Played the landlord in film, *Bunny Lake is Missing*. Wrote *Suite in Three Keys*. Badly weakened by attack of amoebic dysentery contracted in Seychelles.

1966 Played in *Suite in Three Keys*, London, which taxed his health further. Started adapting his short story *Star Quality* for the stage.

1967 Caesar in TV musical version of *Androcles and the Lion* (score by Richard Rodgers), New York. Witch of Capri in film *Boom*, adaptation of Tennessee Williams's play *The Milk Train Doesn't*

Stop Here Any More. Lorn Loraine, Coward's manager, and friend for many years, died, London. Worked on new volume of autobiography, *Past Conditional*. *Bon Voyage* (short story collection) published.

1968 Played Mr Bridger, the criminal mastermind, in *The Italian Job*.

1970 Awarded knighthood in New Year's Honours List.

1971 Tony Award, USA, for Distinguished Achievement in the Theatre.

1973 26 March, died peacefully at his home in Blue Harbour, Jamaica. Buried on Firefly Hill.

QUADRILLE

For
LYNN and ALFRED
with more than thirty years of love
and admiration

Quadrille was first performed at the Opera House, Manchester, on 15 July 1952, and then in London at the Phœnix Theatre on 12 September 1952, with the following cast:

THE REV. EDGAR SPEVIN	John Gill
SARAH, *his wife*	Moya Nugent
GWENDOLYN, *his daughter*	Pamela Grant
WAITER	Michael Allinson
COURIER	Timothy Forbes Adam
THE MARQUESS OF HERONDEN, *Hubert*	Griffith Jones
MRS. AXEL DIENSEN, *Charlotte*	Marian Spencer
CATCHPOLE, *a butler*	Gordon Phillott
THE MARCHIONESS OF HERONDEN, *Serena*	Lynn Fontanne
LADY HARRIET RIPLEY	Joyce Carey
FOSTER, *a maid*	Sybil Wise
FOOTMAN	Rhoderick Walker
AXEL DIENSEN	Alfred Lunt
OCTAVIA, COUNTESS OF BONNINGTON	Sylvia Coleridge
WAITER	Charles Rennison

TRAVELLERS, etc. Allegra Nicole, Derek Prouse, Betty Hare, Gillian Raine, Richard Scott and Dorothy Blythe

Directed by THE AUTHOR with grateful acknowledgement to Miss Fontanne and Mr. Lunt
Scenery and Costumes by CECIL BEATON
Incidental music by NOËL COWARD
Music under the direction of LESLIE BRIDGEWATER

ACT I

ACT II

ACT III

ACT I: Scene I

The scene is the Buffet de la Gare, Boulogne.

The time is May, 1873.

When the curtain rises it is very early morning and the gas-lamps are still burning. The sun has not yet risen but the grey daylight outside is brightening. There are a few tables discernible at which are seated travellers sipping coffee or chocolate. They may murmur to each other occasionally but this is rare because they are sleepy.

A lady in black presides at the buffet bar at the back. She is aided by two waiters who scuttle about between the tables. At a table down right the REVEREND EDGAR SPEVIN *is seated with his wife,* SARAH, *and their daughter,* GWENDOLYN. *He is a harassed, bright little man; over-eager, amiable and, like certain types of dogs, trustingly convinced that everyone is delighted to see him.* SARAH *is as grey as the weather of her native Cumberland.* GWENDOLYN, *aged fourteen, lacks charm to a remarkable degree. She is also a bad traveller.*

GWEN: It is coming on again, Mama.

SARAH: Not *again*, Gwendolyn!

GWEN (*tearfully*): I cannot help it, Mama. I think I am going to die.

MR. S.: Come, come, child, that is no way to speak. Seasickness is not a mortal disease, you know. A great number of people are seasick every day of the week.

GWEN: Oh, Papa!

SARAH: Really, Edgar. There is no necessity to harp on it.

MR. S.: I realise that it is unpleasant while it lasts but it doesn't last long once one is on dry land.

GWEN: It is lasting with me. It is coming on again now. I know it is.

MR. S.: You had better take her, my love.

SARAH: I don't know where it is.

5

MR. S.: I will enquire. (*He calls.*) Waiter – Garçon.

    A WAITER *appears.*

WAITER: Monsieur?

MR. S.: Ma petite fille est souffrante. Où est la lavabo?

WAITER: La deuxième porte à droite, monsieur.

SARAH (*laboriously*): J'espère que c'est bien propre?

WAITER: Ça je ne sais pas, madame. Ce n'est pas mon métier.

SARAH (*rising*): Come along, Gwendolyn.

GWEN: Hurry, Mama – please hurry.

    They exit hurriedly.

WAITER: Encore du café?

MR. S.: Non, merci. Well, perhaps half a cup – Oui, un peu encore.

    The WAITER *fills his cup and darts off to another table. A group of people rise, having paid their bill – and go out on to the platform.*

    As they go, a uniformed COURIER *comes in ushering effusively the* MARQUESS OF HERONDEN (HUBERT) *and* MRS. AXEL DIENSEN (CHARLOTTE). HUBERT *is a handsome man in the late forties. He looks the typical English 'Milor' of the period.* CHARLOTTE *is several years younger than* HUBERT. *She is an exquisitely dressed blonde and very carefully preserved.*

COURIER: This table is reserved, milor.

HUBERT: Thank you.

COURIER: I will call you five minutes before the train leaves and conduct you to your compartment. (*He calls.*) Garçon.

    A WAITER *approaches.*

WAITER: Monsieur?

COURIER: You wish for coffee or chocolate, milor – milady?

CHARLOTTE: Oh dear.

HUBERT: I am travelling incognito. The name is Baxter-Ellis. A plain Monsieur will suffice. Coffee, please. Charlotte?

CHARLOTTE: Yes, coffee – anything.

HUBERT: Coffee, butter, croissants – vite.

WAITER: Bien, monsieur. (*He bows and goes.*)

HUBERT (*to the* COURIER): Thank you for your help.

COURIER: A pleasure, milor – an honour, monsieur. (*He bows and goes.*)

CHARLOTTE (*after a pause*): Oh, Hubert!

HUBERT: My love, my pigeon – you are sure you wouldn't have preferred chocolate?

CHARLOTTE: It was not the thought of coffee that made me sigh.

HUBERT (*placing his hand over hers*): Look at me, Charlotte.

CHARLOTTE (*looking away*): No, Hubert.

HUBERT: I insist. Please.

CHARLOTTE (*reluctantly meeting his gaze*): There.

HUBERT: Remember our pact. Our spoken vow.

CHARLOTTE: Yes, Hubert.

HUBERT: No regrets. Whatever should happen, no regrets. That was a most solemn promise, my dear love.

CHARLOTTE: I know it was – but—

HUBERT: The past is over. We have the present, and the future.

CHARLOTTE: But the past is not over. Not quite over. There will be scenes and troubles, I know there will. Oh, Hubert, I am so afraid.

HUBERT: There will very likely be scenes and troubles, but not between us, we shall be far away. The sky will be blue above us and the Mediterranean will glitter in the sunlight. We will take breakfast on a terrace ablaze with bougainvillæa and scented with jasmine—

CHARLOTTE: Breakfast! Oh, Hubert!

The WAITER *appears with the coffee and croissants.*

HUBERT (*tenderly*): You are sure that you would not have preferred chocolate?

CHARLOTTE: Quite, quite sure.

HUBERT (*to the* WAITER): Merci.

WAITER: A votre service, monsieur. (*He bows and goes.*)

HUBERT: What is done is done. There is no going back now.

CHARLOTTE: How long do you suppose it will be before – before—? (*She breaks off.*)

HUBERT: Before what, my heart?

CHARLOTTE: Before they discover where we have gone? Before they follow us?

HUBERT: I doubt if either of them will follow us, even if they do find out where we are.

CHARLOTTE: But Serena is a woman of strong character. You have frequently remarked upon it.

HUBERT: She has a will of iron.

CHARLOTTE: Oh, Hubert!

HUBERT: Her charm and her wit, which are considerable, mask an executive determination that would shame Napoleon Bonaparte.

CHARLOTTE: Please don't, Hubert. You are frightening me dreadfully.

HUBERT: She has absolutely petrified me for years. It has been most exhausting.

CHARLOTTE: She will undoubtedly follow us and petrify you again.

HUBERT: Never. I have escaped at last. And it is you who have delivered me. Your love is the file with which I have whittled down my prison bars, the knotted sheet by which I have lowered myself to freedom.

CHARLOTTE: Lowered yourself? How can you, Hubert!

HUBERT: A figure of speech, my love – my file – my lantern of hope in a dark and dangerous world.

CHARLOTTE: I sometimes wonder how much you really feel. Your phrases are so extravagant, so fanciful. Do they spring from your depths, these highly coloured words you use, or are they merely decoration, the icing on a cake, the flaking paint on old panelling?

HUBERT: Pray do not suspect me of dry-rot, my dearest.

CHARLOTTE: Am I your dearest? Has anyone ever been your dearest?

HUBERT: Do you anticipate betrayal already? Is your trust in me beginning to fade so soon?

CHARLOTTE: Your manner has been alarming ever since we left London Bridge.

HUBERT: In what way alarming?

CHARLOTTE: Too light, too irresponsible. You have been behaving like a bubble.

HUBERT: It is my lost youth that you have given back to me. I gazed at the smoky station and the hurrying people with new eyes. I listened to the escaping steam, the porters shouting, the whistles blowing, with new ears. I felt I wanted to shout and sing. It was only out of consideration for you that I refrained from bribing the engineer to allow me to drive the locomotive.

CHARLOTTE: Please do not speak of trains. I loathe them.

HUBERT: Forgive me. I had forgotten. How tactless of me.

CHARLOTTE: Railways are my husband's first love, last love and only love. I realised quite soon after our wedding that in marrying me he was committing bigamy. His heart and his allegiance belong to the Illinois Central. My married years have been flattened and deafened by the railways of the world. I too have, at last, escaped, only to find that my deliverer wishes to drive an engine. It is more than I can bear. (*She buries her face in her hands.*)

HUBERT: What can I say to retrieve my hideous blunder? What excuse can I give? The signals were against me and I crashed over the points.

CHARLOTTE: Hubert!

HUBERT: You must forgive this mood of mine, this reclaimed adolescence. Not only forgive but understand it, for after all it is your fault.

CHARLOTTE: How my fault?

HUBERT: Because of your stubborn, unconscious youthfulness.

CHARLOTTE: I am middle-aged, Hubert.

HUBERT: Never. One day, soon or late, you may suddenly be old, but never middle-aged.

CHARLOTTE (*with a smile*): How foolish you are.

HUBERT: Middle-aged is an entracte, a tedious interval between the scenes when men and women of sensibility chatter in a vacuum, aware that what has so far happened is not enough, that there is more to come, that the curtain will rise again.

CHARLOTTE: Last acts are often tragic.

HUBERT: Comic too. A farce sometimes follows the sombre drama, or even a harlequinade, with clowns and columbines and pantaloons and strings of sausages.

CHARLOTTE: I had not envisaged the mellow years of our high romance as strings of sausages.

HUBERT: How touchy you are.

CHARLOTTE (*crossly*): Disillusion has begun already.

HUBERT (*apologetically*): My ill-considered words again, my wilful tongue, it was the sausages.

MR. SPEVIN *approaches their table.*

MR. S. (*diffidently*): Excuse me.

HUBERT: By all means. What have you done?

MR. S.: Intruded perhaps?

HUBERT: Perhaps. But surely not without reason?

MR. S.: You are the Marquess of Heronden?

HUBERT: Yes.

CHARLOTTE (*warningly*): Hubert.

HUBERT: The incognito is as yet less than skin deep. This gentleman could not be expected to salute it.

MR. S.: I recognised you, sir – my lord. I could not fail to. My name is Spevin.

HUBERT: Spevin – Spevin? Is that name then a symbol of clairvoyance? Has it a psychic affiliation of which I am unaware? How could you 'not fail' to recognise me?

MR. S.: The village of Clanbury lies between two hills, my lord. It was my living for several years. Beyond the nearest hill is Heronden. My little daughter Gwendolyn's earliest memories are of the mushrooms in your park.

HUBERT: Not quite her earliest, surely?

MR. S.: To see you here, unexpectedly, among all this foreignness suddenly overcame my natural diffidence and inspired me to speak. Please forgive the impulse, it was too strong to be denied.

HUBERT: I forgive you freely. But having indulged your impulse, having abandoned yourself to this sudden urge, what is it that you wish to say?

MR. S.: I noticed on the steamer that your luggage was labelled 'To Nice'.

HUBERT: A man of uncanny observation. A very reverend detective. I tremble for your flock, Mr. Spevin.

MR. S.: That is the reason for my intrusion. My flock.

HUBERT: I cannot believe that a man so palpably sincere as yourself should deliberately wish to confuse me, but how, in the name of heaven, can a brief conversation with me in Boulogne concern your flock in Clanbury?

MR. S.: It isn't at Clanbury. It was, but it isn't any more.

HUBERT: Surely not a mass evacuation?

CHARLOTTE (*disapprovingly*): Really, Hubert—

HUBERT: It is disconcerting, my dear, to find oneself completely at sea ten minutes after landing.

MR. S.: I am the vicar of the English church at Nice, my lord. My predecessor there died in March.

HUBERT: A treacherous month, even on the Riviera.

MR. S.: My congregations are sparse, mostly residents, and nearly all of them invalids. I was wondering if I could prevail upon you to honour me with your patronage?

HUBERT: You would like me to come to your church? To set an example? To be an incentive to the laggards – that's it, isn't it?

MR. S.: Yes, my lord. It is quite a nice little church, architecturally primitive, of course, but pleasantly situated.

HUBERT: I will make no promises. My doctor has ordered me complete rest, and a public appearance, even among resident invalids, may be too much of a nervous strain. However, if I fail to come, you can count on me for a subscription at least.

MR. S.: It is most gracious of you, my lord, most kind.

HUBERT: The name is Baxter-Ellis.

MR. S. (*astonished*): Baxter-Ellis?

HUBERT: The address, Villa Zodiaque, St. Guillaume des Fleurs.

MR. S.: But I understood—

HUBERT: For various reasons, Mr. Spevin, I am travelling incognito. It is a whim of my doctors. A new name, he said, coupled with new surroundings and different sights and sounds, will work wonders.

MR. S.: I trust that your indisposition is not serious?

HUBERT: Fairly serious, I am afraid. (*He glances at* CHARLOTTE.) A strange form of fever. It can cause considerable inconvenience although it is only rarely fatal.

CHARLOTTE: Hubert – the train – it is nearly time.

HUBERT (*firmly*): Au revoir, Mr. Spevin.

MR. S.: Thank you so much – you have been so kind – so kind.

MR. SPEVIN *bows rather tentatively to* CHARLOTTE *and most definitely to* HUBERT. *He then backs away and returns to his table.*

CHARLOTTE: How could you, Hubert? How could you so fluster the poor little man?

HUBERT: Certain people in the world are cunningly fashioned by the Almighty especially to bore their fellow creatures. Mr. Spevin is one of them.

CHARLOTTE: He was concerned for his church.

HUBERT: Only obliquely. His real motive was less worthy, a craving to hobnob, a desire to wave my title like a banner in the face of his ailing congregation.

CHARLOTTE: How cynical you are.

HUBERT: It is a matter of self preservation. Do you not realise what would happen if he were permitted to achieve his purpose? We should be lost, trapped in fearful gentility. Besides our secret would be discovered, our romance questioned and discussed and handed round the local tea-tables like petit fours.

CHARLOTTE: No English churchgoers will call on us, Hubert. Moral attitudes are more potent even than Marquisates. You seem to forget our sinful state.

HUBERT: Forget it! I was just glorying in it when that tedious ass came and interrupted us.

CHARLOTTE: The next year will be hard for me, harder for me than for you. Society is lenient to men, especially eminent men, but I am a woman and an American.

HUBERT: To be a woman and an American! What greater gifts could God bestow?

CHARLOTTE: It is heartless of you to mock me. You are all I have to turn to now.

HUBERT: Is not my love enough to hold you safe? To secure you from little fears?

CHARLOTTE: It is not your love I doubt, but the world outside it.

HUBERT: We will have no traffic with the world outside it. We will be sufficient to each other.

CHARLOTTE: That is easy to say now, at the beginning. But later, when the excitement has simmered down, what then?

HUBERT: What then indeed!

CHARLOTTE: You are mocking again.

HUBERT: Is it a private hell of recrimination that you visualise? The two of us bitterly pecking out the feathers of the wings that once bore us away so bravely?

CHARLOTTE: There you go again, suffocating me with words.

HUBERT: Although we knelt before no altar, you have taken me for better or for worse.

CHARLOTTE: Let it be for better, Hubert, and please try to discuss our circumstances more simply. Whenever you embark on a sentence I feel as though you were off on a long journey and that I must wave you good-bye.

HUBERT: You are finding me a bore uncommonly soon.

CHARLOTTE: No, no – it isn't that—

HUBERT: Perhaps you would like me to recall Mr. Spevin. His phrases are flat enough.

CHARLOTTE: You are wilfully misunderstanding me.

HUBERT: I will speak in monosyllables from now onwards.

CHARLOTTE: You are unkind.

HUBERT: Dear love, this is our first quarrel. How charming! How exquisite!

CHARLOTTE: You are hopeless.

HUBERT: No, no – on the contrary – I am over the moon with hope and joy.

CHARLOTTE: Hubert!

HUBERT (*lyrically*): To be here with you, alone with you, actually to have the time to squabble. What bliss!

CHARLOTTE: Be quiet, Hubert, I beg of you. Mr. Spevin will hear you.

HUBERT: God bless him!

CHARLOTTE (*firmly*): Be quiet, Hubert. I will have no more of this. You will make us a laughing stock.

HUBERT: There speaks authentic Boston. Passionate courage and the dread of mockery.

CHARLOTTE: You know nothing of Boston. You have never been there.

HUBERT: I have read about it. Since our first meeting, since the first entrancing broad A I heard you utter fell on my ear, I have read nothing else. It is a city of magic to me. I could

describe to you Beacon Hill on a snowy evening; the chill
refinement of Back Bay. You will take me there one day. You
shall be the first to show me the first families.

CHARLOTTE: Not until we are married, Hubert. Not until our
divorces are over and done with and forgotten.

HUBERT: How wise you are, my sweetest heart. No Bostonian
would receive us in our present state. I had foolishly forgotten
their sturdy, New English rectitude. You shall return to your
home a Marchioness.

CHARLOTTE (*covering her eyes with her hand*): Don't, Hubert. It may
never happen.

HUBERT: It must. It shall.

CHARLOTTE: Serena will refuse to divorce you. I feel it in my
bones. That is the fear that haunts me, the dreadful canker in
my happiness.

HUBERT: Serena is a remarkable woman. She can be hard,
forceful and determined, but there is no meanness in her. Also
she has a tidy mind.

CHARLOTTE: A tidy mind?

HUBERT: She loves everything to be shipshape.

CHARLOTTE (*tartly*): Does she, indeed?

HUBERT: Her writing-desk is a model of neatness. Loose ends
exasperate her. Life to Serena is insupportable unless it is spick
and span, and nothing could be less spick and span than having
a husband living abroad with someone else.

CHARLOTTE: Her passion for tidiness in no way prevented her
from rising above your former infidelities with commendable
fortitude.

HUBERT: You wound me, Charlotte. You really do.

CHARLOTTE: I am not quite a fool.

HUBERT: To think that all the time I was concentrating on
Boston for your beloved sake, you were cross-questioning
your friends about my former infidelities. It is heart-breaking.

CHARLOTTE: The fact remains, Serena acknowledged them.

HUBERT: She did no such thing. She placed them in a secret
drawer in her mind marked 'To be resolved later'.

CHARLOTTE (*inexorably*): And they were.

HUBERT: Please, Charlotte, let us change the subject. This is most painful.

CHARLOTTE: Was divorce ever mentioned between you in those other earlier circumstances?

HUBERT: Certainly not. Nothing was ever mentioned between us. It was all tacitly understood.

CHARLOTTE: And will this, too, be tacitly understood? Something to be ignored, to be resolved later?

HUBERT: This is quite different. I have never loved before.

CHARLOTTE: Do not deceive me. I cannot bear it.

HUBERT: It is true. I have never before felt this enchantment, this lifting of the heart. This can never be resolved, later or at any time.

CHARLOTTE (*tearful again*): Oh, Hubert—

HUBERT: I have left Serena. I have left my life behind, gladly, ecstatically, to be with you until my last day. Serena will know that this is final, her instincts are sound and she is honest enough to admit defeat. But what if your husband should elect to play dog-in-the-manger? What if he should refuse to set you free?

CHARLOTTE: Axel will not refuse. He will not care enough. To him I am less than a locomotive.

HUBERT: A tender – a lonely, loving tender.

CHARLOTTE: It is no laughing matter.

HUBERT: It is now. All our past sadnesses are laughing matters. Look into my eyes, my sweetest heart, and see the future mirrored in them, the sun and the stars and the lovely years that are waiting for us.

CHARLOTTE (*overwhelmed*): My darling.

> *They sit staring into each other's eyes. A bell clangs loudly outside. There is considerable activity in the buffet.* MRS. SPEVIN *and* GWENDOLYN *come charging in.* MR. SPEVIN, *in a frenzy of agitation grabs them by the arms.*

MR. S.: Quickly – quickly – the train is going.

SARAH: The door stuck – we couldn't get out.

MR. S.: Never mind, you're out now.

SARAH: She was terribly sick again, poor mite. (*To* GWENDOLYN.) Pick up your bag, dear.

MR. S. (*breathlessly, as they collect their things*): I talked to them.

SARAH: Talked to who?

MR. S.: The Marquess and Marchioness, they were most agreeable.

SARAH: Marchioness indeed!

MR. S.: What do you mean, Sarah?

SARAH: That woman's not the Marchioness. I'd have recognised her on the boat if she had been.

MR. S.: Her veil was lowered. I took it for granted.

SARAH: More fool you. Come along, Gwennie—

> *They rush out on to the platform.*
> *The* COURIER *returns.*

COURIER: The train is about to leave, my lord. If you will permit me I will escort you to your compartment.

HUBERT: Gladly. Charlotte?

CHARLOTTE: I am ready.

HUBERT: Really and truly ready?

CHARLOTTE: Yes, Hubert.

HUBERT: Come then.

> HUBERT *and* CHARLOTTE *follow the* COURIER *out.*
> *There is a further clanging of a bell, the noise of whistles blowing and escaping steam.*

CURTAIN

Scene II

The Heronden house in Belgrave Square.

> *The scene is* SERENA's *private sitting-room.*

> *The time is five o'clock p.m. on the same day as the preceding scene.*

> *When the curtain rises* CATCHPOLE, *an elderly butler, is drawing the curtains back allowing the late afternoon sunlight to flood into the room. It is an exquisitely furnished room for* SERENA *is a woman of great taste. Somewhere on the other side of the Square a street organ is playing 'The Last Rose of Summer'.*

SERENA *enters followed by* LADY HARRIET RIPLEY.

SERENA *is a striking woman. Her clothes are impeccable and there is something in her personality that commands immediate respect.*

HARRIET *is less impressive, of a lighter calibre. She has been a cheerful widow for many years and her life is built on the affairs of her friends and acquaintances.*

SERENA: I declare I am parched after all that horrid dust. Bring tea at once, Catchpole.

CATCHPOLE: Very good, milady.

SERENA: I am not expecting anyone, am I?

CATCHPOLE: I do not think so, milady

HARRIET: What a relief! We can settle down to a nice gossip.

SERENA: My dear Harriet, we gossiped incessantly all the way to Richmond yesterday, all, or nearly all, the time we were there and all the way back to-day. There can be scarcely anyone left to discuss. (*To* CATCHPOLE.) His lordship left for Heronden last evening as arranged, Catchpole?

CATCHPOLE: Yes, milady. There is a note for you on the bureau. His lordship wrote it immediately prior to his departure. He requested me to be sure that you received it safely.

SERENA (*glancing towards the bureau*): Doubtless something he forgot at the last minute. Thank you, Catchpole.

CATCHPOLE (*bowing*): Milady.

He goes out.

SERENA: It was sweet of you to come with me, Harriet. I fear that poor Mama is not exactly enlivening and that house is dreadfully oppressive.

HARRIET: She seemed happy enough, I thought. It is the wretched Miss Godstone who commands my sympathy.

SERENA: Miss Godstone revels in subservience. She was born to slavery.

HARRIET: I should hate it so, being a companion, having to fetch and carry all day long, being utterly dependent.

SERENA: She was even more dependent in her own home. Imagine four brothers and five sisters all crushed into a small rectory in Suffolk. I expect Mama's draughty mausoleum at Richmond must seem a haven of rest by comparison.

HARRIET: Will Hubert be long away?

SERENA: Ten days at the utmost. He has to be back on the twenty-fifth for the Claverings' ball. I may join him towards the end of the week, a breath of sea air will revive me and Heronden is so lovely at this time of the year.

HARRIET: You do not look in need of revival. Your vitality always amazes me. I don't know how you do it.

SERENA: Do what, my dear?

HARRIET: All the things you do do. You are here, there and everywhere. Your charity committees alone would exhaust a more ordinary woman, then there are your other activities. How often have you dined peacefully at home during the last few years?

SERENA (*with a smile*): More often than you realise. At least once a fortnight. Foster brings me a tray in bed. I look forward to it.

HARRIET: Are you happy?

SERENA: What an extraordinary question. Why shouldn't I be?

HARRIET: I have no way of knowing. I merely asked if you were.

SERENA: You are quite irrepressible, Harriet.

HARRIET: Is it offensive to question the happiness of those one is fond of?

SERENA: No, not offensive, just a little startling perhaps.

HARRIET: Why startling?

SERENA: Because it gives a jolt to complacency, I suppose. A sudden query flung at random can pierce habitual armour most disconcertingly. It might even draw blood.

HARRIET (*persistently*): Did it? Did it draw blood?

SERENA (*laughing*): No, Harriet, no. Not even a tiny blue speck.

HARRIET: You admit, however, to being armoured.

SERENA: Of course I do. Our world can be treacherous.

HARRIET: What do you fear that causes you to take such stringent precautions?

SERENA: A million things, and there is nothing stringent about it. A façade is a necessary form of self-preservation. There is no mystery in it. I have little to hide.

HARRIET: What sort of things do you fear?

SERENA: Railway accidents, dogs being run over, going out on a winter's day without a handkerchief.

HARRIET: Now you are being frivolous.

SERENA (*continuing*): —dining at Windsor when the Queen is in one of her moods, standing wedged in the crowd at Covent Garden and watching my carriage drive away empty, having to sit next to Mr. Gladstone at luncheon—

HARRIET: Do stop.

SERENA: Most of all I fear being probed and prodded like some unfamiliar fish on a slab.

HARRIET: I accept the rebuke.

SERENA: It wasn't really a rebuke, and even if it were I know you far too well to hope that it would have the slightest effect. Ah, thank heaven here is tea at last.

> CATCHPOLE *enters with a folding table and a cloth, followed by a young* FOOTMAN *bearing the tea-tray.*

HARRIET: The road just beyond Putney Heath is worse than I have ever known it.

SERENA: Quite abominable. I suppose the urban council is to blame. Someone should write a strong letter to *The Times*.

HARRIET: Perhaps you could persuade Hubert to do so. His name would carry great weight.

SERENA: Hubert never writes strong letters, he seldom writes letters at all if he can avoid it.

HARRIET: He has at least written you one and you haven't even opened it.

SERENA: I can guess only too easily what it contains. Probably instructions for his new riding boots to be sent on to him, or an engagement to play Whist at his club that he has forgotten to cancel. Restrain your curiosity until I have drunk a little tea, Harriet. I promise I will withhold nothing from you.

HARRIET (*irritably*): Really, Serena!

> By this time the tea-table has been set – and CATCHPOLE *and the* FOOTMAN *have withdrawn from the room.*

SERENA (*presiding*): Now then – cream or milk?

HARRIET: Cream if you please.

SERENA (*pouring her out a cup of tea and handing it to her*): There are probably muffins in that covered dish.

HARRIET: Thank you.

SERENA: You look offended. Don't you care for muffins?

HARRIET: I am not offended. I am uneasy.

SERENA: Why?

HARRIET: There is something that I wish to say to you. At least I do not wish to exactly but I feel that it is my duty.

SERENA: That means that it is bound to be unpleasant. I shall have a muffin to fortify myself against the shock. (*She lifts the lid of the dish.*) Oh, how disappointing, it isn't muffins after all, only toast. (*She takes a piece.*)

HARRIET: I have been summoning up my courage to speak—

SERENA: Good heavens, is it as bad as that?

HARRIET: I do not know whether it is bad or not. I merely wish to put you on your guard. But you are so touchy sometimes, Serena. You are quite liable to bite my head off.

SERENA: Not with a mouth already full of toast.

HARRIET: It concerns Hubert.

SERENA: I suspected it did.

HARRIET: I saw him the day before yesterday.

SERENA: So did a number of people; he went to the Horse Show.

HARRIET: This was before the Horse Show, in the afternoon. (*She pauses.*)

SERENA: Well, Harriet, pray continue, I am on tenterhooks. What was he doing? It couldn't have been anything absolutely beyond the pale in the afternoon.

HARRIET: I saw him at the Zoo.

SERENA: He is devoted to the Zoo. So am I. Particularly when the seals are being fed. I dote on seals. They seem so carefree and they always appear to be applauding. If I were an actress I should like to perform to an audience exclusively composed of seals.

HARRIET: Hubert was not alone, Serena.

SERENA: It is difficult to be entirely alone at the Zoo. It is becoming more and more popular. Soon there will be so many people's heads in the way that we shall only be able to see the giraffes.

HARRIET: He was with a woman in a veil.

SERENA: A delicate skin no doubt. Some people freckle so easily.

HARRIET: You don't believe me?

SERENA: I most certainly believe you, as I sent them both on there after the brougham had dropped me off in Regent Street.

HARRIET (*deflated*): Both?

SERENA: The mysterious veiled lady was only poor Naomi.

HARRIET: Naomi?

SERENA: You must remember her, Naomi Charteris, Clara's eldest girl. She is Hubert's cousin once removed. As a matter of fact she was almost entirely removed last November when her horse rolled on her in the hunting field.

HARRIET: But—

SERENA (*mowing her down*): She came up from Kettering to have her teeth done and stayed three days with us. She has had to have a sort of contraption right across her mouth for months, poor child. That is why she wears a veil.

HARRIET: I see.

SERENA: She is a nice enough girl but self-conscious.

HARRIET: I am not surprised.

SERENA: She was never exactly a beauty at the best of times and of course being rolled on did little to improve her. However the doctor and the dentist say that she will be perfectly presentable eventually, so all's well that ends well.

HARRIET: It's no use, Serena.

SERENA: What is no use?

HARRIET: Trying to pull the wool over my eyes.

SERENA: I don't know what you mean.

HARRIET: Hubert's companion at the Zoo was not a gangling girl. She was a mature woman and extremely well dressed into the bargain.

SERENA: I wonder who it could have been, then.

HARRIET: How much do you really mind?

SERENA (*sweetly*): Mind what, Harriet dear?

HARRIET: Hubert carrying on with other women?

SERENA: There is a perennial adolescence about you that is really most endearing. You always give me the feeling, when we are alone together, that we should be brushing our hair and sipping cocoa.

HARRIET: Well, really!

SERENA: After lights out, of course.

HARRIET: I respect your reticence, my dear, in fact I find it highly admirable but I must admit that it hurts me to realise how little you trust me. After all we are very old friends.

SERENA: If you respect and admire reticence so, why do you not accept it without being hurt? I have always had too much pride. It is my besetting sin. It is difficult for me to unburden my heart of its secrets, even to you, one of my closest friends. You will have to forgive me, Harriet, there are no two ways about it.

HARRIET (*wistfully*): In the old days, before we were both married, we used to discuss everything.

SERENA: You did, my dear.

HARRIET: My only desire is to help you, to be of some slight comfort if comfort is required.

SERENA: I know and I appreciate it most deeply. I will set your mind at rest over one thing at any rate. No comfort is required at the moment and if and when it is you will be the first that I shall turn to.

HARRIET (*a trifle waspishly*): At all events you cannot be emotionally upset after all these years.

SERENA: What a curious assumption. Would you like a little more tea?

HARRIET: No, thank you.

SERENA (*after a pause*): Oh dear, you are looking downright sullen. What *am* I to say to you?

HARRIET: I am sure you have a vast reserve of small talk. We could discuss the weather, the Wagner Society, Miss Godstone's chilblains; you might even give me your views on the Albert Memorial.

SERENA: That would not be small talk, it would be high treason.

HARRIET (*rising*): If you think that I have been impertinent I can only assure you that it was quite unintentional and that I am sorry.

SERENA: Really, Harriet, this is too much of a good thing. Please sit down again immediately.

HARRIET: I would prefer to go now. I promised to call on

Lavinia on my way home; she has moved into her new house.
I am already late.

SERENA: I insist on you staying a few minutes longer. I cannot
allow you to leave in anger.

HARRIET: I am not in the least angry.

SERENA: Nonsense, my dear. You are bristling like a hedgehog. If
you happened to brush against Catchpole in the hall you
would lacerate him. Sit down again, please. Hurt feelings
between friends are intolerable. Please, Harriet.

HARRIET (*relenting*): Very well – just for a little longer. (*She sits
down.*)

SERENA: What can I do to coax you back into benevolence?

HARRIET: Nothing.

SERENA: I have it – Hubert's letter! I will read it aloud to you.

HARRIET: I have no desire to hear it.

SERENA: But I want you to. (*She rises, goes over to the bureau, picks
up the letter and returns to the tea-table, slitting the letter open as she
does so.*) You can say riding boots and I shall say Whist at the
club and we will see who wins. (*She sits down and begins to read.*)
'My dear. I am afraid this letter will be a shock to you, but by
the time you receive it I shall be—'

*She stops dead, reads on quickly for a moment, then aware that
HARRIET's eyes are on her, she bursts out laughing.*

HARRIET: What on earth is the matter?

SERENA (*now in perfect control*): He really is impossible.

HARRIET: What has happened?

SERENA (*playing for time*): You'll never believe it!

HARRIET: What is it? Why should the letter be a shock to you?

SERENA: Judge for yourself – listen – (*She pretends to read.*) – 'I am
afraid this letter will be a shock to you but by the time you
receive it I shall be safely at Heronden and out of reach of the
first impact of your fury—'

HARRIET: Good heavens!

SERENA (*still pretending to read*): 'Allow me, my dearest Serena, to
make full and abject confession.' (*She pauses.*)

HARRIET: Go on – go on. What *has* he done?

SERENA (*still pretending to read*): 'I have sold the two small
Romneys and the Gainsborough in the blue drawing-room to

23

Sir Isaac Weissberger. He offered me so fantastic a price for them that I was unable to resist temptation. If you should desire either to divorce me or murder me I am entirely at your disposal. My love, etc., etc.' (*She folds the letter.*) There!

HARRIET: What an extraordinary thing to do.

SERENA: He must be demented.

HARRIET: Surely he is not in immediate need of money?

SERENA: Of course not.

HARRIET: Is the Gainsborough the one with the sheep in the foreground?

SERENA: The Gainsborough is the one with Hubert's great-grandmother in the foreground.

HARRIET: Who on earth is Sir Isaac Weissberger?

SERENA: I don't know. It is a very impressive name, don't you think.

HARRIET: What could have possessed him to do such a thing without even consulting you?

SERENA: There are many things that men do without consulting their wives. This is definitely one of them.

HARRIET: It sounds very fishy to me.

SERENA (*beginning to laugh, with a note of hysteria*): You are quite right. It certainly is fishy! Fishier than anything he has ever done before. Oh, dear—

HARRIET: Why are you laughing in that strange manner?

SERENA: I cannot help myself. (*She laughs with more abandon.*)

HARRIET (*alarmed*): Serena!

SERENA (*searching in her reticule for her handkerchief*): The situation has its humorous aspects.

HARRIET: Situation?

SERENA (*finding her handkerchief and dabbing her eyes*): Do not look so agitated, Harriet. I shall recover in a moment.

HARRIET: I think he has behaved irresponsibly and with utter lack of consideration.

SERENA: Yes, he has really, hasn't he?

HARRIET: And I cannot for the life of me see what there is to laugh at.

SERENA: Hubert's instability, his – unpredictableness, always make me laugh.

HARRIET: Why should he suddenly decide to sell three valuable family heirlooms without rhyme or reason? There must be something behind it.

SERENA: Not necessarily. Hubert's eccentricities are frequently quite motiveless. He has inherited a certain streak of waywardness from his mother.

HARRIET: Old Lady Heronden is not wayward, Serena, she is as mad as a hatter.

SERENA: You need not put it so crudely, Harriet. The family is prepared to admit that she suffers from rather curious delusions on occasion but beyond that they will not budge.

HARRIET: Facts are facts and there is no getting away from them. It is well know that she has imagined herself to be a bird for several years, and before that there were all those extraordinary letters she wrote to Lord Palmerston.

SERENA: The Albatross phase ended just after Christmas.

HARRIET: I'm sure I am very glad to hear of it.

SERENA: I believe that she is now something smaller and more manageable. I had a letter from Teresa only a week or so ago. It was guarded and far from explicit but I gathered from it that the situation had eased considerably.

HARRIET: I still do not see why the aberrations of Hubert's mother should be directly responsible for his abrupt disposal of two Romneys and a Gainsborough. Let me see the letter.

SERENA (*hurriedly*): No, Harriet. That would be a betrayal of confidence.

HARRIET: You have just read it aloud to me.

SERENA: That is entirely different. If Hubert ever knew that you had actually read it with your own eyes he would be dreadfully humiliated. He is extremely sensitive about that sort of thing.

HARRIET: What was really in the letter, Serena?

SERENA (*shocked*): Harriet!

CATCHPOLE *enters with a card and a note on a salver.*

What is it, Catchpole?

CATCHPOLE: Mr. Axel Diensen has called, milady.

SERENA: Mr. Axel Diensen? (*She looks at the card and opens and reads the note.*)

CATCHPOLE: I have shown him into the drawing-room, milady.

SERENA: Just a moment, Catchpole.

HARRIET (*to* CATCHPOLE): Is Mrs. Diensen with him?

CATCHPOLE: No, milady, he is alone.

HARRIET: How very odd.

SERENA (*thoughtfully putting the note back into the envelope*): You had better show Mr. Diensen up here, Catchpole. Solitude in the drawing-room can be depressing.

CATCHPOLE: Very good, milady.

He goes.

HARRIET: I didn't know that you knew the Diensens.

SERENA: I scarcely do. They were staying with Etta Tewkesbury when Hubert and I were there last autumn and I remember speaking a few words to them at the Cameron-Wilkinson wedding in February.

HARRIET: It was Etta who really launched them originally, wasn't it?

SERENA (*absently*): Yes. I believe it was.

HARRIET: She, Mrs. D., comes from Boston, you know.

SERENA: Yes. She murmured it to me almost immediately on shaking hands. The significance of it escaped me at the time but I have since discovered that, in America, to come from Boston is essential.

HARRIET: He apparently is an entirely different proposition. Quite rugged I am told.

SERENA: Rugged?

HARRIET: He is a railway man and very rich indeed. I suppose I shall be snapped at again if I ask what was in the note?

SERENA: He wishes me to meet him secretly at the Zoo.

HARRIET: You are quite impossible to-day, Serena. This time I really shall leave you.

SERENA: Yes, you must. He says he wishes to see me privately on a matter of great urgency.

HARRIET: It is no use trying to tease me and tantalise me. I know perfectly well that it is a formal little note, probably from his wife, inviting you to a ball or to their box at the opera.

CATCHPOLE *enters.*

CATCHPOLE (*announcing*): Mr. Axel Diensen.

AXEL DIENSEN *enters. He is a tall, well-built man in the late forties.*

SERENA (*putting out her hand*): How do you do, Mr. Diensen.

AXEL (*taking it*): I am well, ma'am – thank you.

SERENA: This is Lady Harriet Ripley.

AXEL (*shaking hands with* HARRIET): I am honoured.

HARRIET: As a matter of fact we have met once before, for a brief moment, at that curious charity fête at Twickenham. Do you remember?

AXEL: Yes. I remember.

SERENA: Can I offer you some tea?

AXEL: No, thank you. My time is limited.

SERENA: In that case you had better leave the tea things, Catchpole. Albert can come and clear them away when I ring.

CATCHPOLE: Very good, milady.

HARRIET: I really must go now, Serena, Lavinia will be furious. Good-bye, Mr. Diensen, I hope that we shall soon meet again.

AXEL: The pleasure would be mine, ma'am.

SERENA (*kissing her*): Good-bye, my dear. I will send you hourly bulletins.

HARRIET: How horrid you are.

> CATCHPOLE *ushers* HARRIET *out and follows her, closing the door behind him.*

SERENA: Pray sit down, Mr. Diensen.

AXEL: If you do not object, ma'am, I would prefer to stand, or even walk about.

SERENA: Perhaps you would prefer to return to the drawing-room? It is much larger.

AXEL (*moving to the window*): I am a man of action rather than words. The bulk of my life has been spent in very different circumstances to those in which I now find myself. I am well accustomed to handling men and making decisions and dealing with sudden crises when they occur – but not this sort of crisis.

SERENA: Crisis?

AXEL: Yes, ma'am. A most definite crisis.

SERENA: You alarm me, Mr. Diensen.

AXEL: You read my note?

SERENA: Yes.

AXEL: I said in it that I wished to see you on a matter of great urgency.

SERENA: Yes. I must admit that that puzzled me.

AXEL: You have no idea of what the matter might be?

SERENA: None.

AXEL (*violently*): Hell and damnation!

SERENA: Really, Mr. Diensen.

AXEL: Forgive me, ma'am. The railroads of the west provide inadequate training for the drawing-rooms of Belgravia.

SERENA: Be calm I beg of you. Your outburst startled rather than offended me. I am perfectly prepared to regard hell and damnation in the Biblical sense if it will make you any more comfortable.

AXEL: We are comparative strangers to each other.

SERENA: I fully realise that, but even comparative strangers might be able to discover some stretch of mutual ground, or should I say 'track'? on which to meet, might they not?

AXEL: In this instance they most unfortunately have.

SERENA: Unfortunately?

AXEL (*swinging away from her and striding about*): This is terrible – terrible—

SERENA: I can only hope, Mr. Diensen, for the sake of the American industrial progress, that you deal with your railroad crises with more dispatch than you are dealing with this one.

AXEL: I would rather face a faulty viaduct, a landslide, a collapsed tunnel, a forest fire and an engineers' strike, than tell you what I am obliged to tell you.

SERENA (*beginning to put two and two together*): Come to the point, Mr. Diensen.

AXEL: Has nothing happened to you to-day? Nothing unexpected?

SERENA: Happened to me?

AXEL: You have received no bad news? No news of any kind?

SERENA: I have been visiting my mother in Richmond. She has a slight cold.

AXEL: Since your return you have heard nothing? Received no disturbing message? – no letter?

SERENA: Please say clearly and frankly what you have to say.

Forget that I am a comparative stranger. Treat me as a board
of directors, if you must, but for heaven's sake, speak.

AXEL: Hell and damnation! Hell and damnation!

SERENA: You said that before and it led us nowhere.

AXEL: Lady Heronden. (*He pauses.*) Your husband has left you.

SERENA (*looking at him steadily for a moment and then turning
away*): Yes, yes, I know he has.

AXEL: You *know*?

SERENA: I understand your embarrassment, Mr. Diensen. I see
clearly now what has happened.

AXEL: How long have you known?

SERENA: Only a little while, a few minutes before you arrived. I
think I will sit down if you don't mind, we cannot both of us
stroll about the room indefinitely. (*She sits down.*)

AXEL: I am deeply concerned, ma'am, deeply sympathetic, please
believe that.

SERENA: Thank you, Mr. Diensen, you have my sympathy also.
Hubert, my husband, left me a note which I received on my
return from Richmond. It was brief and mentioned no names.
Your wife I presume was more explicit.

AXEL: Oh no. Her note said little beyond the fact that she had
left me, that by the time I received it she would be far away,
and that she hoped that I would make no attempt to follow
her. She mentioned no names either.

SERENA: Then how did you know, why were you so sure that
my husband was the man she had eloped with?

AXEL: I guessed.

SERENA: Guessed?

AXEL: They have been seeing each other a good deal during the
last few months.

SERENA: Have they? I didn't know.

AXEL: I discovered it only by chance, a few weeks ago; a friend of
mine from Minnesota happened to meet them accidentally.

SERENA: At the Zoo?

AXEL: So you did know.

SERENA: No, that too was a guess. My husband has utilised the
Zoo for a long while.

AXEL: I see.

SERENA: It is more convenient than the Tower of London, and less fashionable than Madame Tussaud's.

AXEL: I think, after all, I will have a cup of tea.

SERENA: I will ring. (*She half rises.*)

AXEL: No, please don't ring, what is there will do.

SERENA: It is by now stone cold and quite black.

AXEL: Milk alone would be preferable to an interruption.

SERENA: I quite agree. (*She empties the remains of tea from* HARRIET's *cup, washes it out with hot water over the slop basin, pours some milk into it and hands it to him.*)

AXEL: Thank you. (*He sits down.*)

SERENA (*pouring some out for herself*): I think I shall have some too.

AXEL: Once during a flood on the Aitcheson and Topeka, the train was stranded and I had to live on milk for two days.

SERENA: How fortunate to be able to procure milk in the middle of a flood.

AXEL: It was a cattle train.

SERENA: I see.

AXEL (*after a pause*): At the risk of being considered impertinent, may I say that you are behaving magnificently?

SERENA: I am not behaving at all.

AXEL: It must be a terrible blow.

SERENA: For you also.

AXEL: I have had longer to think about it. I received my note this morning. I, at least, have had the hours of the day in which to conquer my emotions and accustom my mind to the situation.

SERENA (*drily*): Time is a great healer.

AXEL: But for you the very suddenness of the blow must be shocking.

SERENA: Violent shocks are sometimes accompanied by a merciful numbness. I am told that in the heat of battle, for instance, soldiers frequently lose limbs without being in the least aware of it until afterwards.

AXEL: It is afterwards however that the pain begins.

SERENA: Have you been married for long, Mr. Diensen?

AXEL: Nearly nine years. My wife came from Boston, you know.

SERENA: I had heard of that enviable circumstance.

AXEL: She was an Eliot.

SERENA: How gratifying!

AXEL: Her family have always maintained that in marrying me she married beneath her.

SERENA: How undiscerning.

AXEL: Thank you, ma'am.

SERENA: Perhaps it will be a relief to them that she has eloped with a Marquess?

AXEL: In the circumstances I fear not. They are very strait-laced.

SERENA: Have you arrived at any decision, Mr. Diensen? Have you decided on any specific course of action?

AXEL: Certainly I have. That is the purpose of my visit. There is still time to avert complete catastrophe if we act immediately.

SERENA: Act immediately? What can we do?

AXEL: Go after them and bring them back.

SERENA: We don't know where they have gone!

AXEL: I do. They are at the Villa Zodiaque, St. Guillaume des Fleurs, Alpes Maritimes, France.

SERENA: How on earth do you know? How did you find out?

AXEL: Charlotte, my wife – she was baptised Charlotte by the way.

SERENA: An attractive name, provided it is not allowed to degenerate into Charley.

AXEL: It never has so far.

SERENA: Pray continue.

AXEL: I happened to give her a ruby and diamond necklace some years ago on the occasion of our second wedding anniversary.

SERENA: Very thoughtful.

AXEL: At the moment it is being re-set at a shop in Bond Street. She left secret instructions to her maid to forward it on to her by special courier.

SERENA: I expect she felt that she would be lonely without it.

AXEL: It was to be delivered to a Mrs. Baxter-Ellis at the address I have just told you.

SERENA (*thoughtfully*): Baxter-Ellis – Baxter-Ellis – Ah, now I remember. Some years ago my husband was strongly attracted to a Mrs. Baxter-Ellis. You are quite sure of the name?

AXEL: Quite sure. I cross-examined the maid for two hours this morning. She finally broke down and confessed.

SERENA: I know the Villa Zodiaque. Hubert and I took it for the winter in 1865.

AXEL: You will accompany me there at once?

SERENA: Certainly not.

AXEL: But, Lady Heronden—

SERENA: It would be too humiliating, too – too vulgar. I couldn't consider it.

AXEL: Vulgarity be damned.

SERENA: It usually is, Mr. Diensen.

AXEL: Please, Lady Heronden, please be reasonable.

SERENA: Reasonable!

AXEL: Apart from you and me nobody knows as yet what has happened. The situation can still be saved.

SERENA (*suddenly rising and walking about the room*): This is intolerable – degrading—

AXEL: Do you love your husband, ma'am?

SERENA (*icily*): Really, Mr. Diensen. I think you go too far.

AXEL: Never mind about that – do you?

SERENA: Unlike your wife's maid, I shall not break down under cross-examination.

AXEL: But see here, Lady Heronden—

SERENA: As you said yourself. We are comparative strangers. I am not in the habit of discussing my private emotions with comparative strangers.

AXEL (*grimly*): Well, you'd better break your rule, ma'am.

SERENA: I am sure the railways of America owe a great deal to your blunt speech and your forceful character, Mr. Diensen, but kindly remember that I am not an American railway.

AXEL: You gave me permission just now to talk to you like a board of directors.

SERENA: It had not occurred to me that even *American* executives would be prepared to answer intimate personal questions in full committee.

AXEL: Committees are privileged, ma'am.

SERENA: Even so, privileges should not be abused.

AXEL: We are our own committee, a committee of two, and we are privileged to be in the hell of a difficult situation. Without plain speaking we shall get no place.

SERENA: As far as I can see there is no place to get.

AXEL: That is where you are wrong. The place for us to get is the south of France and quick at that.

SERENA: I have already told you that I have no intention of going to the south of France with you—

AXEL (*beginning to lose patience*): But listen a minute—

SERENA: There is nothing to prevent you going by yourself if you wish to.

AXEL: Don't you realise that we are in the same boat whether you like it or not?

SERENA: I do. And I *dis*like it intensely.

AXEL: Our only chance of averting scandal is to look facts in the face and pool our resources.

SERENA: I feel, Mr. Diensen, that our resources are too divergent to pool successfully.

AXEL: God give me patience!

SERENA: I find blasphemy offensive.

AXEL: That wasn't blasphemy, it was a heartfelt prayer.

SERENA: I really cannot feel that much can be achieved by continuing this conversation.

AXEL: But, Lady Heronden—

SERENA: That is all I have to say, Mr. Diensen.

AXEL: But why this? What have I done to offend you, to banish all reason from your mind?

SERENA: I am not accustomed to being spoken to in that tone.

AXEL (*striding about the room*): Hell and damnation! Hell and damnation!

SERENA: Your vocabulary seems to be as limited as your manners.

AXEL (*violently*): Wrong again, ma'am! Wrong all along the line! My vocabulary is boundless. I can curse the stars out of the sky with rich words that you do not even know exist. I can swear red, blue and purple for twenty minutes without repeating myself once! And it is only my manners that are restraining me from doing so now. They may be rough, these manners of mine which you dismiss with such aristocratic scorn; they may not be polished and shining and false like those of your careful little English world, but they were good enough for my mother and father, and they should be good enough for you too, because they come from the heart and are dictated neither by fashion nor snobbery. They at least prompted me to come to you immediately to-day, to try, quietly and reasonably to discover whether or not we might, in mutual understanding, decide together on a course of action. Then, for some frivolous reason best known to yourself, you suddenly get on to your high horse and start riding me down. I will not be ridden down, Lady Heronden, please make no mistake about that. I am not impressed either by your title, your position, or your traditions. I *was* impressed, up until a few moments ago, by your honesty and your intelligence. For the love of heaven, woman, what has got into you? I didn't ask if you loved your husband out of idle curiosity. It doesn't matter a nickel to me if you love him or not. All I wanted to find out was the degree of your affection for him, whether or not it was still strong enough to save him and his name and his reputation, from public opprobrium.

SERENA (*after a pause*): The meeting is now adjourned.

AXEL: Very well. I only ask your pardon for one thing, my vulgar impertinence in daring to call upon you. (*He bows and goes to the door.*)

SERENA: Mr. Diensen—

AXEL (*with his hand on the door handle*): Yes?

SERENA: Please do not go. The ill manners were on my side, not on yours. I am truly sorry.

AXEL (*still at the door*): It is my habit to speak my mind, ma'am, regardless of the company in which I find myself. This I know to be an error and I have tried to conquer it. My words do well enough when there is no urgency to roughen them, but when there is – Oh Lord! – out they come like a river in full spate, and what little grace I have learned is swept away.

SERENA: Come away from the door, Mr. Diensen. If you flared up again you might vanish through it before I had time to restrain you. You were right in what you said just now. We must pool our resources.

AXEL (*coming away from the door*): Bully for you, ma'am.

SERENA: You asked me if I loved my husband.

AXEL: Forget the question. It is of no consequence.

SERENA (*turning away from him*): The answer is 'Yes' – very definitely 'Yes'. But I love him now without illusion. The years have banked down the fires leaving a pleasant, protective glow. He is a man of charm and wit and sensibility: he has a kind heart and is incurably romantic. His search for romance only began with me, whereas mine ended with him. He is also feckless and irresponsible to an alarming degree and, of course, excellent company. My life without him would be perhaps more tranquil but immeasurably dull.

AXEL: Thank you for your confidence, ma'am.

SERENA: And you? Can you tell me the state of your heart before we start on our journey? It would be a fair exchange. Are you in love with your wife?

AXEL: No, no longer in love with her. Time has banked down my fires also. But I am fond of her, too fond to allow her to break up her life if I can possibly prevent it. Society means much to her – a great deal too much as a matter of fact. The opinion of the world is as necessary to her as the sun is to a rose garden. If the sun withdraws and the wind blows cold, she will wilt considerably.

SERENA: We must both do our utmost to prevent her from wilting, Mr. Diensen. When do you propose to leave?

AXEL: To-night.

SERENA: To-night! Oh dear.

AXEL: I made all the necessary reservations early this afternoon in the hope that you would agree.

SERENA: You have told no one?

AXEL: No one. I have sent my wife's maid back to her home in Derbyshire. I myself have told the household that I am joining my wife on the continent for a few days.

SERENA: Hubert is supposed to be at Heronden, our house in Kent. Nobody will know that he isn't, for a few days at least. I shall explain to my maid and my butler that I am joining him there to-night.

AXEL: Surely your maid will expect to accompany you?

SERENA: Normally she would of course, but fortunately her sister is about to be married in Essex. I have been dreading having to make the gesture of letting her go. Now I welcome it. What time does the boat train leave?

AXEL: Eight o'clock p.m. from London Bridge station.

SERENA: Will you be so kind as to meet me at the barrier at seven-forty-five?

AXEL: I surely will, ma'am.

SERENA: Then that is settled.

AXEL: A deal, ma'am. (*He puts out his hand.*)

SERENA (*taking it solemnly*): A deal. Thank you, Mr. Diensen, for your consideration and also for your efficiency.

AXEL: Thank you, ma'am, for your understanding and your courage.

SERENA: The latter may fail me yet.

AXEL: I doubt that.

SERENA: Shall we succeed, do you think? Will this curious campaign upon which we are embarking so impulsively be crowned with victory? Or shall we return with heavy hearts, shamed and humiliated and unable to meet each other's eyes?

AXEL: We shall at least have tried. To picture defeat at the outset will undermine our determination. We must banish the very idea from our minds. Death or glory, ma'am.

SERENA: A glowing phrase, Mr. Diensen, but in this particular instance, excessive.

AXEL: Until seven-forty-five, ma'am.

SERENA: Until seven-forty-five.

> AXEL *bows and goes out swiftly.*
>
> SERENA, *left alone, picks up* HUBERT's *letter which she has left on the tea-table.*
>
> *She walks over to the window and looks absently out into the Square for a moment. Then she goes over to the bureau, tears the letter methodically into pieces and drops them into the waste-paper basket.*

SERENA (*as she does so*): Hell and damnation! Hell and damnation!

CURTAIN

ACT II: Scene I

The Villa Zodiaque.

The main living-room of the Villa opens on to a terrace. The terrace commands a view of rolling hills crowned by small, sun-washed villages set among olives and cypresses. In the far distance is the blue line of the sea.

The room itself is spacious and pleasantly furnished in a mixture of styles, the predominant of which are sturdy Provençal and Italian rococo. There is naturally a sprinkling of Victoriana but the total effect, although confused, is charming enough.

Two nights and two days have elapsed since the preceding scene.

The time is mid-morning. Sunlight is flooding into the room and HUBERT *and* CHARLOTTE *are lingering over a late breakfast.* HUBERT *is attired in a splendid brocaded breakfast robe,* CHARLOTTE *is in a negligee.* HUBERT *is scanning the pages of* Le Petit Niçois.

HUBERT: It is not that I dislike *The Magic Flute*, Charlotte, it is merely that it goes on for such a long time.

CHARLOTTE: I heard Jenny Lind sing it, she was exquisite.

HUBERT: To me she resembled an agreeably vocal currant bun.

CHARLOTTE: Hubert!

HUBERT: At all events she is not singing it this evening in the Municipal Opera House. It is an undistinguished cast and not even a gala performance.

CHARLOTTE: It would be foolish anyhow for us to be seen together at a gala performance.

HUBERT: Alas yes, but we cannot be furtive indefinitely. I had hoped that my love was strong enough to still your social conscience.

CHARLOTTE: Social fiddlesticks, Hubert. My insistence on discretion is for both our sakes; we are bound to encounter

37

unpleasantness sooner or later and would be silly to meet it halfway.

HUBERT: It shall be as you say, my precious dear. We will stay in our fortress on our enchanted hill and dine on the terrace in the moonlight. The nightingales shall provide our opera; at least they will not sing Mozart.

CHARLOTTE: I cannot bear you not to like Mozart.

HUBERT: For your sake my darling I will adore him, I swear I will: your loving hand shall guide me to his perfections. There will come a time when his every mathematical semi-quaver will be clear pleasure to me, but you must be patient; at the moment my heart is deaf to all music save the sound of your voice. I have very little ear anyhow.

CHARLOTTE: You are talking nonsense again.

HUBERT: When I was young it took me seven months to learn 'On the Banks of Allan Water'.

CHARLOTTE (*rising impulsively and going over to the windows*): It is no use.

HUBERT: What is no use?

CHARLOTTE (*turning*): Pretending.

HUBERT: Pretending what?

CHARLOTTE: That we are happy and carefree, enclosed in a lovely private dream with no outside world to menace us and nothing to worry about.

HUBERT: Is your part of the dream wearing thin already?

CHARLOTTE (*in distress*): Yes – Oh, yes, it is.

HUBERT: A meagre little dream, barely more than forty winks.

CHARLOTTE: You will not admit it then?

HUBERT: Admit what?

CHARLOTTE: That there is a strain in the air.

HUBERT: Do be quiet, my dearest, you are frightening away the morning! It was clear and beautiful an hour ago, now there are clouds coming up over the sea, look, you can see them.

CHARLOTTE: We must go away.

HUBERT: We are away.

CHARLOTTE: Away from here, I mean.

HUBERT: You are very fidgety, Charlotte, we have only just arrived.

CHARLOTTE: There are too many people near us here.

HUBERT: No one that we know, excepting poor old Octavia Bonnington.

CHARLOTTE: *I* do not know poor old Octavia Bonnington.

HUBERT: Then you shall, my tender heart. But I warn you she may alarm you.

CHARLOTTE (*protesting*): Hubert—

HUBERT: She lives in a dank villa just near-by and writes fiercely improper books under a pseudonym. None of her relations will have anything to do with her.

CHARLOTTE: Then why should we?

HUBERT: Because she is old and lonely and incurably sentimental. It would give her so much pleasure to welcome two runaways, two ecstatic social outcasts. We will call on her immediately, to-day.

CHARLOTTE: We will do no such thing.

HUBERT: Come, Charlotte, you must not be selfish. We have happiness to spare, we are bathed in illicit bliss! The least we can do is to share it.

CHARLOTTE: Share it! You must be mad.

HUBERT: Think what it would mean to her, an elderly eccentric living alone with an ageing pug and a curiously thick-set Major-Domo.

> CHARLOTTE *twists her hands with irritation.*

CHARLOTTE: Hubert – Oh, Hubert!

HUBERT (*enlarging on his theme*): Imagine her excitement! She would hear the sound of our carriage wheels in the drive and, . peering through quite dreadful curtains, she would see us descend from it. She would sense in an instant, from the way I touched your hand as I helped you to alight, from the tenderness of your smile as you closed your parasol, that we were in love—

CHARLOTTE: Please stop, Hubert, I can bear no more.

HUBERT: In a moment she would be in the hall, holding out her arms to us, warming her chilled old heart in the flow of our passion: the pug would bark wildly, the parrots would shriek – I forgot to tell you that she has two vast macaws – rapture would flood through the house. And all because two lovers, two abandoned, wayward lovers, had suddenly appeared out of the bright sunlight.

CHARLOTTE (*nearing the end of her tether*): Once and for all, Hubert, will you stop talking! Your fantasies are driving me mad, your endless words beat upon my nerves until I want to scream. I will *not* consent to call upon this Octavia whatever-her-name-is—

HUBERT: Bonnington.

CHARLOTTE (*moving about the room*): Oh – oh – oh!

HUBERT: Why do you say 'Oh – oh – oh!' my treasure?

CHARLOTTE: Because I am lost. Because I am unhappy.

HUBERT: To the devil with Octavia Bonnington. Let her remain for ever in her sad tower gazing at an empty road.

CHARLOTTE: Oh, Hubert—

She bursts into tears.

HUBERT: Why do you weep so frequently, my angel? It is infinitely distressing to me.

CHARLOTTE: I have already told you. I am unhappy.

HUBERT: How can you be unhappy in Paradise?

CHARLOTTE: Perhaps because I am beginning to realise that it is a fool's Paradise.

HUBERT: Charlotte!

CHARLOTTE (*with spirit*): It is true. I am bewildered and insecure. I am deafened and blinded all the time by your exuberant romanticism. Our situation is difficult and, for me, haunted by the dread of humiliations. Your continued refusal to share my fears, your resolute determination to float through the air indefinitely, terrifies me. I am beginning to suspect that you are not in love with me at all, you are merely in love with the idea of being in love with somebody, anybody—

HUBERT: If I kissed you, would you forget my infamies?

CHARLOTTE: No.

HUBERT *approaches her.*

HUBERT: And forgive my verbosity?

CHARLOTTE: I do not wish you to kiss me.

HUBERT: Why not?

CHARLOTTE: Because it is not the moment. Mid-morning is no time for foolishness.

HUBERT: If it is the light that is worrying you we could draw the curtains.

CHARLOTTE: Really, Hubert!

HUBERT (*tenderly*): Please let me press my lips on yours, my darling.

CHARLOTTE: It would solve nothing and merely confuse me.

HUBERT: It would solve everything, for a little while and then we could quarrel again later in the day.

CHARLOTTE: No, Hubert.

HUBERT (*taking her in his arms*): Yes, Charlotte.

He kisses her.

CHARLOTTE (*surrendering*): Oh, my love—

HUBERT: Whisper that again

CHARLOTTE (*almost inaudibly*): Oh, my love.

With his mouth nearly touching hers.

HUBERT: Are you still lost?

CHARLOTTE: Hubert—

HUBERT: Still unhappy?

CHARLOTTE: Please – please—

HUBERT: Come away – come back to the night for a little—

He kisses her again lingeringly and passionately.

They both stand locked in each other's arms oblivious to sight or sound.

SERENA *and* AXEL *come quietly in from the terrace and stand for a moment looking at them.*

SERENA (*breaking the silence*): It is almost time for luncheon, Hubert.

HUBERT *and* CHARLOTTE *break away from each other.* CHAR-LOTTE *gives a slight scream.*

HUBERT: I find this difficult to forgive, Serena.

SERENA: I am glad to know that we still have something in common.

CHARLOTTE: Axel!

SERENA: There seemed to be no one about in the front of the house so we came round by the terrace.

HUBERT: There is a bell outside the front door, an exceedingly loud bell.

SERENA: To be awakened from a dream by a bell is always disagreeable.

AXEL: Here is your necklace, Mrs. Baxter-Ellis – re-set and delivered as you requested by special courier.

CHARLOTTE (*dimly*): Thank you.

HUBERT: Why have you come, Serena?

SERENA: I should have imagined the reason to be fairly obvious.

HUBERT: On the contrary I find it most obscure. What could you possibly hope to achieve by this, this tasteless twofold intrusion?

SERENA: Let us dispense with artificial bluster, Hubert. The situation is both difficult and delicate.

HUBERT: It is also irrevocable.

SERENA (*calmly*): Surely not so irrevocable as to preclude all discussion.

HUBERT: My dear Serena—

> SERENA *takes off her gloves.*

SERENA: Please say something, Mr. Diensen. The conversational burden so far has rested almost exclusively on my shoulders. It really is not quite fair.

AXEL: I am at a loss, ma'am, and when I am at a loss all but the crudest phrases elude me.

SERENA: We are all at a loss, which is not surprising in the circumstances. (*To* CHARLOTTE.) Perhaps you would like to speak to your husband privately, Mrs. Diensen?

CHARLOTTE: I have nothing to say to my husband now or at any other time.

SERENA: I hope that you will reconsider that decision later on. Sullen silence is not only unco-operative but extremely irritating. There is a great deal to be discussed. Is there not, Mr. Diensen?

AXEL: There surely is, ma'am.

SERENA: Thank you. That was at least a contribution, if only a minor one.

HUBERT: There is nothing to be discussed, Serena, except by our lawyers. Please understand that once and for all. Even your famous high-handedness cannot transform what is essentially an emotional situation into a debate.

SERENA: As far as I am concerned the situation is not in the least emotional, and I intend to discuss it fully from every angle. That is why we are here, is it not, Mr. Diensen?

AXEL: That is so, ma'am. (*To* HUBERT *and* CHARLOTTE.) This is all a hell of a mess and we are here to get it settled one way or another.

HUBERT: It is already settled one way, there is no other.

AXEL: You are a God-damned adulterer, sir.

SERENA: An accurate statement, Mr. Diensen, but over-emphatic. Please remember your promise.

AXEL: I am sorry.

SERENA (*conversationally*): Mr. Diensen promised me on the steamer and again in the train to restrain his temper, Hubert. He is a man of naturally strong feeling; he is also, as you may observe, physically in the pink of condition. I beg of you in your own interest as well as in the interest of general decorum, not to try his patience too far.

HUBERT: I am no more impressed by Mr. Diensen's physical prowess than I am by his uncouth manners.

SERENA: Do remember that, having eloped with Mr. Diensen's wife, you are in no position to criticise his manners. I would be very much obliged if you would pour me out a glass of wine: the journey was hot and dusty and I feel quite exhausted. (*She sits down.*)

There is silence while HUBERT *goes over to a side table upon which is a decanter of wine and some glasses. He pours out some wine and brings it to* SERENA.

HUBERT (*coldly*): A little wine, Mr. Diensen?

AXEL: Thank you. I will help myself.

HUBERT: Do by all means. Charlotte?

CHARLOTTE: No thank you.

AXEL goes to the side table and pours himself a glass of wine.

SERENA: What time is luncheon? I am exceedingly hungry.

HUBERT: You intend to stay to luncheon?

SERENA: We intend to stay indefinitely.

HUBERT: I fear that that is out of the question. There are not enough rooms to begin with, and the domestic staff consists merely of one old woman and her husband and a girl who comes down from the village three times a week to do the cleaning.

SERENA: You seem to forget, Hubert, that I know this villa well. In the earlier, more halcyon days of our married life, we took it for a whole winter. During that time we managed to put up a number of people including that unpleasant nephew of yours who ultimately had to be sent to the Colonies. There is ample accommodation for six guests not counting the room at the back with the stove in it.

HUBERT: Serena—

SERENA: As for the domestic staff, that is merely a question of organisation.

HUBERT (*bitterly*): You would reduce the sun and the moon and the stars in their courses to a question of organisation.

SERENA: Indeed I would if the Almighty had not so successfully forestalled me.

AXEL: Bully for you, ma'am.

SERENA: Thank you, Mr. Diensen.

HUBERT: Without wishing to appear inhospitable, Serena, I fear that I must state firmly and emphatically that you and Mr. Diensen are *not* going to stay in this villa indefinitely. You are not even going to stay for luncheon.

CHARLOTTE: Hubert, I really think—

HUBERT: Hush, my treasure.

SERENA: Considering that that is virtually the only sound that has emerged from your treasure since our arrival, it is unkind of you to discourage her.

HUBERT: You have always been a hard and determined woman, Serena.

SERENA: Not quite always. In our earlier years I was malleable enough but the skies were clear then and the breezes gentle: later, when the bleak winds of disillusion blew cold, my heart froze a little and my character suffered a sea change. It was only to be expected.

HUBERT: What was your object in making this tactless excursion? What could you hope to gain by it?

SERENA (*sipping her wine, rather wearily*): I do not hope to gain anything, Hubert. I cherish no romantic notions of winning you back to me. All I am trying to do is to salvage a little of our mutual dignity.

AXEL: Lady Heronden is perfectly right, Charlotte.

CHARLOTTE (*with spirit*): I am sure she is according to her lights. Apparently she is always perfectly right. Perhaps if she had not been so . . . so frigidly correct for so many years, this situation would never have occurred.

AXEL: Please come out on to the terrace – I wish to speak to you alone.

CHARLOTTE: I have already said that I have nothing to say to you.

AXEL: But I have a great deal to say to you.

HUBERT: Say what you like, Mr. Diensen. Charlotte has given away her heart, I suspect for the first time. It is a gallant, loving, shining heart, untarnished by compromise: none of your plans or arguments can move it now. She has flitted from your self-made world. She will never return.

AXEL: If I had not already been warned about your high-flown phraseology, sir, I should think you were plumb crazy.

HUBERT: You would think so, anyhow. We speak different languages.

AXEL: I have always found the language of common sense sufficient for my needs, and common sense, in this particular instance, has made at least three facts clear to me. The first is that Charlotte is returning to England with me immediately, if I have to carry her there by force; the second is that apart from your noble heritage and your verbal felicity, you are nothing but an irresponsible, frivolous libertine . . .

HUBERT (*angrily*): Now look here, Mr. Diensen . . .

AXEL (*overriding him*): The third fact is that if you are unwise enough to indulge in any further equivocation and fiddle-faddle, it will give me immense pleasure to knock you senseless.

> *At this moment* MR. SPEVIN *appears nervously on the terrace and taps on the shutter. Everybody jumps.*

HUBERT: Good God!

MR. S.: Am I intruding, my lord? There seemed to be no one about in the front of the house so I came round by the terrace.

HUBERT (*recovering himself*): Please come in, Mr. Spevin.

MR. S.: You honour me, my lord, by remembering my name. So kind – so very kind. (*To* CHARLOTTE.) I hope that your ladyship is rested after that long and tedious journey? (*To* AXEL.) We met in the buffet at Boulogne, you know, after a most disagreeable crossing. My little girl was dreadfully seasick, poor mite, but she is now as gay as a cricket.

AXEL: Bully for her.

MR. S. (*puzzled*): I beg your pardon?

HUBERT: Mr. Diensen is an American, Mr. Spevin.

MR. S.: How interesting, how very interesting, the New World, so vital. One of my parishioners is married to an American, from a place called Philadelphia.

AXEL: I have heard of it, sir.

MR. S.: The name is Potter. Perhaps you have run across the family at one time or another?

SERENA (*to* AXEL): You might conceivably have run over one or two of them, might you not, Mr. Diensen?

MR. S. (*puzzled again*): I fear that I—

SERENA (*gently*): Mr. Diensen is a railway man and that was a foolish little joke.

MR. S. (*with an eager smile*): Oh, I see – I see. I will tell Mrs. Potter. She is a woman of ready humour.

SERENA: My husband has omitted to introduce us. I am Lady Heronden.

MR. S. (*flustered, darting a look at* CHARLOTTE): Oh, I – er – I – I'm afraid I—

SERENA: An understandable mistake, Mr. Spevin. My husband escorted Mrs. Diensen to the buffet at Boulogne while Mr. Diensen took me directly to the train. Like your daughter, I too was a little under the weather.

MR. S.: My wife was quite right after all. She was positive that – er – Mrs. Diensen was not your ladyship. We argued about it quite heatedly all the way to Paris.

SERENA: Perhaps you will take a glass of wine with us?

MR. S.: No – no – thank you so much – I really must be getting back. I merely called on the chance of finding you at home. (*To* HUBERT.) I hope you will forgive the informality?

HUBERT (*stiffly*): Delighted, Mr. Spevin—

MR. S.: I happened to be passing the house on my way home from a triste little mission. Poor Lady Bonnington—

SERENA: Good heavens! Is she still alive?

MR. S.: Oh yes, but alas, her little pug passed over.

SERENA: How sad.

MR. S.: He was very old, of course, but she was devoted to him. She asked me to conduct a brief burial service in the garden. I could hardly refuse, could I? She was so very upset.

HUBERT: I trust that the macaws are still extant?

MR. S.: Oh yes, they attended the service. (*After a slight pause.*) I was wondering if I might ask a small favour? I do so hope that you will not consider it presumptuous on my part, but—

SERENA: What is it, Mr. Spevin?

MR. S. (*with a rush*): One of my parishioners, a Mrs. Edgar Venables, has lent us her garden to-morrow afternoon for a jumble sale in aid of the choir outing. There is to be a raffle and competitions and some quite amusing races. It would give such tremendous cachet to the whole affair if you and his lordship would honour us with your presence and perhaps, I only say perhaps, consent to give the prizes?

HUBERT (*firmly*): Now look here, Mr. Spevin—

MR. S.: It is all on a very small scale of course, nothing grand or distinguished, but it is English. I often describe my little church as an English island in a foreign sea. It means a great deal to me. You do understand, do you not?

SERENA (*decisively*): Of course we do, Mr. Spevin, and we shall be charmed to come to your jumble sale.

HUBERT (*protesting*): Serena—

SERENA: *And* give the prizes. What time would you like us to arrive?

MR. S.: I am quite overwhelmed by your kindness, Lady Heronden. About four-thirty. I think everything will be well under way by then. Do you really mean that you will come?

SERENA: Certainly. We will all come. Will we not, Mr. Diensen?

AXEL: Whatever you say, ma'am.

SERENA: And afterwards you shall show us your 'English island in a foreign sea'.

MR. S.: I can never express my gratitude, never. My wife will be in the seventh heaven. I can scarcely wait to tell her. Thank you – thank you a thousand times – so kind – so very kind!

> MR. SPEVIN, *spluttering with excitement, bows to everyone and goes out via the terrace.*

HUBERT: I have no intention of going to a church jumble sale to-morrow or at any other time. In fact I have no intention of seeing Mr. Spevin ever again in my life. He has already obtruded himself on my privacy twice in thirty-six hours and I have been reasonably civil. That is enough.

SERENA: In that case I shall go alone and make excuses for you. After all it is merely what I have been doing for over twenty years.

HUBERT: Once and for all, Serena, will you kindly leave this house and take Mr. Diensen with you? Your presence here is acutely embarrassing. I regret that you should be inconvenienced, I regret your possible unhappiness. To you too, Mr. Diensen, I tender my most sincere apologies. More than that I cannot say. I cannot even say that I am sorry because the ecstatic beating of my heart would strangle the words in my throat. Come into the garden, Charlotte, this room is suffocating me.

CHARLOTTE: But, Hubert—

AXEL: Stay where you are, Charlotte.

HUBERT (*seizing her by the hand*): Come, my dear love, come out under the sky, away from the dangerous endeavours of those who so implacably wish us well.

> HUBERT *takes* CHARLOTTE *out on to the terrace.*
>
> AXEL *makes a movement as if to follow them.* SERENA *sits down again and proceeds to remove her hat.*

SERENA: You are quite content to let them go, Mr. Diensen? Out under the sky?

AXEL: Certainly, ma'am. They'll be back soon. It is beginning to rain.

> *They look at each other. Then they smile.*

THE LIGHTS FADE

Scene II

Early the next morning.

AXEL is seated at the breakfast table. He is thoughtfully sipping a cup of coffee and smoking a cigarette. After a moment or two SERENA comes in.

SERENA: Good morning, Mr. Diensen.

AXEL (*rising*): Oh! Good morning. (*He is about to crush out his cigarette.*)

SERENA: Pray do not stop smoking on my account, I like the smell of tobacco.

AXEL: Would you care for some fresh coffee?

SERENA: No, thank you, I have already breakfasted in my room. (*She walks over to the window.*) A lovely day, not a cloud, not a breath of wind. We at least have that to be thankful for.

AXEL: I trust that you slept well?

SERENA: Quite well, thank you, but not enough. Yesterday was a difficult day, it began early and ended very much too late. I feel a little tired.

AXEL: You betray no signs of it.

SERENA: Thank you, Mr. Diensen.

AXEL: May I take this opportunity of saying how profoundly I admire you?

SERENA: Thank you again. You are most encouraging.

AXEL: Not merely as a woman, that goes without saying, but as an executive.

SERENA: You overwhelm me, Mr. Diensen.

AXEL: Your handling of this whole damned business is beyond praise. From the moment we arrived yesterday until the early hours of this morning you have displayed qualities of endurance, patience and determination that Abraham Lincoln would have envied.

SERENA: Mr. Lincoln abolished slavery, I have merely been fighting to re-establish it.

AXEL: There is bitterness in your voice.

SERENA: There is bitterness in my heart, Mr. Diensen.

49

AXEL: Eliminate it, ma'am, it will stain your shield. This is a trivial adventure.

SERENA: Is it? I wonder.

AXEL: Measured against the world's deeper sorrows of course it is. We must not, even in the interests of self-justification, magnify our comedy into a tragedy. Tragedy inflicts deeper wounds than those we have suffered. Our cause is reasonable enough, I grant you, but it is hardly a crusade, merely an assertion of pride.

SERENA (*with a faint smile*): Bully for you, Mr. Diensen.

AXEL: Are you laughing at me?

SERENA: No more than at myself.

AXEL: A healthy sign at any rate.

SERENA (*turning again to the view*): Do you see that village on the hill?

AXEL (*joining her at her window*): Yes.

SERENA: Just to the right of it, below the little church, there is a clump of cypresses.

AXEL: I see it.

SERENA: It marks an old enclosed garden where the wall has crumbled at one end and you can look out over the olive groves to the sea. Many years ago, when Hubert and I had this house, we escaped from our guests one evening after dinner and drove up there by ourselves in the moonlight. We were much younger then, of course – it was a year before my son died. It was an evening I shall always remember, a special enchantment, detached from everything else. Would it be a healthy sign if I laughed at that too?

AXEL: Perhaps not a guffaw, ma'am, just a grateful smile.

SERENA: Have all American railway magnates so light a touch?

AXEL: Every man jack of them.

SERENA (*coming away from the window*): Do you think we are wasting our time?

AXEL: Maybe, who knows?

SERENA: It was your impulse that brought us here.

AXEL: I accept full responsibility.

SERENA: What spoils will the day yield to us, have you envisaged them?

AXEL: Courage, ma'am.

SERENA: Each of us leading home in triumph a whimpering hostage! Poor pickings, Mr. Diensen.

She turns away.

I do not think that I can face the humiliation.

AXEL: Is your resolution fading?

SERENA: I do not know. I only know that I feel curiously degraded.

AXEL (*vehemently*): This is horrible, horrible!

SERENA: What do you mean?

AXEL: To see you disintegrating before my eyes, crumbling away like the walls of your enchanted garden.

SERENA: Your simile is unattractive.

AXEL: So is this shocking access of weakness in you. A whiff of memory, a light stab of nostalgia, and down you topple from your pedestal—

SERENA (*tartly*): Please be quiet, Mr. Diensen. You are aggravating me considerably.

AXEL: To think that a few cypress trees could wreak such havoc in so sturdy a heart! It is mortifying.

SERENA: I withdraw my recent implication regarding your lightness of touch. At the moment your misplaced badinage has all the subtlety of a herd of buffalo.

AXEL: That is better.

SERENA (*suddenly very angry*): I refuse to accept your arbitrary decisions as to what is better or worse.

AXEL (*meekly*): As you say, ma'am.

SERENA: But kindly remember that we are still, to all intents and purposes, strangers to each other.

AXEL: Bravo! The stench of powder and the clash of steel!

SERENA: And if you imagine that our present circumstances have, in any way, established a basis of whimsical intimacy between us, I assure you that you are very much mistaken.

AXEL: Stuff and nonsense.

SERENA: I beg your pardon?

AXEL: So you should, Lady Heronden, so you should.

SERENA: Well, really—

AXEL: This damned high horse of yours is a thought too frisky. You mustn't allow him to bolt with you.

SERENA (*icily*): Mr. Diensen—

AXEL: Whereas you undoubtedly have every right to lose control of your temper with your erring husband, you have no right whatsoever to lose it with me.

SERENA: How dare you speak to me like that!

AXEL: Dare, Lady Heronden? What do you imagine I have to fear from your intricate high-bred tantrums? So we are still strangers to each other, are we? And any assumptions of friendliness, of 'whimsical intimacy' on my part must therefore be branded as impertinence. You alone it seems are to have the privilege of deciding our mutual status!

SERENA: Once and for all, Mr. Diensen, I will not be spoken to like this.

AXEL: Stuff and nonsense! I said it once and I say it again. Also poppycock, fiddlesticks, and hell and damnation!

> *He stamps out on to the terrace.*
> SERENA *puts her hand out as though to restrain him and then withdraws it and stands looking after him, biting her lip.*
> CHARLOTTE *enters. She stops short on seeing* SERENA.

CHARLOTTE: Oh!

SERENA: Good morning.

CHARLOTTE (*stiffly*): I am looking for Axel, my husband.

SERENA: I am delighted to hear it.

CHARLOTTE: Do you happen to have seen him?

SERENA: He is in the garden, I believe.

CHARLOTTE: Thank you. (*She goes towards the window.*)

SERENA: Just a moment, Mrs. Diensen—

CHARLOTTE (*stopping*): Forgive me, Lady Heronden, but I fear that we have nothing to say to each other.

SERENA: On the contrary, I should think that, taken all in all, we have many mutual interests – by now.

CHARLOTTE: This is an impossible situation and the sooner it is ended the better.

SERENA: I quite agree. That is why I wished to talk to you.

CHARLOTTE: Surely everything has been said that could possibly be said?

SERENA: You mean that a decision has been reached?

CHARLOTTE: No, I do not. I mean that I cannot stand any more. I am near breaking point.

SERENA: Where is Lord Heronden?

CHARLOTTE: I have not the least idea. I have not seen him since – since last night.

SERENA: Please sit down, Mrs. Diensen.

CHARLOTTE: I would rather not.

SERENA: Will you answer me one question?

CHARLOTTE: That depends upon what the question is.

SERENA: Do you really love my husband?

CHARLOTTE: Does it matter to you whether I love him or not?

SERENA (*gently*): Please answer my question. I want most earnestly, to know the truth.

CHARLOTTE: Why should you concern yourself with that kind of truth? So long as you get your own way, so long as scandal is averted and the situation saved from your point of view, why should it be of the faintest interest to you whether I love Hubert or not?

SERENA: Because, although you may not believe me, his happiness is of great importance to me.

CHARLOTTE (*with a bitter little laugh*): Happiness! Really, Lady Heronden.

SERENA: You must remember that I have been married to him for many years. I know him well.

CHARLOTTE: He is in love with me.

SERENA: I am fully aware of that. He was in love with me once, you know.

CHARLOTTE: A very long time ago.

SERENA: He, however, has been in love several times since. There was a German actress called Lotte Schell; she had large, china-blue eyes and was very sentimental. Then there was a Mrs. Railston; she had an excellent figure but was married, unfortunately, to a card-sharper. I believe they went to South Africa eventually.

CHARLOTTE: There is no necessity for you to give me a list of your husband's mistresses.

SERENA: I think you should at least know their names if only for reference. He is bound to allude to them from time to time. Then there was Hermione Grace—

CHARLOTTE: Lady Heronden—

SERENA (*ignoring her interruption*): She was the widow of an Indian colonel. Hubert was devoted to her for nearly two years. She died ultimately in Harrogate and left him a set of Benares brass-ware, a large luncheon gong and a musical box that played three tunes and had a picture of Loch Lomond inside the lid. I am afraid we still have it somewhere.

CHARLOTTE: What is your object in telling me all this?

SERENA: Merely to prove to you that with Hubert the state of 'being in love' is impermanent.

CHARLOTTE: I see.

SERENA: And to discover what, if anything, you have to put in its place when the time comes?

CHARLOTTE: The time may not come. Hubert may continue to be in love with me.

SERENA: Pigs might fly, Mrs. Diensen, but as a general rule they don't.

CHARLOTTE: You have been at some pains to explain Hubert's fickleness, presumably with the object of frightening me, of making me doubt the genuineness of his feeling for me, but there is one fact that you have overlooked, a very significant fact.

SERENA: And what is that?

CHARLOTTE: He has never, with the other ladies that you mention so glibly, made any personal sacrifices, has he? He has never, for instance, left you before? Never been prepared to jettison his name and position and reputation for any one of them. He has done this for me, Lady Heronden, and there can have been no other reason except that he loved me enough to consider it worth while.

SERENA: Perhaps the others were more foolish than you, or more kind. Perhaps they were willing to accept him on more generous terms.

CHARLOTTE: I do not know what you mean.

SERENA: You are demanding a great deal of him, you know. He will require substantial dividends later on.

CHARLOTTE (*angrily*): And what of his demands of me? I am making the same sacrifices, am I not?

SERENA: No, not quite the same. You have less to lose and more to gain.

CHARLOTTE: And what do you mean by that?

SERENA: If I were willing to divorce Hubert and your husband were willing to divorce you, you could eventually marry Hubert and return to America as the Marchioness of Heronden. It would still be a name of considerable social value even with the shadow of past scandal on it.

CHARLOTTE: You shock me, Lady Heronden. You really do.

SERENA: Don't be silly, Mrs. Diensen.

> HUBERT *comes in from the hall.*

Ah, there you are, Hubert. We were wondering what had become of you.

HUBERT: I have been for a long walk.

SERENA: Mrs. Diensen and I have been having a little chat.

HUBERT (*gloomily*): How nice.

CHARLOTTE: It was not nice, it was abominable. I feel defiled.

SERENA: That is natural enough in the circumstances.

CHARLOTTE (*breaking down*): Hubert – what am I to do? Where am I to turn? I can bear no more of this. For heaven's sake take me away, do not let me ever have to speak to her again – I can bear no more – I can bear no more—(*She bursts into tears.*)

HUBERT (*to* SERENA): There now. You have made her cry again.

SERENA: I claim no credit for that. She has wept at regular intervals from two o'clock yesterday afternoon until the early hours of this morning.

HUBERT: Do you blame her?

SERENA: No, Hubert. I do not blame her. She has every right to cry if she feels like it. I only wish that she would not feel like it quite so often.

HUBERT (*to* CHARLOTTE): My dearest heart, please try to control yourself.

CHARLOTTE: Don't come near me.

> AXEL *comes in from the terrace.*

AXEL: What is happening?

SERENA: Your wife has broken down again.

AXEL: Now see here, Charlotte—

CHARLOTTE: Leave me alone. I do not wish to speak to you. I do not wish to speak to anybody.

AXEL: In that case might I suggest that you go upstairs and lie down? You cannot appear at Mr. Spevin's jumble sale with red eyes.

CHARLOTTE: I am not going upstairs, and I am not going to the jumble sale either.

SERENA: It was agreed last night that we would all go to the jumble sale. Outward appearances at least must be upheld.

CHARLOTTE: I don't care any more what happens.

SERENA: Give her some wine, Mr. Diensen, she is becoming hysterical.

CHARLOTTE (*making a supreme effort and speaking quietly*): I do not want any wine. I want to know what you have decided to do, Hubert. I want to know now.

HUBERT: But, Charlotte—

CHARLOTTE: You have not spoken to me since last night. You have been for a long walk. During that time you must have arrived at some conclusion, made some sort of decision.

HUBERT: You mistrust my love for you. I can hear it in your voice. You are betraying me in your heart. I can feel it! I can feel it!

AXEL: Well, I'll be damned!

SERENA: Please, Mr. Diensen.

CHARLOTTE: Your wife has won, has she not, Hubert? You knew she would from the very beginning; she always has and she always will, is not that the truth? Is it not that that prevented you from speaking to me this morning and sent you off on your lonely walk; the realisation that it was no use fighting any more, that she was too strong for you, that you were bound by all the years of her dominance to give in, to surrender unconditionally, to squirm on the ground with your legs in the air like a beaten, faithful spaniel?

SERENA: An only moderately faithful spaniel.

HUBERT: The conversation has taken an ugly turn. I resent it. Your eyes are suddenly hard, Charlotte. There is a steely note

56

in your voice that I cannot recognise. You are dragging Boston
into Arcadia.

AXEL: If this is Arcadia, give me Kansas City.

SERENA: Please be quiet, Mr. Diensen.

CHARLOTTE (*ignoring all interruptions*): Your wife asked me a
question a short while ago, a question that I did not answer.
She asked me if I really loved you. Well, I answer it now, and
the answer is No.

HUBERT (*horrified*): I forbid you to say another word. This is
madness!

CHARLOTTE: I believed I loved you with every fibre of my being.
I was willing to sacrifice my reputation, to endure social
ostracism in order to spend the rest of my life with you, but
not now, not any more. The scales have fallen from my eyes, I
have seen you in your true colours. They are pale colours,
Hubert, and they fade too easily in the glare of conflict. Ever
since your wife and my husband arrived in this house
yesterday I have watched you twisting and turning, retreating
and evading. You have wit and charm and a noble heritage
indeed; but your character is watery.

HUBERT: Watery! May God forgive you.

CHARLOTTE (*with dignity, to* AXEL): I will return to London with
you whenever you wish, Axel. I will also endeavour, in every
way I can, to right the wrong I have done you. But please
remember one thing, will you? It was not your love that I
betrayed, merely your pride. Forgive me, Lady Heronden, for
so nearly shattering the admirable façade of your married life.
It would have been a cruel thing to do as it is so obviously all
you have left.

> CHARLOTTE *sweeps out, leaving an uncomfortable silence behind
> her.*
>
> HUBERT *breaks it.*

HUBERT (*bitterly to* SERENA): I hope you are satisfied.

SERENA: I am far from satisfied.

HUBERT: You have achieved your object. With implacable,
fiendish vandalism, you have rent the fabric of romance into a
thousand pieces; you have trampled brutally on a dream,
stamping it into the ground, mangling it beyond recognition.

You have ridden roughshod through my private heart swaggering and looting and burning until there is nothing left but emptiness and desolation. You are not a woman, Serena, you are a Juggernaut. I shall never forgive you for this. Never – never – never until the grave closes over me.

> HUBERT *stamps out on to the terrace.*

SERENA (*sits down*): I feel very tired.

AXEL: A little wine?

SERENA: Thank you.

AXEL (*pouring it*): We have won.

SERENA: Yes.

AXEL: I wonder if all victories carry with them such a curious sense of deflation?

SERENA: I expect so.

AXEL (*handing her a glass of wine*): This should be a moment of exultation.

SERENA: I know.

AXEL: It should make this rather acid Red wine taste like champagne.

SERENA (*sipping it*): It still tastes like rather acid Red wine.

AXEL: Have you forgiven me for my boorishness a little while ago?

SERENA: Yes. Have you forgiven me?

AXEL: Yes.

SERENA: And Charlotte, and Hubert?

AXEL: Yes, I suppose so. But I have not forgiven Fate.

SERENA: Why do you say that?

AXEL: Do you not know, Lady Heronden?

SERENA (*firmly*): No. Nor do I wish to. Perhaps after all we were wrong to have come, perhaps it would have been wiser to have let them go.

AXEL: For their sakes or our own?

SERENA: It would at least have been more dignified.

AXEL: Is dignity so all important?

SERENA: Oh yes – yes. To me it is. Vulgarity humiliates me. These last few days have made me so ashamed.

AXEL: And yet vulgarity can be warm, sometimes, warm and

lively and human. Dignity on the other hand is cold always. I am surprised that you set such store by it.

SERENA: There are different kinds. Please do not be too hard on dignity; it has much to recommend it.

AXEL: Did he really love Charlotte, do you suppose? Does he really love her?

SERENA: Oh no. It is all a question of degree, of capacity. Hubert has never really loved anybody. Not even me.

AXEL: Then he is a sad and dull man. An insensitive fool.

SERENA: I cannot permit you to speak like that of my recently reclaimed husband. It is most unsuitable.

AXEL: He must have loved you, ma'am, in your early married years when you were young together and the privileged world was at your feet, when he was handsome and gay and you were so beautiful.

SERENA: It pains me to have to confess that I was not beautiful, Mr. Diensen. I was gauche and skinny, my legs were too long and my shoulders bony. My eyes were good but alas, on the small side. In later years, however, I am glad to say that I improved.

AXEL: You certainly did.

SERENA: I am grateful for your vehemence. It is most comforting.

AXEL: And he never loved you, this poor lordling?

SERENA: He thought he did. He treated the idea of me most ardently, most tenderly, but it was his idea, not mine. The whole of our life together has been his idea really; I have merely carried it out. Even to coming here and spanking him and putting him in the corner. He relied upon it and expected it in his innermost heart, I am sure he did.

AXEL (*gently*): You had a son and he died?

SERENA: Yes. I had a son and he died.

AXEL: And nothing more? Nothing else – ever?

SERENA: A comfortable and civilised life, Mr. Diensen, and, during the last few years at least, an excellent cook.

AXEL: I congratulate you.

SERENA: Thank you.

At *this moment* OCTAVIA, COUNTESS OF BONNINGTON, *appears*

on the terrace. Her age might be anything between sixty and eighty.
Her hair is snow white and her skin leathery brown from exposure to
the sun. She is wearing a shapeless old russet-coloured tea gown and
sandals. She also wears three ropes of valuable pearls and several
expensive bracelets. She tiptoes into the room unobserved by SERENA
and AXEL. *She scrutinises them carefully through a lorgnette which*
she carries suspended by a wide black ribbon round her neck.

OCTAVIA: They were right then, my wild, fervent voices!

AXEL (*turning swiftly*): Good God!

SERENA (*rising hurriedly*): What on earth—?

OCTAVIA: Do not move, either of you. I absolutely forbid it.
Stand there where you are, shining with your secret radiance.
It is so sweet to see, so very, very sweet.

AXEL: You may not be aware of it but this is a private villa,
madame.

OCTAVIA: I know it well. It lies ghostly and empty for long
stretches of time, and then suddenly, hey presto! it comes to
life again. Lights appear in the windows and smoke curls from
the kitchen chimney, which incidentally needs sweeping, and I
listen on my hill for the sound of lovers' voices.

AXEL: Madame, I really feel that—

OCTAVIA: If I have offended you I apologise. But I was unable to
resist the impulse to come. My instincts tugged at me and I
had to obey them, I had to see for myself if it was true.

SERENA: I fear there has been some mistake.

OCTAVIA: No mistake. No mistake at all. And I was so afraid that
there would be, that they'd lied to me; you know what they
are, always prone to over-egg the pudding, always given to
exaggeration.

AXEL: We have no idea, madame, what you are talking about.

OCTAVIA: Never mind, they were right this time. All is well. Oh,
indeed, there is no mistake. Every twitter, every whisper was
correct. How happy I am, not only for you but for myself.

SERENA: Who was right? And about what?

OCTAVIA: You are naturally shy and a little bewildered. That is
only to be expected, the first vital step is so breath-taking, but
once taken there is no return; you will find that the awareness
of that is most soothing.

SERENA (*stiffly*): I am Lady Heronden.

OCTAVIA: Of course you are, my dear. I recognised you immediately. I knew your grandmother well in the old days; a lovely creature! So charming in some ways and so excessively disagreeable in others. Is she still alive or has God taken her?

SERENA: She died seventeen years ago.

OCTAVIA: They all go, all my old cronies, rustling away into the shadows like leaves. Do you know that I have outlived forty-three of the girls I was at school with? At moments the realisation of it fills me with splendid elation and then back swings the pendulum and I am plunged in loneliness. My little pug Lancelot died the day before yesterday which was a sad shock, although the end had been clearly in sight for some months. He was nearly fourteen years old, which in doggy language means a very great age indeed. But let us not talk of my troubles, let us talk of you, the gallantry of your magnificent gesture, the gauntlet you have so defiantly flung in the teeth of the world.

AXEL: I hate to disillusion you, madame, but—

OCTAVIA: Pray cast evasion to the wind, let us be utterly frank with each other. I am Octavia, Lady Bonnington.

SERENA: Ah! I am beginning to understand.

OCTAVIA: But perhaps you would be more likely to know me by my pen-name, Lucien Snow. There now – does not that wake an echo?

AXEL: I fear, madame, that—

OCTAVIA: I wrote *The Faraway Lovers, Mariposa, The Story of an Eager Heart* – Mariposa is the Spanish for butterfly, you know – and *Tender Was She*. That was the story of a high-bred English girl who ran off into the Sahara with a Bedouin. It was banned by all the public libraries but went into several editions.

SERENA (*firmly*): This is Mr. Diensen, Mr. Axel Diensen.

OCTAVIA (*scrutinising* AXEL *through her lorgnette*): How foolish people are, are they not? So determined to get hold of the wrong ends of sticks. All the villagers near me have described you as an English 'Milor' and you my dear – (*She turns to* SERENA.) – as petite and blonde with blue eyes!

SERENA: Lady Bonnington—

OCTAVIA: Do not deny anything I implore you. Do not attempt

to repudiate the lovely flame that has fused your hungry
hearts together. As a matter of fact it would be a waste of time
for you even to try. I am an old woman and my life is nearly
done, but I am neither deaf nor blind. I can still hear the
beating of wings, still see the stars in lovers' eyes. I stood on
the terrace a moment ago feeling the vibrations between you,
the air tremulous with unspoken longing—

SERENA: Please stop, Lady Bonnington. This is extremely embarrassing.

OCTAVIA: Embarrassing! What rubbish! You have burnt your
bridges as I did once long ago. You have turned your backs on
stale modesties and petty conventions. You are now free to
plunge laughing into the mountain streams, to ride naked
together across the meadows—

AXEL: Just a minute, ma'am—

OCTAVIA (*ignoring him*): This is a land where love is understood
and revered and seen in its right perspective. Embarrassing
indeed! The word belongs to London and fogs and fusty
drawing-rooms; there is no place for it here.

SERENA (*helplessly*): Oh dear – what *are* we to do?

OCTAVIA (*suddenly taking* SERENA's *hands in hers*): Do not be angry
with me, I beg of you, for flashing in upon you like a mad
bird.

SERENA: It is not a question of being angry, Lady Bonnington, it
is merely that—

OCTAVIA (*sympathetically*): I know – I know – I understand more
than you think I do.

SERENA: I am afraid you don't – you see—

OCTAVIA: I have thought about you so much since you arrived.
If I go up on to my roof I can see the lights of this villa quite
clearly. I have imagined you wandering together in the garden
under the stars and standing hand in hand on the terrace
gazing out over the sea. It has given me such deep pleasure to
think of you here, so near me, starting out together on the
loveliest adventure of all. I promise you I will not come again
unless you invite me: I make no plea for company for I am
well accustomed to being alone. But if you should happen to
wander up the hill at any time, the gates of my house are just

before you come to the village, on the right: there is a little
placard with 'Villa La Joie' written on it, a trifle faded I fear,
but you cannot possibly miss it. A bientôt. Stay true to
yourselves and to one another. That is all that really matters.

*She waves her hand, goes swiftly out on to the terrace and
disappears.*

SERENA (*sinking down*): How dreadful that was! How perfectly
dreadful!

AXEL (*staring after her*): Poor lady – Poor old girl.

SERENA (*laughing, a trifle nervously*): She is mad, raving, raving
mad.

AXEL (*raising his glass*): I drink to her all the same.

SERENA: Mr. Diensen!

AXEL: I drink to her frantic imagery, to her wild, fervent inner
voices, to her dead pug dog and to her kindly, lonely heart.

SERENA: Have you become raving mad also?

AXEL (*putting his glass down with a bang on the table*): Yes, ma'am, I
believe I have. So help me God I believe I have!

He walks out of the room slamming the door behind him.

THE LIGHTS FADE

Scene III

The same evening.

SERENA, CHARLOTTE, HUBERT *and* AXEL *are sitting about
the room drinking coffee. The atmosphere is a trifle strained. They
are all in travelling clothes.*

SERENA (*to* CHARLOTTE): More coffee, Mrs. Diensen?

CHARLOTTE (*dimly*): No, thank you.

SERENA (*reminiscently*): Poor Mr. Spevin.

HUBERT: There is no necessity to pity Mr. Spevin. He is
absolutely delighted with himself and thanks to your misguided interest in his unpleasant little church, he will probably
bore the life out of us indefinitely. We shall be inundated with

letters by every post, asking for subscriptions and telling us news of his congregation.

SERENA: We can read them aloud. It will be something to do in the evenings.

AXEL: If I may say so, Lord Heronden, I thought that your speech at the drawing of the raffle ticket was a model of brevity and elegance.

HUBERT (*disagreeably*): Thank you very much.

AXEL: You spoke with such ringing sincerity and your reference to the church being 'An English island in a foreign sea' was so apt that it fully merited the burst of gratifying applause it received.

HUBERT: I find your attempts at humour heavy-handed, Mr. Diensen.

AXEL (*equably*): That is what Charlotte always says.

SERENA: There is no point in continuing to be disagreeable, Hubert. We cannot sit in dead silence and we might just as well talk about the jumble sale as anything else.

HUBERT: Why the devil doesn't the carriage come?

SERENA: It was not ordered until half-past nine.

HUBERT: I find this situation absolutely intolerable.

SERENA: I quite agree. But it cannot be helped, can it? Therefore the only thing to do is to make the best of it.

HUBERT: Would you care to take a stroll in the garden, Charlotte?

CHARLOTTE: Certainly not, thank you.

SERENA: More coffee, Mr. Diensen?

AXEL: No, thank you, ma'am.

SERENA: Hubert?

HUBERT: No, thank you.

SERENA (*after a long pause*): It will be interesting to discover, when we reach London, how the Tichborne case is progressing. I haven't seen a newspaper for days.

HUBERT: Damn the Tichborne case!

SERENA (*to* CHARLOTTE): I do think that on the whole there has been far too much fuss made over the Shah of Persia's visit, don't you?

CHARLOTTE (*listlessly*): Yes – yes, I suppose so.

SERENA: They have rushed him to the Opera and the Albert Hall and the Abbey, they even took him in the Underground railway to Madame Tussaud's. The poor little man must be exhausted. He was probably impressed though. I don't expect they have them in Persia.

HUBERT: What?

SERENA: Underground railways.

HUBERT: I doubt if they have an Albert Hall either.

SERENA (*persevering*): I wonder if the Lathburys' ball was a success. It took place last night.

HUBERT (*grimly*): Did it?

SERENA: They apparently took an endless amount of trouble over it. Harriet told me that—

HUBERT (*vehemently*): For the love of God have done, Serena. It is no use trying to behave as though nothing has happened. We are all on edge. The very air we breathe is acrid with disillusion and emotional strain and there is no sense in stubbornly making believe that it is not. It is perfectly understood that when we arrive back in London no stain, no blemish shall be allowed to deface the shining, united front we present to our foolish friends. All that is agreed. You are the conqueror: you have dictated the terms of surrender and we, the cringing vanquished, will abide by them. But we are not in London yet; we still have time, a few hours, in which to lick our wounds and prepare our bland and expressionless faces for the parade. Leave us in peace and quiet then for just those few hours. Be merciful in your hideous triumph! Or is that too much to ask?

AXEL (*angrily*): Kindly refrain from using that tone to Lady Heronden in my presence.

HUBERT: Go back to your wild west, Mr. Diensen. Return to your Colonial wigwams! And mind your own business!

> HUBERT *stamps out of the room.*
>
> AXEL *makes a movement to follow him but* SERENA, *with a gesture, restrains him.*

SERENA: No brawling, I beg of you, Mr. Diensen. Please sit down.

AXEL: But—

SERENA: My husband has always had an overdeveloped gift for oratory. I believe that when he was young his initiation speech in the House of Lords caused quite a sensation.

AXEL: I'll bet it did.

SERENA: You, as a railway man, will agree I am sure, that all high-powered locomotives must be allowed to let off steam occasionally.

CHARLOTTE (*rising*): If you will excuse me, Lady Heronden, I will retire to my room. I have not quite finished packing my dressing-case.

AXEL (*urgently*): Stay here, Charlotte. Your dressing-case can wait.

CHARLOTTE: I cannot stay here. What Hubert said about the strain is only too true. It is suffocating me.

   She goes out hurriedly.

SERENA: Please do not let me keep you here if you wish to follow your wife upstairs, Mr. Diensen.

AXEL: I would like a little more coffee if there is any.

SERENA: There is, but it is not very hot.

AXEL: It will do.

SERENA (*pouring coffee into his cup*): My efforts to ameliorate the situation have been dismally unsuccessful, I fear.

AXEL: You did your best, ma'am.

SERENA: Not quite my best. I can be more subtle than that.

AXEL: I have no doubt of it.

SERENA: Perhaps I did behave a little badly, but I found the temptation irresistible. They both looked so hang-dog.

AXEL: You are a truly remarkable woman.

SERENA: Please smoke a cigarette. Instinct tells me that you are longing to.

AXEL: Thank you. It is true that tobacco can be soothing in moments of crisis.

SERENA: There is no longer any crisis. Merely anticlimax.

AXEL (*lighting a cigarette*): Uncomfortable though, however you describe it.

SERENA: Yes, very uncomfortable. I think we must be prepared for certain stresses and strains during the next few months. Our victory was too swift perhaps.

AXEL: I shall always remember this episode, this strange adventure we have shared.

SERENA: I too, Mr. Diensen. (*After a silence.*) You will be returning to America shortly?

AXEL: Yes. I am impatient to be gone. The social life of London that Charlotte so enjoys is to me nothing but a restless vacation. I have only endured it for her sake. I want to get back to work.

SERENA: You have always worked? All your life?

AXEL: Yes, ma'am. It has become a habit like smoking; I cannot give it up. My father was an engineer on the early railroads. He drove trains in the dangerous years, through Indian ambushes and storms and blizzards and droughts. We lived in a little village in Illinois which is now a thriving town. I started work when I was thirteen.

SERENA: Thirteen?

AXEL: I was a news-butcher!

SERENA: What is that?

AXEL: A cheeky, shrill-voiced little boy who prances through the rolling trains selling newspapers and questionable magazines and pea-nuts and chewing-tobacco. I learned the facts of life early. Later, of course, I rose from the ranks, but those first years were useful. I was a fairly bright lad, ma'am.

SERENA (*with a smile*): I would never doubt that for an instant, Mr. Diensen.

AXEL: I worked on freight trains, passenger trains and cattle trains. To me the future always lay at the end of a line. The Iron Horse was my Godhead; as cruel and unpredictable as any of the Gods of Antiquity. He dragged me back and forth across the prairies and deserts and mountains of my country. He took my father from me and two of my brothers. He also, more benevolently, disposed of an uncle in Wisconsin who left me eighteen thousand dollars in his will. That was the beginning of fortune. It seemed to me then as it seems to me now that the destiny of America lies in the increasing power and expansion of her railroads – the annihilation of distance – the drawing together of isolated peoples – the – (*He breaks off.*) I

am boring you. This is my hobby horse, my iron hobby horse.
You must not encourage me.

SERENA: Please go on, Mr. Diensen.

AXEL: You are kind, very kind.

SERENA: I am interested.

AXEL: That is kinder still.

SERENA: Pray continue.

AXEL: There is so much that I would like to say to you but my
intention falters.

SERENA: Why should it?

AXEL: I envy your husband his gift of words. To you, whose ears
are attuned to so much glittering hyperbole, my homespun,
rough-shod phrases must sound sadly uninspired.

SERENA: Come, come, Mr. Diensen, this continual harping on
your verbal inadequacy comes perilously near affectation. I am
not entirely imperceptive and although our acquaintanceship
has been brief I have already suspected that your far-away
railroads provided you with ample opportunities for reading.

AXEL: You have seen through me, ma'am. Your sharp mind has
unmasked my pitiful little secret.

SERENA: Nonsense, Mr. Diensen. You are too assured to cherish
pitiful secrets.

AXEL: Assured! Why, at this very moment the ground is shaking
beneath my feet. You are undermining the very foundations of
my character.

SERENA: Such exaggeration rings false, but I presume you meant
it to.

AXEL: Come to my country one day, ma'am. Your own true
quality would immediately recognise its valour and forgive its
young vulgarities. It is a great territory, still untamed and rich
with promise; even richer in variety. From the white frame
houses of New England to the Florida swamps; from the
painted streets of Charleston to the adobe villages of California
there is so much diversity, so much to fire your imagination.
Oh, Lord, the whole of life seems newly washed, seen from
the open door of a caboose.

SERENA: Caboose?

AXEL: The tail end of a freight train, the last car of all, a small shaky cabin with a twisted iron ladder climbing to the roof, that is the home of the brakeman. There he sits, hour in hour out, watching the trees marching along and the cinders and earth and sands of America slipping away beneath the wheels. He can watch the sun set over the gentle farmlands of Wisconsin and rise over the interminable prairies of Nebraska and Illinois and Kansas. Those flat, flat lands bring the sky so low that on clear nights you can almost feel that you are rattling along through the stars. It is rougher going in the mountains where there are sharp curves and steep gradients and the locomotive strains and gasps and fills the air with steam and sparks; tunnels close round you, infernos of noise and sulphurous smoke, then suddenly you are in the open and can breathe again and there are snow-covered peaks towering above you and pine forests and the sound of waterfalls. Over it all and through it all, the familiar, reassuring noise of the train; a steady beat on the level stretches when the wheels click over the joints in the rails but changing into wilder rhythms when you clatter over bridges and crossings and intersections. The railroad is my dream, ma'am, the whole meaning of my life, my pride and all my hopes for the future – come to my country one day. Let me take you in a private car from Chicago to the West, a car specially designed by George Mortimer Pullman. The luxury of it will soothe and startle you; sofas and chairs of damask of the most violent patterns but infinitely comfortable; dark, grinning servants to wait on you; fresh iced celery from Kalamazoo. Rainbow trout from the Rocky Mountains, and outside the wide windows of your drawing-room you shall see the New World passing by . . .

SERENA: I will remember your invitation, Mr. Diensen, even though my circumstances may never allow me to accept it. I will also remember . . . (*She stops abruptly and turns away.*)

AXEL: What is it that you were about to say? What made you stop short so suddenly?

SERENA: It was of no consequence.

AXEL: Please do not withdraw, Lady Heronden. It seemed to me that perhaps, at last, we were becoming friends.

SERENA: We will always be friends, Mr. Diensen.

AXEL: Do you mean that, ma'am?

SERENA: Yes, I do.

AXEL (*looking at her*): The carriage will be here at any moment now.

SERENA: I know.

AXEL: Good-bye, Lady Heronden.

SERENA: Good-bye, Mr. Diensen.

She puts out her hand. He bends down and kisses it, then he goes over to the window and stands looking out at the stars with his back to her. HUBERT *comes in wearing an overcoat and hat.*

HUBERT: Françoise and Jean have gone on in the wagonette with the luggage. The carriage is waiting.

AXEL: Where is Charlotte?

HUBERT: She is waiting too. It is time to go.

SERENA (*rising*): Very well.

HUBERT: I think you both might have the grace to look a little more cheerful in your triumph; the atmosphere is full of regrets.

SERENA: I am not feeling particularly triumphant, Hubert.

HUBERT: You should, my dear, you really should. You have got your own way. But then you always do, don't you!

He goes out.

SERENA (*as he goes*): Not quite always. Come, Mr. Diensen.

SERENA *sweeps out followed by* AXEL *as*

THE CURTAIN FALLS

ACT III: Scene I

A year later.

SERENA's *sitting-room in Heronden House, Belgrave Square.*

When the curtain rises, the french windows are wide open, warm afternoon sunlight is flooding into the room and a hurdy-gurdy is playing outside in the square.

SERENA *is seated at her escritoire writing a letter. Occasionally she pauses to think of a word. Suddenly she rises and goes swiftly to the window; she fumbles in her reticule for some coins, then throws them to the organ-grinder and waves her hand gaily. She returns to her letter smiling, adds a couple of words to it and is sealing it up when* HUBERT *comes into the room. She gives a slight start and slips the letter into her bag.*

HUBERT: Ah – there you are, my dear.

SERENA: You say that as though you expected me to be somewhere else. I am usually here at this time of day.

HUBERT (*absently*): Yes – yes, I know you are. (*He wanders over to the windows.*) Those damned street organs should not be allowed.

SERENA: On the contrary I think they should be encouraged.

HUBERT: In heaven's name why?

SERENA: The sound has a certain charm.

HUBERT: I find little charm in being unable to hear myself speak.

SERENA: I can well understand that, my dear, but on the whole you contrive to hear yourself speak a great deal more than most people.

HUBERT: Charm indeed! The ghastly instrument is out of tune.

SERENA: Perhaps it is but that is part of its appeal. A muffin bell also is out of tune, even the cry of a lavender seller may not be vocally accurate but there is a sweetness in it, an evocative quality. London would be sad without her gentle noises.

HUBERT: Stuff and nonsense!

SERENA: Poppycock! Fiddle-faddle! and hell and damnation! (*She laughs.*)

HUBERT (*startled*): Serena!

SERENA (*meekly*): Yes, Hubert?

HUBERT: What on earth is the matter with you?

SERENA: Nothing, nothing at all.

HUBERT: You seem to be in a strange mood.

SERENA: You also are in a strange mood, more irascible, less cheerful than mine. Has anything happened to upset you?

HUBERT (*shortly*): No.

SERENA: You lunched with poor Roderick?

HUBERT: Yes.

SERENA: He generally amuses you.

HUBERT: Well, he didn't to-day.

SERENA: Poor Roderick.

HUBERT: Why do you always say 'Poor Roderick'?

SERENA: There is something in his determined buoyancy that commands my pity.

HUBERT: He has everthing that his heart could desire.

SERENA: Perhaps that is why.

HUBERT: Wit, money, good looks, an understanding wife—

SERENA: I detect a sting of envy in your voice. Do you find me obtuse?

HUBERT: No, Serena. I most certainly do not.

SERENA: Would you say that, on the whole, our marriage had been a success?

HUBERT: What an extraordinary question!

SERENA: Leaving aside the unfortunate episode of last year, would you say, all things considered, that our long years together had been reasonably happy?

HUBERT: Of course I would.

SERENA (*lightly*): It's not quite enough, is it?

HUBERT: What on earth do you mean?

SERENA: 'Till death do us part'. I have always thought that that particular phrase was didactic and a trifle ingenuous. Life provides so many reasons for parting, death only one.

HUBERT: What is in your mind, Serena? What has prompted this abrupt soul-searching?

SERENA: Hardly soul-searching, merely a light, introspective summing-up.

HUBERT: Summing-up of what?

SERENA: Debits and credits, gains and losses. Surely all well-conducted businesses lay aside a certain time each year for stock-taking?

HUBERT: And how do you find that we stand at the moment? How are our securities?

SERENA (*gaily*): Gilt-edged, Hubert, a trifle static but wonderfully gilt-edged.

HUBERT: Splendid.

SERENA: Yes, it is, isn't it?

HUBERT: You are leaving for Heronden this evening?

SERENA: Yes, on the seven-fifteen train.

HUBERT: I presume that Alfred knows?

SERENA: Yes, he is meeting me with the dog-cart at Deal.

HUBERT: Why the dog-cart? It will be dark by the time you arrive.

SERENA: There is a moon to-night, a full moon, didn't you know? The sea will be calm and I shall be able to see the lights on the French coast, so near, so very near.

HUBERT: There may be a fog, or at least a heavy sea mist. There frequently is at this time of year.

SERENA: There won't be to-night.

HUBERT: I am willing to admit that you are a brilliant organiser, Serena, but surely even you must stop short at arranging the climate.

SERENA: I am so glad that you think I have been efficient. You would give me a kind reference, wouldn't you, if you had to? Honest, sober, industrious and—

HUBERT: What *are* you talking about?

SERENA: I am not sure that I know.

HUBERT: I am afraid I shall not be able to get down before Saturday. I have to dine with that fellow Mallory on Friday.

SERENA: Which fellow Mallory?

HUBERT: You know perfectly well. I told you about him last week. He is an Irishman.

SERENA: How delightful.

HUBERT: He is also a first-class shot.

SERENA: The Irish nearly always are, aren't they? I suppose they have to be.

HUBERT: That is what I wanted to talk to you about.

SERENA: Shooting?

HUBERT: No, Mallory.

SERENA: Oh.

HUBERT: I have decided to go to East Africa with him.

SERENA (*astonished*): Hubert!

HUBERT: He is a professional big-game hunter; he is organising an expedition into the interior, and has invited me to join it.

SERENA: So you really think you will enjoy that?

HUBERT: Why on earth shouldn't I?

SERENA: You have always been so careful of your creature comforts. I find it difficult to imagine you charging through tropical jungles with a gun.

HUBERT: You don't hunt big game in tropical jungles.

SERENA: Nonsense, my dear, of course you do. I was reading about it in *Blackwood's*. There are swarms of insects and deadly snakes and the air is so stifling that you gasp for breath. I should think you would positively loathe it. When I remember the fuss you made about the heat at Lords only last week—

HUBERT: I am leaving at the end of the month.

SERENA: I see. How long will you be gone?

HUBERT: I am not sure. Six months at least.

SERENA: So it is all decided.

HUBERT: Yes. (*There is a pause.*) Do you mind?

SERENA (*absently*): No – no, Hubert. I don't mind. Why should I?

HUBERT (*apologetically*): I had to say definitely whether I would go or not. Mallory has to plan the whole business and there isn't much time.

SERENA: Will it be a large expedition?

HUBERT: About a dozen all told, I believe.

SERENA: Anyone you know?

HUBERT: No, I don't think so.

SERENA: And you like this man Mallory well enough to spend six months in his company?

HUBERT: He is an engaging fellow. Occasionally witty and always agreeable; and there will be the others.

SERENA (*turning away*): Yes, yes, of course there will.

HUBERT: Are you angry?

SERENA: No, not in the least.

HUBERT: It was perhaps inconsiderate of me to decide to go without consulting you.

SERENA: Were you afraid that I might raise objections? Put difficulties in the way?

HUBERT: No, not exactly. I expect I was a little afraid that you might laugh me out of it.

SERENA: Poor Hubert.

HUBERT: Why do you say that?

SERENA: Chained to a dragon.

HUBERT: You over-dramatise yourself, my love. You are no dragon; merely a woman of extreme sensibility who has become suddenly bored with her own social rectitude. Poor Serena.

SERENA: How perceptive you are!

HUBERT: I regard you, my dear, with the most fearful respect.

SERENA: Tempered, I hope, with at least a residue of affection?

HUBERT: Will you miss me when I have gone?

SERENA: I have missed you for years.

>   CATCHPOLE *enters.*

CATCHPOLE (*announcing*): Lady Harriet Ripley.

>   HARRIET RIPLEY *comes in.*

SERENA: My dear Harriet! (*They kiss.*) Bring the tea, will you, Catchpole?

CATCHPOLE: Very good, milady.

>   *He goes out.*

HARRIET: How are you, Hubert? (*She shakes hands with him.*)

HUBERT: Well, thank you, Harriet, monotonously well.

HARRIET: Well, that is more than I am – this heat is completely exhausting me. You must be longing to get down to Heronden, Serena.

SERENA: I am, indeed.

HARRIET (*sitting down and proceeding to take off her gloves*): I hear that you had luncheon with poor Roderick to-day, Hubert. How is he?

HUBERT: Poor Roderick has just made eight thousand pounds on the Stock Exchange, his horse, Tantivy, has won four races in three weeks, and his mother-in-law returned to Argyllshire yesterday.

HARRIET: No wonder Elsie looked so excitable at the Royal Academy this afternoon. She was talking at the top of her voice and darting from picture to picture like a bluebottle. She *does* wear the most ramshackle hats does she not? You would think with all her money that she *might* make a little more effort, wouldn't you?

> CATCHPOLE *and a* FOOTMAN *enter with the tea things.*

Ah, here is tea – thank heaven! I am quite prostrate.

SERENA: Are you dining in, Hubert?

HUBERT: No, I am meeting Harry at Boodles' at six o'clock. I must go and change.

SERENA: Surely you will have a cup of tea first?

HUBERT: No, my love. I detest tea and I am sure you and Harriet have much to gossip about.

SERENA: Indeed we have. I feel, Harriet, that you should be the first to know that Hubert is leaving me.

HARRIET: Serena!

SERENA: He is going to hunt big game in Africa.

HARRIET: Good gracious! Will you like that, Hubert?

HUBERT: Of course I shall. Why shouldn't I?

HARRIET: It seems so unlike you somehow. I cannot imagine you stalking solemnly for days and days across the African veldt.

HUBERT: I am not going anywhere near the African veldt.

HARRIET: But you of all people! You who set such store by the luxuries of life—

HUBERT (*exasperated*): Both you and Serena seem to regard me as a sort of spineless sybarite, an ageing ninny who is afraid of getting his feet wet. Let me hasten to assure you that you are both entirely mistaken. I am sick and tired of this stuffy insular groove in which I have been stuck fast for years. I long with all my heart and soul to get out into the open for a little; to lie under the stars by a flickering camp-fire, to fill my lungs with fresher, cleaner air, to rest my eyes on new and strange horizons.

HARRIET: Well, at any rate I hope the weather will be nice.

HUBERT: The weather will *not* be nice, Harriet. It may be violent and unpredictable, it may be hot, cold, dry and wet to excess, but it will never, *never* be nice!

> *By this time* CATCHPOLE *and the* FOOTMAN *have arranged the tea-table – and withdrawn from the room.*

SERENA: There is no occasion to bellow at Harriet, my dear. She was merely wishing you well.

HUBERT: I know she was, Serena. I am quite sure that you both wish me well, but I would be more appreciative of your well wishing if it were neither pitying nor patronising. Up to now, it has been both. As I shall probably not see you again before you leave for the station, I will say good-bye now.

SERENA: Very well, dear.

HUBERT: Good-bye for the moment, Harriet.

HARRIET: Good-bye, Hubert. I still hope that you will not live to regret this rather bizarre enterprise.

HUBERT (*ignoring her*): You may expect me on Saturday, Serena.

SERENA (*returning from far away*): Saturday? Oh, yes – of course – Saturday.

HUBERT: Tell Alford to meet me with the trap. I will arrive on the two-thirty from Cannon Street.

SERENA: Yes, Hubert.

HUBERT: And if Hannibal's foot has showed no signs of improvement you had better send for the vet.

SERENA: Yes, Hubert.

HUBERT: That is all, I think, except for Wilcox and his damned thistles, but I will deal with him myself.

SERENA: Yes, Hubert.

HUBERT: Good-bye, Serena. (*He turns to go.*)

SERENA (*with a sudden note of urgency in her voice*): Oh, Hubert—

HUBERT (*turning back*): What is it?

SERENA: It is only that I do wish you well, Hubert, neither pityingly nor patronisingly, but with all my heart – truly I do.

HUBERT (*surprised*): Why – Serena—?

SERENA: Good-bye, Hubert. (*She rises quickly and kisses him on the cheek.*)

> HUBERT *goes out – and she returns to the tea-table.*

HARRIET: You look flushed.

SERENA: Flushed?

HARRIET: Almost as though you were feverish.

SERENA: I think I am a little feverish.

HARRIET: My dear!

SERENA: Do not be alarmed. It is a mental state more than a physical one.

HARRIET: Why? What has caused it?

SERENA (*laughing*): I have not the remotest idea. Is not that extraordinary?

HARRIET (*suspiciously*): Most extraordinary.

SERENA: Perhaps it is something to do with the climate.

HARRIET: Has anything happened? Anything disturbing?

SERENA: No, I can't think of anything. I saw Mr. Disraeli driving along the Mall this morning. He looked a trifle yellow I thought, but it didn't disturb me at all. After all he has looked fairly yellow for years, has he not?

HARRIET: Never mind about Mr. Disraeli for the moment.

SERENA: Of course I did wave to him which I would never have done to Mr. Gladstone.

HARRIET: Where did you have luncheon?

SERENA: With Etta in Kensington. Ronald and Elizabeth were there, and that moist young man from the German Embassy whose name I can never remember.

HARRIET: Gerhardt von Spiegal, I expect. He always goes everywhere.

SERENA: I cannot imagine why, can you?

HARRIET: He is supposed to be very intelligent.

SERENA: He betrayed no tell-tale signs of it at luncheon. All he did was to eat a great deal and discuss the Princess of Wales's fringe.

HARRIET: Go on.

SERENA: At three o'clock I met Alice at Peter Robinson's and stood by in mute dismay while she chose the most hideous curtain material. Perhaps that is what sent my temperature up!

Then I came home, and Miss Francis arrived to do my nails. That is all, really.

HARRIET: I must say I do not know what we should all do without Miss Francis.

SERENA: She is certainly an excellent manicurist.

HARRIET: She is also a positive mine of information.

SERENA (*a little coldly*): Is she indeed?

HARRIET: Did she say anthing about that rumpus at the Massinghams'?

SERENA: No.

HARRIET: You should have asked her. It is a fascinating story.

SERENA: I do not encourage Miss Francis to gossip.

HARRIET: Then you should, my dear, you miss a great deal.

SERENA: You really are incorrigible, Harriet.

HARRIET: She can be very entertaining if she chooses. After all, most of our friends employ her.

SERENA: Unwisely, it would seem.

HARRIET: It was she who first told me about the Diensens last year.

SERENA (*looking up*): The Diensens?

HARRIET: She, Mrs. Diensen, ran off, you know, to the south of France with a man called Baxter-Ellis, and her husband had to go and fetch her back. I believe there were the most appalling scenes, but it was all hushed up.

SERENA: And how did the redoubtable Miss Francis find out about it?

HARRIET: Through Mrs. Diensen's maid, apparently. Do you mean to say you didn't know?

SERENA: No. I am singularly innocent about that kind of thing. I always understood that they were a devoted couple.

HARRIET: But you saw quite a lot of them. You must have guessed that something was amiss?

SERENA: They dined here once or twice, that is all.

HARRIET: If you ask me, I think *he* is a bit of a dark horse.

SERENA (*dreamily*): A dark Iron Horse.

HARRIET: What did you say?

SERENA: Nothing.

HARRIET: He is back in England, you know, without her!

SERENA: Is he really?

HARRIET: Violet Trevor saw him at Kew Gardens last week, with a mysterious woman.

SERENA: Heavily veiled, I trust?

HARRIET: As a matter of fact, I believe she was.

SERENA: Toast?

She hands her the hot dish.

HARRIET: No, thank you.

SERENA: That chocolate cake comes from Buszard's. It is quite delicious.

HARRIET (*shaking her head*): According to Miss Francis they are actually in process of being divorced. She is living in Boston with her family while it is all arranged.

SERENA: How wise.

HARRIET: Personally my sympathies are with her. I always found him rather a bore, didn't you?

SERENA: Deadly.

HARRIET: I have come to the conclusion that I detest rugged characters.

SERENA: They can be disconcerting.

HARRIET: Did Hubert like him?

SERENA: Immensely. They used to go for long walks together.

HARRIET: Long walks?

SERENA: Hubert has always been fascinated by trains, you know. I remember him talking a great deal about them on our honeymoon. Of course the whole industry has made vast strides since then and Mr. Diensen was able to bring him up to date as it were.

HARRIET: I see.

SERENA: We really should try to learn more about railways, they so often bring out the best in a man.

HARRIET: How can you be so ridiculous!

SERENA: Would you like some more tea?

HARRIET: No, thank you. (*After a slight pause.*) Will you mind Hubert going to Africa?

SERENA: We must ask Miss Francis, she will be bound to know.

HARRIET: No, but seriously, do you?

SERENA: Of course not.

HARRIET: It was rather a sudden decision, wasn't it?

SERENA: I believe that he has had the idea in his mind for some time. I am sure that it will do him a great deal of good. Take him out of himself.

HARRIET: It will also take him out of harm's way.

SERENA: Harm's way?

HARRIET: It is no use pretending that you don't know what I mean.

SERENA: I am not pretending. I have not the least idea what you mean.

HARRIET (*with a little laugh*): Really, Serena!

SERENA: What are you hinting at, Harriet?

HARRIET: Hubert has a new 'friend'.

SERENA: That does not surprise me. He is naturally gregarious.

HARRIET: This one is brunette and very vivacious. I am told that she has a charming singing voice, untrained, you know, but absolutely true.

SERENA: Hubert often pretends to have an ear for music, but he hasn't really, so it won't matter much whether her voice is true or not.

HARRIET: Do you seriously mean to tell me that you know nothing about Hubert and this Mrs. Mallory?

SERENA (*sharply*): Mrs. what?

HARRIET: Mallory. She is Irish, so is her husband. Apparently they are rather rolling stones, always travelling about the world. Charles Barrington met them in Egypt last year. I don't think he formed a very favourable impression of them.

SERENA: Why?

HARRIET: It seems that he, Mr. Mallory, is none too scrupulous over money matters.

SERENA: And the wife? Is she unscrupulous too?

HARRIET: Very, I believe.

SERENA: Oh, poor Hubert!

HARRIET: That is what I meant when I said that the trip to Africa would take him out of harm's way.

SERENA: I see it all now.

HARRIET: Is he leaving soon?

SERENA: Yes, at the end of the month.

HARRIET: That should be a great relief to you.

SERENA (*laughing*): It is! Oh, it is!

HARRIET: Why are you laughing?

SERENA: Because I feel gay. I have felt gay all day.

HARRIET: You are certainly in a very strange mood.

SERENA: Hubert said that only a little while ago. I was listening to a hurdy-gurdy playing in the Square, and all at once everything seemed to be vibrant and sweet and full of furtive excitement.

HARRIET: Furtive excitements? What *do* you mean?

SERENA: If he had come into the room a moment later he would probably have discovered me hopping about the floor kicking my legs in the air like a ballet dancer.

HARRIET (*slightly scandalised*): Serena!

SERENA: How do I look Harriet? Tell me – be a mirror and tell me true. From where you are sitting can you see any crow's feet, any wrinkles?

HARRIET: How absurd you are. Of course I can't.

SERENA: But if I bend closer, there – like that. (*She bends towards* HARRIET.) Now – how do I look?

HARRIET: Candidly, my dear, you look unbalanced.

SERENA: That does not matter. It is the texture that counts. My skin is still soft, is it not? Soft enough at any rate.

HARRIET (*sternly*): Soft enough for *what*, Serena?

SERENA: Soft enough to compensate a little for the hardness of my character.

HARRIET: What rubbish you talk.

SERENA: Do you think there is still time? Do you think it is not too late?

HARRIET: Something must have happened to make you behave like this. What is it?

SERENA: The hurdy-gurdy, perhaps; or the sudden vision I had of poor Hubert filing away so diligently at his chains.

HARRIET: Chains?

SERENA: The stubborn romantic, the eternal troubadour, still eager to sing his lilting ballads to anyone who will listen. Oh, how dull I have been to him! And how cruel! Have some bread and butter.

HARRIET: I do not want any bread and butter. I only want to know what has happened to you.

SERENA: Nothing, Harriet, I promise you. Nothing at all.

HARRIET: But why should you suddenly accuse yourself of being cruel to Hubert, when you know perfectly well that but for your amazing patience and tolerance your married life would have broken up years ago?

SERENA: Would the world have come to an end if it had?

HARRIET: No. The world wouldn't have come to an end, but it might have laughed at you, and that would have been intolerable to your pride.

SERENA: How right you are, Harriet. And what a terrible indictment!

HARRIET: Indictment?

SERENA: Yes – oh, dear me, yes! To deny the spring of the year for fear of mockery! What a fool I have been.

HARRIET: Spring of the year, indeed! What nonsense! Hubert is a middle-aged philanderer and old enough to know better.

SERENA: Charm is independent of age. He will always have charm.

HARRIET (*searchingly*): Do you still love him?

SERENA (*with a smile*): Yes. I think that for the first time, I love him enough.

HARRIET: And what can you possibly mean by that?

SERENA: What a becoming hat, Harriet. Is it new?

HARRIET: There are moments when I could willingly slap you, Serena.

SERENA: Dear Harriet. Are you quite sure you won't have some more tea?

HARRIET: You infuriate me, and what is more, you do it deliberately.

SERENA: Just half a cup?

HARRIET (*rising*): No, thank you. I have to go.

SERENA: Tell me more about Mrs. Mallory.

HARRIET: I have told you all I know.

SERENA: Tell me other things, then. Tell me more about Miss Francis. She fascinates me. I see her suddenly in a new light; a refined, suburban truffle-pig, burrowing her way into her clients' confidences, unearthing their sad little secrets, polishing them up to a nice shine, and then selling them round the town.

HARRIET: Miss Francis is a perfectly respectable, hard-working woman, and she earns her living honestly.

SERENA (*with finality*): Good-bye, Harriet.

HARRIET (*startled*): Serena! What do you mean?

SERENA: You said you were going, and I said good-bye. What is there odd about that?

HARRIET: You said it so abruptly.

SERENA: I wish I could make amends.

HARRIET: What for?

SERENA: For being so – so unsatisfactory. We have been friends for so many, many years, and I have given you so little. Dear Harriet!

HARRIET: Good heavens! There are tears in your eyes!

SERENA (*smiling*): I know.

HARRIET: You *are* unhappy about something. I knew it!

SERENA: No, no. On the contrary, I am very happy indeed. (*She unpins a brooch from her gown.*) I want you to have this. (*She holds it out to her.*)

HARRIET (*astounded*): Serena!

SERENA: It belonged to my great-great-great-grandmother. I believe she was very skittish.

HARRIET: But why should you suddenly wish to give it to me?

SERENA: To remember me by.

HARRIET: Are you going away?

SERENA: Yes. The seven-fifteen from Cannon Street. Alford is meeting me at Deal with the dog-cart. I am devoted to Alford, but he is getting dreadfully old. It is very sad, is it not, when people get dreadfully old – so soon? Please take the brooch.

HARRIET (*taking it*): It is exquisite – I hardly know what to say. (*She kisses her.*) Thank you, Serena – I shall treasure it always.

SERENA: That is what I wanted you to say.

HARRIET: You are sure that you are quite well? That there is nothing wrong?

SERENA: Quite, quite sure.

HARRIET (*still puzzled*): Good-bye, my dear.

SERENA: Good-bye, Harriet.

> HARRIET *goes out.*
>
> SERENA *stands looking after her for a moment, then she goes over to the bell-rope and pulls it.*
>
> *The hurdy-gurdy starts to play again a few streets away.* SERENA *smiles and begins to waltz slowly round the room.*
>
> CATCHPOLE *enters.*

CATCHPOLE: You rang, milady?

SERENA (*stopping her dance*): Yes, Catchpole. Has his lordship gone to the club?

CATCHPOLE: He left a few minutes ago, milady.

SERENA (*producing from her bag the letter she was writing at the beginning of the scene*): Will you give him this when he comes in to-night? I shall be gone, and it is rather urgent.

CATCHPOLE (*taking it*): Very good, milady. Will that be all?

SERENA: Yes, Catchpole. That will be all.

> CATCHPOLE *goes out and closes the door behind him.*
>
> SERENA *begins to dance again as the lights fade on the scene.*

Scene II

The Buffet de la Gare, Boulogne.

> *The scene is the same as in Act I, Scene I. Various travellers are seated at various tables, the waiters are scurrying about, and the dawn is grey outside the windows. At a table downstage* MR. *and* MRS. SPEVIN *and* GWENDOLYN *are seated.*

MR. S.: If it is labelled, the porter will be sure to find it.

MRS. S.: The label might have come off.

MR. S.: I understood you to say that you had tied it on firmly. In that case it will not come off.

GWEN: Mama—

MRS. S.: Be quiet, Gwendolyn, and drink up your tea.

GWEN: If I do, I shall be sick again.

MR. S.: Try not to think about it.

MRS. S.: There is no need to snap at the child!

MR. S.: I did not snap at her. I merely suggested that she might concentrate on something else for a change. (*To* GWENDOLYN.) Where is your nice book, dear?

GWEN: In the pilgrim-basket – the one that's lost.

MR. S.: We have no proof that the pilgrim-basket is lost, Gwendolyn.

GWEN: Mama says it is.

MR. S.: Even your mama has been known to make mistakes occasionally.

MRS. S.: Has she indeed?

MR. S.: I happened to see the porter take it out of the train with my own eyes.

MRS. S.: So did I. But I haven't seen it since.

MR. S.: For heaven's sake stop fussing, Sarah!

MRS. S. (*bridling*): Fussing, indeed! I like that, I must say! All Gwennie's things are in that basket; her two summer dresses, her dancing shoes, all her underclothes, to say nothing of her books and her precious pencil box, and all you do is to sit there guzzling tea.

MR. S. (*with admirable control*): I am not *guzzling* tea, Sarah, any more than you are. I am sipping it in a perfectly ordinary manner.

MRS. S.: You ought not to be sipping anything until the luggage is safely on board. Here am I at my wits' end with Gwennie being sick one minute and having hiccups the next, and you just go on behaving as though nothing had happened. Why don't you at least go and look for the porter?

MR. S.: Because I shouldn't be able to find him if I did. He agreed to meet us with the luggage on the lee side of the funnel in half an hour's time. That was ten minutes ago. If the pilgrim-basket isn't there, we will send him to look for it. The boat doesn't sail for ages yet.

MRS. S.: Downright carelessness, that's all it is—

MR. S. (*with sudden firmness*): If you have finished your tea and Gwennie will not drink hers, you had better both go on board and leave me in peace.

MR. S. (*outraged*): Well, really—!

MR. S.: Here are your tickets. (*He plonks down two tickets on the table*.) If you take my advice you will find two chairs on the upper deck and sit in them. I shall stay here and read my newspaper.

MRS. S.: Of all the selfish, inconsiderate . . .

MR. S.: Do as I say, Sarah. I will join you later. And if the basket is lost, it is lost, and as far as I am concerned, good riddance to it!

> *With a snort of rage* MRS. SPEVIN *snatches up the tickets from the table, grabs* GWENDOLYN *by the hand – and churns away with her.*
>
> MR. SPEVIN *opens a French newspaper and settles himself to read it with a sigh of relief.*
>
> *A* COURIER *comes in, followed by* SERENA *and* AXEL. *He leads them to the table, the same table at which* HUBERT *and* CHARLOTTE *were sitting in the first scene.*

COURIER: This is your reserved table, sir.

AXEL: Thank you.

COURIER: I will call for you when the Paris train is about to leave and conduct you to your compartment. (*He calls.*) Garçon!

> *A* WAITER *appears.*

WAITER: Monsieur?

COURIER: You wish for coffee or chocolate, sir – milady?

AXEL: Serena?

SERENA: Coffee, please. With milk.

AXEL: Black for me, black and hot and strong.

COURIER: Croissants – an omelette, perhaps?

AXEL: No omelette – just the rolls.

COURIER: Bien, monsieur. (*To* WAITER.) Croissants, café, vite. Un noir, un blanc, allez.

WAITER: Oui, monsieur!

> *He scurries away.*

COURIER: I trust that milady and monsieur had a pleasant crossing?

AXEL: Lyrical, thank you.

SERENA: I had no idea the Rubicon could be so calm.

COURIER: Pardon, milady?

SERENA: Thank you so much for your courtesy.

COURIER: A pleasure, milady.

AXEL: Her ladyship is travelling incognito. The name is Baxter-Ellis, Mrs. Baxter-Ellis.

COURIER: Entendu, monsieur.

AXEL: Thank you.

COURIER: At your service!

He bows and goes away.

SERENA: What a kind man, and so handsome!

AXEL (*looking at her adoringly*): I could hardly take my eyes off him.

SERENA: Do you always like your coffee black and hot and strong?

AXEL: Yes. It is part of my character – no compromise.

SERENA: How admirable! And how reassuring!

AXEL (*placing his hand over hers on the table*): Do you need reassurance?

SERENA: Oh yes. I'm a prey to agonising fears.

AXEL: What sort of fears, ma'am? Can you name them, or are they the more dangerous kind, unformed and intangible?

SERENA: Quite tangible, based on mistrust.

AXEL: Serena!

SERENA: Not of you, but of Fate; the irrelevant malignancy of the Gods. There might be an earthquake, for instance, the ground might suddenly open and swallow you up before my eyes.

AXEL: Boulogne has not suffered a really serious earthquake for several years.

SERENA: You might have a heart attack.

AXEL: I am having one now. The pain is exquisite!

SERENA: Your heart *is* strong, though, isn't it?

AXEL: It was, but it isn't any more. It is now weak and vulnerable. Before our journey is over you may have to pluck a feather from your hat and burn it under my nose.

The WAITER *appears with the coffee and rolls.*

WAITER: Il y a assez de temps avant le départ, si monsieur desire une omelette.

AXEL: He is a cruel man. He wishes to shame me. His instincts have already told him that I do not understand his damned language.

SERENA: If you want an omelette, nod; if you don't, shake your head and say 'Merci'.

HUBERT: But Merci means thank you.

SERENA: With a shake of the head it means no.

AXEL (*shakes head*): Merci.

WAITER: Bien, monsieur!

> *He goes.*

SERENA: There now!

AXEL: I too have my fears.

SERENA (*pouring out the coffee*): Name them, and they will slink away.

AXEL: The principal one is that you may, in time, become irritated by my roughness, exasperated by my ignorance of your own ingrained tradition and by my lack of grace.

SERENA: I have also dreaded that contingency.

AXEL: You have?

SERENA (*calmly*): I have envisaged desperate possibilities; moments of acute humiliation when you suddenly attack a soufflé with a knife and fork, or spit into the fireplace without saying Excuse Me. You might also get drunk regularly on Saturday nights and knock me about! When one elopes with an uncivilised ruffian one must be prepared for anything. Here is your coffee, I hope it is black enough.

AXEL (*taking the coffee cup*): I promise never to spit into the fireplace. We will have cuspidors in every room.

SERENA: You may become irritated and exasperated with me first. My 'ingrained tradition' may infuriate you one day and turn your heart away from me.

AXEL: I will love you for ever, until the end of time.

SERENA: You said that in Kew Gardens only the other day. Do you remember?

AXEL: You said the same, word for word.

SERENA: You were seen there by a friend of Harriet's! It seems that you were accompanied by a mysterious lady, heavily veiled. I do hope it was the same day!

> *At this moment* MR. SPEVIN, *who has suddenly caught sight of* SERENA *over the top of his newspaper, rises from his table and comes eagerly across to them.*

MR. S.: Lady Heronden!

SERENA (*startled*): Good heavens!

MR. S.: What a delightful coincidence! Mr. Diensen.

AXEL: How do you do, sir.

MR. S.: Fancy our meeting again so unexpectedly, here of all
places – is it not extraordinary?

AXEL: Miraculous.

MR. S. (*to* SERENA): I trust that his lordship is well?

SERENA: I am afraid he is a little under the weather this morning.

MR. S.: Oh, I am so sorry! Nothing serious, I hope?

SERENA: No, Mr. Spevin, nothing serious. He will recover in
next to no time.

MR. S. (*to* AXEL): And Mrs. Diensen?

AXEL: My wife is in America. She had to visit her lawyers, a
family matter.

MR. S.: Ah yes, I see. (*After a slight pause.*) We are on our way
home to England for a week or so. My daughter Gwendolyn
has been seedy for some time, poor child; the Riviera climate
never really agreed with her, so we are taking her to my sister
in Abergavenny.

SERENA: The contrast alone should work wonders.

MR. S.: The Welsh air is very bracing; it will soon bring the roses
back to her cheeks. It is her stomach you know.

SERENA: No, I fear I didn't.

MR. S.: The poor mite seems unable to keep anything down.

SERENA: How worrying for you!

MR. S.: Are you on your way to Paris?

AXEL: We are returning to the Villa Zodiaque.

MR. S.: How delightful! Such a view!

SERENA: Our last visit was so brief, but so agreeable, that we felt
that we really must go back.

MR. S.: Poor Lady Bonnington will be so pleased. She leads such
a lonely life. Does she know you are coming?

AXEL: If I know anything of her inner voices, she'll meet us at
the station.

MR. S.: Well, well, well, I must not keep you! My wife and
Gwendolyn are already on board. They will be wondering

what has happened to me. I hope for the child's sake that the sea is calm.

AXEL: It is, Mr. Spevin. Calm as a mill-pond; the air too is tranquil and sweet and there is no threat in the sky. In fact the whole world is benign to-day, gay and smiling.

SERENA (*warningly*): Mr. Diensen!

AXEL: On such a morning as this even Gwendolyn should be able to keep at least something down!

SERENA (*holding out her hand*): Good-bye, Mr. Spevin, and bon voyage!

MR. S.: Thank you so much, your ladyship. My wife will be so sorry to have missed you.

SERENA: Remember me to her.

AXEL: Good luck, Mr. Spevin.

MR. S. (*backing away*): Thank you – thank you – such a pleasure to have seen you again – such a great pleasure. . . .

He grabs up his hat from his table and goes out.

AXEL: Poor Gwendolyn.

SERENA: I remember her at the jumble sale. She wore glasses, her petticoat showed beneath her dress and she won the egg and spoon race.

AXEL: The sun is coming up, the dawn of our first day together.

SERENA: Yes – yes, I know.

AXEL: If this were a dream you would tell me, wouldn't you? You wouldn't let me go on sleeping in foolish bliss until some clanging bell dragged me awake?

A bell rings outside on the platform.

SERENA: There it is. There's your bell.

AXEL: I am still sleeping. Now I know that I shall never wake.

SERENA: Oh dear!

AXEL: What is it?

SERENA: Was it wise of us to choose the Villa Zodiaque, I wonder, or was it an error in taste?

AXEL: We have to go there, taste or no taste – it is where we fell in love.

SERENA: This year has been so long I can scarcely remember.

AXEL: I can. Every moment is burned into my brain, every gesture you made, every word you uttered.

SERENA: Did you know – about me, I mean? Did you hear, behind my words, the pounding of my stricken heart?

AXEL: Yes.

SERENA: Oh!

AXEL: Do you resent such unmannerly eavesdropping?

SERENA: I tried so hard to keep my secret. What waste of time!

AXEL: Every moment of our lives has been waste of time till now.

SERENA: Stuff and nonsense, my darling.

AXEL: You haven't eaten a thing.

SERENA: Neither have you.

AXEL: We shall be hungry in the train.

SERENA: I know. I am looking forward to it.

There is the sound of an engine whistle.

AXEL: That is a warning.

SERENA: Do your beloved American locomotives whistle so hysterically?

AXEL: No, ma'am, they sound a deeper note, more mournful. They have vaster distances to travel, wilder territories to cross and heavier, more virile responsibilities: they have no time for shrill, Gallic petulance.

SERENA: The New World. The Brave New World! Will it accept me, do you think? Or shall I be an anachronism?

AXEL: Your earlier adventures contributed much to its quality, part of your blood is there, so you have a stake in it.

SERENA: You are all the guarantee I need.

AXEL: You will find memories of old England in the most outlandish places.

SERENA: I can scarcely wait ...

AXEL: Do not doubt the warmth of your welcome. We are young in heart and eager to enchant our visitors.

SERENA: If only you and I were younger! If only there were more time—

AXEL: There is time enough, my dear love. Time and to spare. Come.

SERENA rises from the table. AXEL takes her hand. There are sounds of whistles blowing, steam escaping, and the clanging of bells.
The COURIER appears in the doorway.

AXEL *offers* SERENA *his arm; she takes it, and with her other hand gathers up her dress. . . . There is a flood of sunshine as they go out on to the platform.*

CURTAIN

'PEACE IN OUR TIME'

To INGRAM FRASER

MY DEAR INGRAM,

I am dedicating *'Peace in Our Time'* to you as a very small gesture of gratitude for all the invaluable help and technical advice you gave me when I was constructing and writing it. The infinite pains you took to plan and map 'Operation Bulldog'—the imagined re-invasion of Occupied England by the Free British, the American, the Free French and the Dominion Forces made it possible for me to visualise the end of the play clearly. Also, without your knowledge of 'Resistance' activities and your quick and precise eye for detail, much of the dialogue might have been muddled and obscure. As it is, thanks to you, I think that within its imagined limits it is fairly accurate. At any rate the operative phrase in all this is 'Thanks to you'.

N. C.

'*Peace in Our Time*' was first produced in Brighton at the Theatre Royal, on 15 July 1947 and then in London at the Lyric Theatre on 22 July 1947, with the following cast:

ALMA BOUGHTON	Helen Horsey
FRED SHATTOCK	Bernard Lee
JANET BRAID	Elspeth March
DORIS SHATTOCK	Maureen Pryor
MR. GRAINGER	Trevor Ward
MRS. GRAINGER	Sybil Wise
NORA SHATTOCK	Beatrice Varley
LYIA VIVIAN	Hazel Terry
GEORGE BOURNE	Kenneth More
BEN CAPPER	Manfred Priestley
WOMAN	Stella Chapman
CHORLEY BANNISTER	Olaf Pooley
BOBBY PAXTON	Derek Aylward
ALBRECHT RICHTER	Ralph Michael
PHYLLIS MERE	Dora Bryan
MAUDIE	Irene Relph
GLADYS MOTT	Daphne Maddox
ALFIE BLAKE	Brian Carey
GERMAN SOLDIER	Charles Russell
HERR HUBERMAN	Richard Scott
FRAU HUBERMAN	Betty Woolfe
IST GERMAN SOLDIER	Anthony Peek
2ND GERMAN SOLDIER	Lance Hamilton
BILLY GRAINGER	Philip Guard
DOCTOR VENNING	Michael Kent
LILY BLAKE	Dandy Nichols
MR. WILLIAMS	William Murray
STEVIE	Alan Badel
ARCHIE JENKINS	John Molecey
MR. LAWRENCE	George Lane
KURT FORSTER	Michael Anthony
MRS. MASSITER	Janet Barrow

YOUNG GERMAN SOLDIER	Anthony Peek
1ST S.S. GUARD	Douglas Vine
2ND S.S. GUARD	Peter Drury

Directed by ALAN WEBB
Under the supervision of THE AUTHOR
Décor by G. E. CALTHROP

The entire action of the play takes place in the saloon bar of a public house called 'The Shy Gazelle', situated somewhere between Knightsbridge and Sloane Square.

———

ACT I
Scene I. *November, 1940. About eight-thirty in the evening.*
Scene II. *June, 1941. About two-thirty in the afternoon.*
Scene III. *January, 1942. Between nine-thirty and ten in the evening.*
Scene IV. *February, 1942. About nine-thirty in the evening.*

ACT II
Scene I. *January, 1945. Nine o'clock in the evening.*
Scene II. *February, 1945. Between five-thirty and six in the evening.*
Scene III. *Three days later. About two-thirty in the afternoon.*
Scene IV. *May 1945. Early afternoon.*

ACT I: Scene I

The time is about eight-thirty in the evening. November 1940.

The whole action of the play takes place in a small public house situated somewhere between Knightsbridge and Sloane Square. The name of the pub is 'The Shy Gazelle'. The scene throughout is the saloon bar. Looking at the scene from the audience the bar is on the left stretching from downstage to upstage. At the back there is a small alcove leading to the kitchen and also, by way of a staircase the end of which can just be seen, to the upper parts of the house.

At the back on the right there is a small door leading to a passage and the back door. In this passage are the Ladies' and Gentlemen's lavatories.

On the right-hand wall there are two windows and, below them, the door into the street.

Behind the bar downstage on the left is a window which opens into the public bar. It is a serving window and is usually open.

FRED SHATTOCK, the manager of 'The Shy Gazelle', is an amiable, gregarious man of about fifty. He was gassed slightly in the 1914–18 war and has been in the publican business since 1919 when he came out of the army and married NORA. NORA SHATTOCK is quiet but firm. She is a year or two younger than FRED; her hair is grey and her manner efficient. Her accent betrays the fact that she could have come from nowhere in the world but South London. FRED's accent is not quite so marked, he has read a good deal over the years and has definite views. DORIS, their daughter aged twenty-one, is a pretty girl with a quick mind. She has been trained as a stenographer and she helps behind the bar in her spare time.

When the curtain rises they are all three serving behind the bar as the saloon is rather full. DORIS is downstage dealing, through the service window, with unseen customers in the 'Public'.

Drinking at the bar are the following people: LYIA VIVIAN, a rather spectacular-looking woman of thirty-five. She is a cabaret artiste of some repute. She was born and brought up in the hunting Counties and is what might be technically described as 'a lady'. Morally she was a casualty of the early 'twenties during which hectic period she threw her bonnet over rather too many windmills. With her is GEORGE BOURNE, *a pleasant-looking man in the late thirties. He has been her lover sporadically for two years; is well dressed, wealthy and apparently completely idle.* JANET BRAID *is a plainly dressed, ordinary-looking woman of about forty. She has a pleasant speaking voice but one cannot help feeling that the light has gone out of her. The reason for this is that her only son Angus has recently been shot down and killed in the Battle of Britain.* CHORLEY BANNISTER *comes under the heading of 'Intellectual', not in the fullest sense but merely in so far as he is well read, intelligent and edits a highbrow magazine called* Forethought. *His conversation is affected and inclined to be over-provocative. He is devoid of moral integrity and easily frightened. He can, however, be witty on occasions.*

    MR. *and* MRS. GRAINGER, *a commonplace couple, are seated at one of the tables by the window. There is also an anonymous couple – a man and woman – at the bar. These are the usual customers. For various reasons, mostly geographical, they patronise 'The Shy Gazelle'. They all live within the radius of a mile or so. From time to time other unnamed customers come in to the pub, have a drink or two and go away again.*

    There is a low buzz of general conversation. ALMA BOUGHTON *comes in from the street. She is a well-dressed, talkative woman in the late thirties.*

ALMA: Hello, Janet!

JANET: Hello, Alma.

ALMA (*going to the bar*): Good evening, Nora. Hullo, Fred.

FRED: Hallo, Mrs. Boughton – I thought you weren't coming back until Thursday.

ALMA: I got through quicker than I expected – Leeds was awful – bitterly cold, you know they've requisitioned the Queen's, Nora?

NORA: Trust them – they always go for the best hotels.

FRED: The usual?

ALMA: Yes, please – very little soda though – I'm frozen.

    FRED *hands her a small glass of whisky.*

JANET: Was the train journey as bad as you thought it was going to be?

ALMA: No, surprisingly good as a matter of fact – I had a carriage to myself as far as Birmingham. (*She sips her drink.*)

FRED: Train on time?

ALMA (*with a slight laugh*): Of course – perfect efficiency.

DORIS (*at the serving window*): Two mild and one rough. That'll be two and sevenpence please.

MR. GRAINGER: Another port, dear?

MRS. GRAINGER: No, thank you.

ALMA: If I thaw in this coat I shall catch my death when I go out. (*Crosses up centre and hangs coat.*)

MRS. GRAINGER: You have one if you want to – there's no hurry.

MR. GRAINGER: I think I will at that. Make it a mild and bitter please, Mrs. Shattock.

NORA: One mild and bitter. Any news of your boy?

MR. GRAINGER: Yes – funnily enough we had a post-card from him only this morning.

NORA: One of those printed ones, I suppose?

MR. GRAINGER: Yes – it said he was well enough.

NORA: Well, that's something to be thankful for, isn't it?

MR. GRAINGER: It certainly is, Mrs. Shattock.

MAN: Good-night, Mrs. Shattock.

    Man and woman exit.

LYIA: What's the time, George?

GEORGE (*glancing at his wrist-watch*): Quarter to.

LYIA: Time for one more before I give my all to my fascinating public.

GEORGE: Two more, please, Fred.

FRED: Righto. (*He pours two gins and lime.*)

ALMA: Show still going well? (*Crosses to downstage right of bar.*)

LYIA: Packed – they don't laugh much but they seem to enjoy themselves. The dinner show's the worst – they sit like stuffed carp. After midnight it's better and they relax a bit.

NORA: I don't envy you and that's a fact. (*Crosses to bar.*)

LYIA: I don't envy myself.

NORA: Mr. Grainger had a post-card from his son – he's still there – in the Isle of Wight.

GEORGE: He'll probably stay there indefinitely, I should think.

JANET: Have you got any cigarettes, Fred?

FRED: Running a bit short, but there's always a packet for you as long as we have them – Players?

JANET: Yes, please.

ALMA: Would you like one of these?

JANET: No, thanks – I can't bear cork tips.

ALMA: Have you been working all day?

JANET: Yes – it passes the time.

ALMA: How's it going?

JANET: I've got about five more chapters to do.

ALMA: How wonderful to be able to do something creative – particular in these times.

JANET: The sort of nonsense I am writing at the moment isn't creative – there's no light in it really and no pleasure – as I said just now it just passes the time.

CHORLEY (*to* NORA): You're sure Mr. Paxton didn't ring up or leave a message or anything? (*Crosses to bar.*)

NORA: Quite sure, Mr. Bannister. I haven't heard of him or seen him for days.

CHORLEY: If there is one thing in the world I detest it is people who make appointments and fail to keep them.

JANET: There's more than one thing in the world that I detest.

CHORLEY: You must admit it's tiresome though, isn't it? I've been sitting here drinking myself into a coma since seven-thirty.

NORA: You've only had two, Mr. Bannister – they weren't even doubles.

CHORLEY: I apologise, Nora – I meant to cast no aspersions on the hospitality of this most amiable tavern. I will have a double now – as a penance. Do you want a drink, Janet? Mrs. Boughton? I've been guzzling alone for too long – it's bad for my soul.

ALMA: One whisky and soda then – if it's to save your soul.

JANET: No more for me, thank you, Chorley. I've got to go home after the nine o'clock news and do some more work.

CHORLEY: I could never work after the nine o'clock news, it's so dreadfully negative.

JANET: If only that were all it was.

CHORLEY: As a matter of fact, I find it increasingly difficult to work at all these days – the air is so full of rumours and tidings and implications – it's like living in a perpetual hail storm.

JANET (*drily*): The magazine is doing as well as ever though, isn't it – now that you have readjusted some of its opinions?

CHORLEY (*with a touch of asperity*): No opinions have been readjusted – *Forethought* says what it thinks.

JANET: You mean it says what you think?

CHORLEY: Why not? I am the editor. I run it.

JANET (*turning away*): Why not indeed?

LYIA: Being an editor just at this particular time is rather tricky, isn't it, darling?

GEORGE: Lyia means on account of the paper shortage.

CHORLEY (*crossly*): Lyia means very little anyway except when she is moaning into a microphone – and not very much then.

LYIA: Why Chorley – that was downright snappy? George, darling, oughtn't you to call him out or knock him down or something for being so rude to your love?

GEORGE: When we were at Oxford I used to knock him down constantly – it never did the slightest good.

CHORLEY: It was most unfair, you were much younger than I was.

LYIA: Poor Chorley.

CHORLEY: My income is adequate, Lyia, and my position in the world of literature unassailable – I resent being described as 'Poor Chorley'.

JANET: How stimulating it must be to know that your position in the world of literature is so unassailable.

CHORLEY: Janet – you are quite definitely biting the hand that only a moment ago offered you a drink.

JANET: I didn't accept it.

LYIA: Leave him alone, Janet – he is obviously in a very irritable mood. (*To* CHORLEY.) Is Bobby Paxton standing you up again?

CHORLEY: Sometimes you go too far, Lyia.

LYIA: He's a very smooth character, Bobby, very smooth indeed. You'd better be careful, Chorley.

CHORLEY: Your rather dubious position as a cabaret singer, my dear, does not entitle you to poke your erstwhile patrician nose into other people's business.

LYIA (*laughing*): The operative phrase in that sentence was 'erstwhile patrician' – I rather like it.

CHORLEY: I have yet to be persuaded that the hunting shires are really a suitable nursery for histrionic ability.

LYIA: I haven't any histrionic ability, darling – as you said yourself just now all I can do is to moan through a microphone.

CHORLEY: I grant that you have a certain appeal for a limited section of the public, Lyia – many amateurs do.

GEORGE (*sharply*): This time *you* have gone too far, Chorley. I am still younger than you and still capable of knocking you down. Lyia is *not* an amateur. What she does she does damn well.

LYIA: Oh George, how lovely – you really are quite cross, aren't you?

GEORGE: Come on – it's time to go.

CHORLEY: George! It would be very foolish for you to knock me down. I think you had better remember that.

NORA: Now, now, now – we don't want anybody to get upset.

GEORGE: Quite right, Nora – don't worry. (*To* CHORLEY.) The veiled threat in what you just said did not escape me, Chorley. Personally I think it was rather indiscreet of you.

> *He takes* LYIA's *arm and they are about to leave when a good-looking, well-dressed man comes in from the street.* GEORGE *and* LYIA *stay where they are without moving. The low-toned conversation of* MR. *and* MRS. GRAINGER *stops abruptly.* DORIS, *who is leaning through the service window, chatting to someone unseen, looks over her shoulder, stops talking and closes the serving window. The man,* ALBRECHT RICHTER, *goes over to the bar.*

ALBRECHT: Good evening.

FRED: Good evening, sir.

ALBRECHT: Whisky and soda, please.

FRED: Double or single?

ALBRECHT: Single, please.

In silence FRED *pours him his drink and hands him the siphon.*
ALBRECHT *mixes it himself.*

FRED: That'll be one and sixpence, please.

ALBRECHT (*paying*): Thank you. (*He raises his glass pleasantly.*)
Here's how! (*Taking out his cigarettes.*) Have you a light?

FRED *gives him one and turns away.*

Thank you!

ALBRECHT *looks smilingly round at everyone. Nobody speaks. He
drinks his whisky and soda with rather a quizzical expression on his
face, then, as though quite unaware of the silence, he puts his glass
down on the bar.*

Well – good-night, Mrs. Shattock.

NORA: Good-night.

ALBRECHT (*to* FRED): Good-night.

FRED: Good-night, sir.

ALBRECHT *goes out shutting the street door firmly behind him.
The silence continues for a few moments.* NORA *breaks it.*

NORA (*to* FRED): What did you want to call him 'sir' for?

FRED: He's a customer, isn't he?

DORIS (*returning to the serving window*): He hasn't got a bad face
really.

NORA: I don't care what kind of a face he has.

LYIA: Poor beast – I feel rather sorry for him.

JANET (*coldly*): Why?

LYIA: It's always horrid being unpopular.

ALMA: It's not our fault.

CHORLEY: It's not his fault either.

JANET: That's very magnanimous of you, Chorley.

CHORLEY: In any situation a little tolerance is not a bad thing.

JANET: I disagree.

CHORLEY: All right, all right – put it on the basis of common
sense—

JANET: I have yet to be convinced that timid expedience is
common sense.

CHORLEY: My dear Janet, I fear that you have yet to be
convinced of a great many things.

JANET (*with sudden anger*): Please don't let's discuss it – Fred, I would like another drink, please, after all – Alma?

ALMA: All right.

FRED: Same again?

JANET: Yes, please.

FRED (*pouring the drinks*): Time for the nine o'clock, Nora – turn it on, will you—

    NORA *goes to the wireless at the top end of the bar and turns it on.*

LYIA: We really ought to go, George.

GEORGE: Stay and hear the headlines. I've got Bert outside with his taxi.

LYIA: Very well.

    Big Ben strikes nine o'clock.

NORA (*as it strikes*): It's funny to think that they can still hear that all over the world.

    At the end of the clock striking the Announcer's voice is heard.

VOICE: This is the B.B.C. Home Service. Here is the news. This evening's communique contains details of a U-boat action in the Atlantic where a large convoy was attacked shortly before dawn to-day. There has been no air activity during the past twenty-four hours. As previously announced, the Military Parade to celebrate the re-opening of Parliament will take place to-morrow. Spectators who have reserved seats in the special stands are reminded to be in their places before 8.30 a.m. Late arrivals will not be seated. The Military Parade will move off from Hyde Park Corner at 9.30 a.m. precisely, proceeding by way of Constitution Hill, the Mall, Trafalgar Square and Whitehall, to Westminster. After passing the reviewing stand at Buckingham Palace, the Parade will be followed at 9.42 precisely by a procession of State carriages escorted by a guard of honour. In the first open landau will be seated the Führer. The carriages following will contain Air Chief Marshal Goering, Dr. Goebbels and high-ranking Army, Navy and Air Force officers—

        THE LIGHTS FADE

Scene II

June, 1941.

   It is about two-thirty in the afternoon.

   FRED *is behind the bar assisted by* PHYLLIS MERE. DORIS *is unable to help during the day owing to her duties as receptionist at the Savoy. Lunches are just being finished in the upstairs room; occasionally* MAUDIE *comes down with a tray and collects some drinks from* FRED.

   The bar is empty except for MR. *and* MRS. GRAINGER, *who are sitting silently at their usual table. There are two glasses of beer in front of them.* MR. GRAINGER *is reading an evening paper.* MRS. GRAINGER *is smoking a cigarette and gazing into space.*

   PHYLLIS MERE *is talking through the serving window.*

PHYLLIS (*to an unseen customer*): Go on!

   There is an unintelligible murmur from the other side of the window.

Well, I never – what sauce! (*Further murmuring.*) Okay. (*To* FRED.) Two more mild, please, Mr. Shattock.

FRED (*drawing them*): Righto.

PHYLLIS (*continuing the conversation*): Well, it's no good arguing with them, is it? Look what happened to poor Mr. Roach. . . . (*Pause for murmuring.*) Well, he didn't do nothing really, you know . . . that is, nothing to speak of. . . .

FRED: Here you are . . . two mild.

PHYLLIS: Thanks, Mr. Shattock. . . . (*Through the window.*) Let me see, that'll be – one and eight and one and eight – three and fourpence, please. (*After a slight pause, money is handed through the service window,* PHYLLIS *puts it in the till.*) It's very nice of you, I'm sure . . . all right . . . cheerio for now. (*To* FRED.) That was Mr. Lawrence and his friend, the one that drives a taxi – he was telling me about some trouble he had last night at Earls Court.

FRED: What kind of trouble?

PHYLLIS: The usual.

FRED: Anyone get hurt?

PHYLLIS: Yes.

FRED: One of them?

PHYLLIS: Yes – he was an officer and he come up to Mr. Lawrence's friend, the one that drives a taxi, and tells him he wants to go to Maida Vale, see? Well, Mr. Lawrence's friend has only just enough petrol left to get himself home to Wandsworth and so this Jerry officer starts ticking him off and threatening, like, and then Mr. Lawrence's friend lets him have one smack in the jaw and down he goes in the gutter, medals and all, and then Mr. Lawrence's friend drives away double quick.

FRED: Did anyone see?

PHYLLIS: No, it was one of those quiet streets round by the Grove.

FRED: Mr. Lawrence's friend had better look out for himself if that officer got his number.

PHYLLIS: He says he couldn't have, what with it being dark and everything and then lying on his face. . . .

FRED: Well, you'd better keep quiet about it, anyway.

PHYLLIS: Yes, Mr. Shattock.

FRED: And tell Mr. Lawrence to, too, the next time he comes in. And his friend.

PHYLLIS: What about Saturday, Mr. Shattock?

FRED: Well, what about Saturday?

PHYLLIS: Doris doesn't work at the Savoy after one o'clock so she'll be home. You said I could have the afternoon off.

FRED: All right, all right.

PHYLLIS: Thanks ever so, Mr. Shattock.

    MAUDIE *comes in from upstairs with tray of glasses.*

MAUDIE: Here's this lot, Mr. Shattock.

    MAUDIE *goes back up stairs.*

PHYLLIS (*looking through the hatch*): There's nobody in the 'Public' – shall I close down?

FRED: Better wait a few more minutes – it's not quite time yet.

    PHYLLIS *lounges against the service window and hums a little song.*
    MR. GRAINGER *comes over to the bar with his paper.*

MR. GRAINGER: Care to have a look?

FRED: Sure you can spare it?

MR. GRAINGER: Yes – I've finished with it.

FRED: Any news?

MR. GRAINGER: There's a bit about the King and Queen.

FRED: What?

MR. GRAINGER: It says they're going to stay there indefinitely. The whole Royal Family.

FRED: At Windsor?

MR. GRAINGER: Yes – there's a picture of the Queen and Princess Elizabeth in the park. You can see the guards watching them in the background.

FRED: How does she look – the Queen? (*He searches through the paper.*) Here it is.

MR. GRAINGER: She looks sad, doesn't she? – but her chin's up.

FRED: They won't find it easy to get our King and Queen down.

> PHYLLIS *looks over* FRED's *shoulder.*

MR. GRAINGER: It makes me feel sick. And that's a fact.

> *Two people, a man and a woman, come down from the dining-room upstairs and cross the bar to the street door.*

MAN (*as they go*): Good afternoon.

FRED (*mechanically*): Good afternoon, sir.

> *They go out.*

Heard anything from your boy?

MR. GRAINGER: He's still there – that's all we know.

> *The street door opens and* ALMA BOUGHTON *comes in. She looks a little strained.*

ALMA: Am I too late for a brandy, Fred?

FRED: No, Mrs. Boughton. It's not three yet, anyhow.

ALMA: Good.

MR. GRAINGER (*to* ALMA): Good afternoon.

> PHYLLIS *hums.*

FRED (*pouring* ALMA *some brandy – to* PHYLLIS): Turn it up, Phyllis. (*To* ALMA.) Anything wrong?

ALMA: No – nothing at all.

MR. GRAINGER: Well, I'll be pushing off. See you to-night. (*He goes over to the table.*) Ready, Mother?

MRS. GRAINGER (*rising*): Yes, dear.

ALMA: Good afternoon.

> *They go out into the street.*

ALMA *watches them go.*

ALMA: They are an extraordinary little couple, aren't they? I see
them here all the time. They never seem to get drunk or say
anything much or even speak to each other. What do they do?

FRED: Nothing. They live in two rooms just off Sloane Square –
in 1939 they had three sons. Now all they've got left is one in a
concentration camp in the Isle of Wight. They go to the
pictures sometimes.

ALMA (*raising her glass*): Here's luck, Fred. We can't say 'Happy
days' any more, can we?

FRED: You're dead right, we can't.

ALMA: Will it ever come to an end, do you think?

FRED: The war?

ALMA: No – all this.

FRED: I suppose it must, some time or other, but whether we'll
be here to see it is another matter.

ALMA: I'd like to be here to see it – I'd like to be here to see it
more than anything in the world.

FRED: So should I.

ALMA: Give me another, will you?

FRED (*raising his eyebrows*): Righto.

ALMA: Don't look shocked, Fred. I haven't taken to the bottle
seriously.

FRED: You're looking a bit peaky. Is anything wrong?

ALMA: You asked me that before.

PHYLLIS *hums again.*

FRED: I know. (*He turns to* PHYLLIS.) You can close the window
now, Phyllis, and run upstairs and give Mrs. Shattock a hand.

PHYLLIS (*closing the service window*): Okay, Mr. Shattock.

She goes off upstairs.

ALMA (*smiling*): I haven't anything to say, really – nothing
particularly private, that is.

FRED: Whatever we say nowadays is private – it's wiser.

ALMA: Yes, I suppose it is.

FRED: What's upset you?

ALMA: Just an incident – the sort of thing that happens every day.

(*She sips her brandy.*) You know that as a buyer for John Mason and Co. I have to go traipsing about all over the place?

FRED: Yes.

ALMA: There's a Mr. Oakley – he's a nice little man, half Jewish, he dyes furs. I had to go and see him this morning – he has a little place halfway down the Edgware Road. There were two S.S. guards standing outside the shop and another one inside. They'd just taken him, Mr. Oakley, away.

FRED: What for – did they say?

ALMA: Questioning! That might mean anything.

FRED: Did they knock him about?

ALMA: No, apparently not. I tried to comfort poor Mrs. Oakley as well as I could – she was convinced that they were going to torture him to death and that she would never see him again.

FRED: There haven't been many cases like that yet.

ALMA: Yet . . . ?

FRED: Yes – that's the word.

ALMA: You don't think that 'Good behaviour' policy will last?

FRED: Do you?

ALMA: I think it all depends how things go. It's certainly working the way they want it to – the 'Good behaviour' policy I mean – they're getting more and more converts every day.

FRED: Some people are born silly.

ALMA: They think they're being sensible, not silly at all.

FRED (*wearily*): Perhaps they are.

ALMA (*shocked*): Fred!

FRED: Now, don't misunderstand me, Mrs. Boughton. I don't want to have any truck with them, but I can't help seeing people's point every now and then – life's got to go on, hasn't it?

ALMA: Your son's life didn't go on, did it? He was shot down in the Battle of Britain.

FRED: All right – all right – don't let's go on about it.

ALMA: Janet Braid's only son was killed, too – I don't suppose either she or Nora would like to hear you talking like that.

FRED: I'm not talking like anything, Mrs. Boughton – I'm just trying to see things clearly, to get my mind straight. I hate the bastards, same as everybody else does, there isn't any argument about that.

ALMA: On the contrary there is a great deal of argument already about just that.

FRED: Not here there isn't.

ALMA: Are you sure?

FRED: I can't be answerable for my customers' opinions, can I?

ALMA (*turning away*): Oh, Fred.

FRED: Well, can I, now? – be fair—

ALMA: It isn't a question of being fair – it's a question of holding on to what one believes in – what one has always believed in.

FRED: I've always believed in one thing, Mrs. Boughton, and that was that the people of this country were the finest people in the world.

ALMA: Don't you still believe that?

FRED: Of course I do – in a way, but you see—

ALMA: I don't see.

FRED: Now listen, Mrs. Boughton.

ALMA: I'm listening.

FRED (*with a tremendous effort*): As I see it, it's like this. We were the finest people in the world – see . . . but we were getting too pleased with ourselves. We all swore in 1918 that we'd never have another war. Then gradually, bit by bit, we allowed our politicians and our newspapers and our own selfishness to chivvy us into this one. Even as late as 1938 we were dancing in the streets because a silly old man promised us 'Peace in our time'. We knew bloody well there wasn't a dog's chance of 'peace in our time'. Then suddenly in 1939 we woke up and found ourselves in the soup, no guns, not enough aeroplanes, half the Navy we should have had. Then what happens? In spite of blood and toil and sweat and fighting on the beaches and in the streets, we get licked. See! We lost the Battle of Britain – not because our flying boys didn't do their best but because of our – stupidity, they hadn't got a chance. They got shot down – my son and hundreds of other people's sons. Now we've been conquered. Do you see now why I don't any longer quite believe all the things I was brought up to believe? Do you, Mrs. Boughton?

ALMA: That was very bitter and impressive, Fred. But it didn't impress me.

FRED: I don't want to impress anybody.

ALMA: Do you think it would have been better for us if we had won the Battle of Britain?

FRED: Of course I do.

ALMA: I don't.

FRED: Mrs. Boughton!

ALMA: It might have been better for America and the rest of the world, but it wouldn't have been better for us.

FRED: Why not?

ALMA: Because we should have got lazy again, and blown out with our own glory. We should have been bombed and blitzed and we should have stood up under it – an example to the whole civilised world – and that would have finished us. As it is – in defeat – we still have a chance. There'll be no time in this country for many a long day for class wars and industrial crises and political squabbles. We can be united now – we shall have to be – until we've driven them away, until we're clean again. I think I'd like another brandy.

FRED (*pouring them*): You know the trouble with you women is, you're too emotional.

ALMA: Are you so sure that intellectual thinking is so vastly superior to emotional thinking?

FRED (*handing her her brandy*): I'm dead sure it is.

ALMA: I often wonder. I should think on the whole that emotion has contributed more over the centuries to the world's happiness than intellect.

FRED: To the world's trouble too.

ALMA: How's Nora?

FRED: She's all right – a bit miserable of course – Churchill's death upset her terribly.

ALMA: There was an emotional mind – he contributed much.

FRED: I'm glad they didn't hang him – being shot seems cleaner somehow, more dignified.

ALMA: Yes – that was clever of them.

FRED: I wonder how much he minded – when it came to the point, I mean.

ALMA: I expect he minded a great deal. He was not the type who would treat defeat or death intellectually.

FRED: All right – all right – you win.

ALMA (*with great sincerity*): Fred, be careful, won't you? Please don't think that I don't see your difficulties – I do. You have to be outwardly civil to everybody who comes here – that's common sense. But don't give in – don't ever let them win you round with their careful words and their 'Good behaviour' policies. They're our enemies – now and for ever. If other people find it expedient to be nice to them – do remember that they don't count, those thinking, broken reeds – they're only in the minority in this country and they'll never be anything else.

> NORA *comes down the stairs at the back.*

NORA: Why, Mrs. Boughton – what a surprise! We don't often see you at this time.

ALMA: I've taken to drinking heavily in the middle of the day, Nora. It's the beginning of the end.

NORA: I wonder we don't all drink ourselves silly and that's a fact.

FRED: Quite a nice idea – as long as we have anything to drink. Anybody left upstairs?

NORA: Yes, two tables – Miss Vivian and Mr. Bourne at one and him and Mr. Bannister at the other.

FRED: Him? – I never saw him come in.

NORA (*laconically*): I did.

ALMA: Who's him?

FRED (*lowering his voice*): You know – our friend – our faithful watch-dog – the pride of the Gestapo, Herr Albrecht Richter.

ALMA: Oh – the City Slicker.

NORA: Shhh, Mrs. Boughton – he may be coming down at any moment.

ALMA: So Chorley Bannister is having lunch with him, is he?

FRED: Yes – they're great pals.

ALMA (*contemptuously*): Typical.

> LYIA VIVIAN *and* GEORGE BOURNE *come down from upstairs.*

GEORGE: That was a jolly good lunch, Nora – I don't know how you do it.

LYIA: Hallo, Alma.

ALMA: Hallo.

LYIA (*after a slight pause*): You both look very mysterious – there's quite an atmosphere – Are you two plotting anything?

ALMA: Yes – the overthrow of the Third Reich.

FRED (*sharply*): Mrs. Boughton, please.

GEORGE: Good for you – nice work if you can get it.

NORA: It's foolish to talk like that, Mrs. Boughton – even in fun. It's inconsiderate, too – we have to earn our living, you know.

ALMA: I've been drinking brandy, Nora – it stimulates the emotions. (*She looks at* FRED.)

LYIA: Come on, George – I shall be late for my rehearsal. (*As a piece of general information.*) I'm putting in two new numbers to-night.

ALMA: In English or German, Lyia?

LYIA: Take me away quickly, George – she's got that battling 'Women of England' glint in her eyes. She's as bad as Janet.

> CHORLEY BANNISTER *comes in.*

CHORLEY: Nobody could be as bad as Janet – because the worst thing in the world is a bore, and poor Janet is most definitely and triumphantly a bore.

ALMA: I don't agree.

NORA (*going behind the bar*): Have you got that list for me, Fred?

FRED: Yes – I made it out – it's by the till.

> ALBRECHT RICHTER *comes in. He is putting his wallet in his pocket, having paid the bill.*

ALBRECHT (*to* ALMA): Good afternoon, Mrs. Boughton.

ALMA: Good afternoon. (*She leans across the bar.*) Any hope of any cigarettes?

FRED: I've got a few packets of Abdullas, that's all.

ALBRECHT (*affably*): I have some Virginians – Craven A – would you like them?

ALMA: No thank you, very much – I only smoke Turkish or Egyptian.

FRED (*handing her a packet of Abdullas*): Here you are, Mrs. Boughton.

ALMA: Thanks – good-bye, Fred – good-bye, Nora – I'll probably see you later.

ALMA *goes out.*

ALBRECHT: Can I offer anybody a drink? Miss Vivian – Mr. Bourne? (*To* FRED.) It's not too late, is it?

FRED: It's just on three.

LYIA: No, thank you – I have a rehearsal.

ALBRECHT: Mr. Bourne? – Chorley?

GEORGE: Thanks – all right.

LYIA: Oh, George!

GEORGE: One quick brandy like Epp's Cocoa would be both grateful and comforting.

CHORLEY: The same for me.

LYIA: You are tiresome, darling – I shall be so late and Paravicci will get in a rage and it will be hell.

GEORGE: Five minutes – that's all—

ALBRECHT (*to* FRED): One, two, three— (*He looks at* LYIA.)

LYIA: Oh, all right.

ALBRECHT: Four brandies, please.

FRED: Four brandies.

ALBRECHT: Perhaps you and your wife would do me the honour of drinking with me?

NORA (*after a slight pause*): No, thank you very much. I never drink. (*To* FRED.) I'm going up to help Phyllis and Maudie with the tables.

FRED: Righto. (*To* ALBRECHT.) I don't drink either, thanks all the same.

> NORA *goes off upstairs.*
> FRED *serves the brandies to the others who gather round the bar.*

ALBRECHT: Who is Epps?

GEORGE (*laughing*): Epp's Cocoa – it's an advertisement that I remember when I was a little boy – 'Epp's Cocoa – Both grateful and comforting'.

ALBRECHT: I see.

LYIA: It's really a code sign, Mr. Richter. George is very high up in the Secret Service – aren't you, darling?

ALBRECHT (*steely for a moment*): What is that?

GEORGE: Yes – my number used to be 8134X – but I was promoted only last week and I am now 8135Y.

LYIA: Why indeed! (*She giggles.*)

CHORLEY: That was a hideous little joke, Lyia – you should be ashamed of yourself.

ALBRECHT (*smiling*): You are pulling my leg, I see.

LYIA: Why, Mr. Richter, how can you be so suspicious?

ALBRECHT: As a matter of fact, Mr. Bourne, I really am very interested. What do you actually do?

GEORGE: Sweet Fanny Adams.

ALBRECHT: What is that?

GEORGE: It's idiomatic – a polite expression for something quite different – like Lebensraum.

ALBRECHT (*with a set smile*): I still do not quite understand, but I gather that you are still joking.

GEORGE: It's a national characteristic, Mr. Richter – whatever happens to us in England we always make jokes.

ALBRECHT: In certain circumstances that might be a little dangerous, might it not?

GEORGE: It might indeed.

ALBRECHT (*lifting his glass*): Heil Hitler.

> ALBRECHT *drinks. There is silence.* CHORLEY *begins to lift his glass and then stops.*

GEORGE (*gently*): That was a mistake, Mr. Richter – a psychological error.

ALBRECHT (*icily*): In what way?

GEORGE: It places us in an embarrassing position.

ALBRECHT: You are a defeated nation. Isn't that an embarrassing position?

GEORGE: Exceedingly. But defeat – among other things – is an attitude of mind. We haven't all of us fully acquired it yet.

ALBRECHT: Then I can only advise you – for your own good – to acquire it as quickly as possible.

CHORLEY: This is all very unpleasant – and quite unnecessary.

ALBRECHT (*with a great effort*): I quite agree. I agree with Mr. Bourne too. For me to expect you to drink with me to my Führer was indeed a psychological error. It was what you describe in England I believe as 'Rushing the fences'. I should be delighted to honour any toast that you care to propose. (*He smiles.*) What shall it be?

GEORGE (*raising his glass*): Epp's Cocoa.

ALBRECHT *laughs charmingly and they all raise their glasses and murmur 'Epp's Cocoa' as the lights fade.*

Scene III

January, 1942.

The time is about ten o'clock in the evening, just before closing time.

Behind the bar are FRED, NORA *and* DORIS. ALMA *is at the downstage end of the bar. At upstage end* CHORLEY BANNISTER *is drinking with* BOBBY PAXTON. BOBBY *is a sleek, rather good-looking young man, there is something vaguely repellent about his personality.*

In addition to these people whom we already know there are several strangers. GLADYS MOTT, *fairly obviously a tart, is having a drink with a German soldier.* HERR HUBERMAN *and* FRAU HUBERMAN *are chatting in German. They are a youngish couple, possibly clerks in one of the ministries. At the table below the door a toutish-looking man,* ALFIE BLAKE, *is reading a sporting paper. In front of him is a glass of beer which he is trying to make last as long as possible.*

When the curtain rises there is a low buzz of conversation, occasionally GLADYS MOTT *giggles rather loudly.*

JANET BRAID *comes in from the street and goes over to join* ALMA *at the bar.*

ALMA: Hallo – I thought you weren't going to turn up.
JANET: Dolly Brand and I went to a film – it went on for hours – all about Frederick the Great.
ALMA: An unpleasant character, I always thought.
JANET: I'm not at all sure that that isn't subversive propaganda, dear.
ALMA: Practically every word that falls from my lips is subversive propaganda, I find. What do you want to drink?
JANET: What is there?

ALMA: No whisky, no gin, very little beer and some rather curious rum.

JANET: Very little beer sounds safest.

ALMA: I think Fred would rather you had rum. He's hoarding the beer to the last drop.

JANET: All right.

ALMA: Fred – a rum for Mrs. Braid.

FRED: Righto – good evening, Mrs. Braid.

JANET: Good evening, Fred.

> GLADYS MOTT *gives a loud laugh.*

That girl seems to find life in occupied England quite hilarious.

FRED: Our Gladys is in good spirits to-night – she's had a windfall.

ALMA: What sort of windfall?

FRED: Well, her 'Steady' – you know – that stout gent from Hamburg who runs that factory I can't pronounce the name of – well, he's been over to Paris for a trip and brought her back a packet of stuff – scent and stockings and what not – she's on top of the world.

JANET: She has no racial inhibitions I see.

FRED: Anything as long as they're Aryans.

ALMA: I suppose one must draw the line somewhere.

> *During this conversation* FRED *has given* ALMA *her rum.* CHORLEY *and* BOBBY *come down from the upper end of the bar.*

CHORLEY: Hallo, Janet – I wanted to see you.

JANET: What a surprising statement, Chorley – I am overwhelmed.

CHORLEY: You know Grant Madison, don't you?

JANET: Yes.

CHORLEY: Is it true that he's written a new play and is going to re-open His Majesty's with it?

JANET: I don't know – I haven't seen him for ages.

CHORLEY: Bobby wants to be in it.

BOBBY: Hullo!

CHORLEY: Do you think you could help?

JANET: Why don't you ring him up yourself – he's in the book.

CHORLEY: I gave him a bad review in *Forethought* for the show he was doing before the Occupation. He's never forgiven me.

JANET: You are putting me rather on the spot, Chorley – I really don't want to appear disagreeable, but you see—

CHORLEY: I suppose he's on your black list – is that it?

JANET: No, not exactly – let's say my grey list – but I really don't approve of the way he's behaved and I certainly don't approve of his re-opening His Majesty's.

CHORLEY: I see no reason why he shouldn't and every reason why he should. The Theatre has got to go on, actors and scene designers and musicians have to earn their livings.

JANET: Yes – I know all that – this is a personal feeling—

CHORLEY (*irritably*): I really think, Janet, that you carry your censorious attitude too far. (*Firmly.*) This country was invaded and occupied. That was a tremendous and most horrible shock, not only to our deep personal feelings but to our national pride and our patriotism.

JANET: You don't consider national pride and patriotism to be deep personal feelings?

CHORLEY: No, I most emphatically do not. They are conditioned by environment and education and habit and propaganda. Patriotism is not an inevitable, fundamental part of human nature. New born babies are not patriotic.

JANET: Really Chorley, the assurance with which you talk nonsense is quite remarkable.

CHORLEY: I am not going to lose my temper with you, Janet. If only I could make you see that to accept circumstances, without prejudice, and to adjust yourself accordingly, is far more admirable and helpful than stubbornly wallowing in a morass of archaic, abstract idealism.

JANET: My son died for that archaic, abstract idealism.

CHORLEY: Rubbish! Forgive me, Janet, but that really is sentimental rubbish. Your son died because he was young and adventurous and liked flying through the air at breakneck speed and pitting his wits and fighting skill against the enemy.

JANET: I don't think he wanted to die.

CHORLEY: I am not decrying his courage. He accepted the risk at the outset – thousands of young men did likewise, but it is highly inaccurate to imagine that either he or they did it for

'Dear old England' or 'Nelson' or 'Magna Carta', or 'Good Queen Bess'!

JANET (*smiling*): You're very intelligent, Chorley, extremely articulate and quite inexpressibly silly.

CHORLEY: It's no good attempting to talk sense to you – you're hopeless.

JANET: Oddly enough I'm not, but we'd better leave it at that, I think, and get back to the point at issue. You want me to introduce a friend of yours to a man who was once a friend of mine and of whom I now most strongly disapprove.

CHORLEY: It is that high and mighty disapproval of yours that is the point at issue.

JANET: My disapproval is not high and mighty. It is carefully considered and, according to my personal view of the general situation, completely logical.

CHORLEY: Hasn't it occurred to you that your personal view might be swayed by hysteria rather than logic?

JANET: No, Chorley. I am not the hysterical type. If I had been I should have slapped you violently in the face two minutes ago.

CHORLEY: Really, Janet – I see no point in our continuing this ridiculous squabble—

JANET: It is neither ridiculous nor a squabble. As a matter of fact it is very important, but I would like to make myself clear. Grant Madison, and others like him, epitomise acceptance and defeat. He did nothing particularly shameful at first, beyond a rather unbecoming eagerness to prance on to the stage before his conquerors at the earliest possible moment. It was a little later that he began to slip. There was that Christmas broadcast – do you remember? Quite innocuous in itself, but he happened to be introduced and signed off by Lord Haw Haw. Then there was that little supper party at Ciro's – admirably publicised – at which Herr Ribbentrop was present. These are just some of the more obvious reasons for my disapproval of him, Chorley, and I disapprove of you for exactly the same reasons, except that you, being less of a public figure, are less publicly contemptible. I think that is all my mounting hysteria permits me to say at the moment. Come on, Alma – let's go.

JANET *and* ALMA *go out.*

CHORLEY: God for Harry, England and St. Agnes!

> *Enter* GEORGE *and* LYIA.

LYIA: Good evening, Chorley – hallo, Bobby.

BOBBY: My dear, you've missed quite a scene.

LYIA: Oh, what a shame – who with and what about?

CHORLEY: Be quiet, Bobby. It was only poor Janet strangling herself with her old school brassiere. It's made of two Union Jacks tied together. You know Grant Madison, don't you, George?

GEORGE: Of course I do – why?

CHORLEY: He's re-opening his Majesty's with his new play and there's a wonderful part in it for Bobby. You wouldn't like to be a dear and suggest him for it would you? I daren't because he spits venom every time he sees me.

GEORGE: All right, Chorley – I'll call him up.

CHORLEY: I was always devoted to you, George.

GEORGE: That calls for a drink. We all have our price, you know.

CHORLEY: What do you want?

GEORGE: I *want* a clear and exquisite Dry Martini made with Gordon's Gin and flavoured with lemon peel, but I'll *settle* for a rum and synthetic pineapple juice.

CHORLEY: Lyia?

LYIA: The same, darling, I'm afraid.

CHORLEY: Bobby?

BOBBY: Why not? We can only die once.

CHORLEY: Fred – four of those repellent rum cocktails, please.

FRED: Righto, Mr. Bannister. (*He proceeds to mix the drinks.*)

> *The light which has been concentrated on the lower end of the bar spreads and becomes general. The conversation becomes general too. This convivial hum dies away into silence when the street door opens and* ALBRECHT RICHTER *comes in accompanied by two Gestapo men in uniform.*

ALBRECHT (*coming over to the bar*): Good evening, Mr. Shattock. I am sorry to inconvenience you. This is merely a routine matter. Good evening, Mrs. Shattock.

NORA: Good evening.

> *The uniformed men proceed round the saloon asking questions in low tones and demanding identity cards.*

CHORLEY (*affably*): Good evening – would you care for a drink?

ALBRECHT: No, thank you – not at the moment. Is there anyone in the public bar, Miss Shattock?

DORIS (*looking through the serving window*): Yes – one or two.

ALBRECHT: Will you please tell them to stay where they are until I have checked up.

DORIS (*through the serving window*): Stay where you are, boys – Robin Hood's here with his merry men.

HERR *and* FRAU HUBERMAN: Heil Hitler!

ALBRECHT: Thank you.

DORIS: Not at all – anything to oblige.

NORA (*reprovingly*): Doris!

> *The uniformed men have arrived at the downstage table.*
>
>   ALFIE BLAKE *jumps up and begins searching through his pockets.*

ALFIE (*agitated*): Strike me if I haven't gone and lost me bloody card.

FRED: Tried all your pockets?

ALFIE: Tell 'em who I am, Fred, for God's sake.

FRED: He's all right, Mr. Richter – it's Alfie Blake – one of our steadies – I've known him for years.

ALBRECHT (*going over to* ALFRED): Nevertheless, he will have to produce his identity card.

ALFIE: I 'ad it on me when I come out – I swear I 'ad.

DORIS: Try looking in your mac—

ALFIE (*searches in his mackintosh pocket and finally finds the card*): Thanks, Dorrie – oh dear! – That give me quite a turn. (*To the men.*) Here you are, cocks.

> *The uniformed men examine his card minutely and then cross over to the bar.*

GEORGE: Do you do this in every pub in the district?

ALBRECHT: Yes, but not regularly – just every now and then.

CHORLEY: What do you hope to find?

ALBRECHT: We don't *hope* to find anything or anyone particularly. As I said before, it's merely a matter of routine.

LYIA: How's the war going?

ALBRECHT: Do you not listen to the radio or read the newspapers?

LYIA: Yes, darling – that's why I'm asking you.

ALBRECHT: I am flattered if you think that I know more than the public information services.

LYIA: You might *say* more.

CHORLEY: I doubt it – Albrecht can be very evasive.

GEORGE: Are you sure you won't have a drink?

ALBRECHT: Do you think that that might loosen my tongue?

GEORGE: Could be.

ALBRECHT: Very well. (*To* FRED.) I'll have a gin and water, please.

FRED: I'm afraid we haven't got any gin.

ALBRECHT: Not even for special customers?

FRED: No, only rum and fruit juice – like what they're having.

ALBRECHT: All right – that'll do.

>   FRED *mixes another cocktail.*

I might be able to remedy the gin situation for you.

NORA (*without enthusiasm*): Very kind of you, I'm sure.

ALBRECHT: A small amount at any rate – enough for you to put aside for Mr. Bannister, Mr. Bourne, Miss Vivian and – even me.

GEORGE: Special customers?

ALBRECHT (*with a smile*): Exactly.

FRED (*about to protest*): Well, you see, Mr. Richter, it's like this—

GEORGE: Don't argue, Fred— (*Firmly.*) It's very kind of Mr. Richter to suggest it.

FRED: Yes, but you see I wouldn't like to be unfair to the public—

LYIA: Don't be so tediously upright, Fred, there's a dear.

NORA (*with great determination*): We really couldn't do it, I'm afraid, Mr. Richter – but thank you very much all the same.

ALBRECHT (*stiffly*): I quite understand.

CHORLEY: Really, Nora – I think you are being both tactless and silly.

FRED: It's a question of principle, Mr. Bannister.

ALBRECHT: Would you have felt the same about it if I had been an Englishman? I am curious to know.

FRED: If you had been an Englishman you wouldn't have made the suggestion.

LYIA: You wouldn't have been able to get the gin either.

ALBRECHT: Would you be kind enough to answer me a question, Mr. Shattock?

FRED: What is it?

ALBRECHT (*suavely*): You, I take it, represent a certain class in this country – shall we say the middle class – that is so, is it not?

FRED: I don't represent anybody – I'm what I am.

ALBRECHT: Nevertheless for the sake of argument we can assume that you – being what you are – are an ordinary middle-class Englishman.

FRED: I'm a publican – that might mean any class.

CHORLEY: Don't be so tiresome and obstructive and suspicious, Fred. Mr. Richter isn't trying to trap you.

FRED: How do I know?

NORA (*grimly*): Let the gentleman ask his question, Fred.

ALBRECHT: The question is this – in your opinion how long will it take ordinary hard-working people like yourselves to be reconciled to the inevitable?

FRED: Inevitable? How do you mean?

ALBRECHT: Owing to the fortunes of war and superior equipment, determination and power, my country has taken possession of yours, and will remain in possession for many years – possibly for ever – this is inevitable.

FRED: Is it?

ALBRECHT: Obviously.

FRED: Do you think that our Dominions overseas and our friends in America are going to allow you to occupy this country indefinitely?

ALBRECHT: They will have no choice in the matter. If only you British had trained your minds to be less insular and more realistic you would understand that your friends in America are a small minority. Three-quarters of the United States are not in the least concerned to-day as to whether Great Britain survives or not. Before you were conquered you were still a potent force in the world. Now you are not. America is fully occupied with a war against us in the Atlantic and the Japanese in the Pacific. Both these she will eventually lose—

FRED: Is that inevitable too?

ALBRECHT: Quite. (*Preserving his suavity.*) You mentioned – a trifle optimistically – your Dominions overseas. Taking them in order of their possible importance to you. Canada is the nearest; but Canada is too closely allied to the United States both geographically and ideologically to move independently. Australia is thirteen thousand miles away. New Zealand is equally far and equally negligible. South Africa will support your cause only for as long as General Smuts holds the reins. His successor will support ours. That we have already arranged. There remains a few scattered Colonies. Malaya and Borneo which will be under Japanese domination within a few weeks. India which, as usual, is in a state of racial and economic chaos – I am not painting this gloomy picture maliciously, Mr. Shattock – I am merely trying to convince you of the actual facts of the case.

FRED: Like so many foreigners, Mr. Richter, you speak English much better than you understand it.

ALBRECHT: I see that I have failed.

FRED: Even supposing all you say is true – even if we are in the soup up to our necks – what do you expect me to do about it? What's all this in aid of?

ALBRECHT: I know that you are too stubborn to believe me, Mr. Shattock, but I assure you that my intentions are friendly.

FRED: All right – so what?

ALBRECHT: I asked you just how long, in your opinion, would it take ordinary, decently educated, hard-working people like yourself to become reconciled to the situation.

FRED: Never, Mr. Richter. Nor our children after us, nor their children's children.

ALBRECHT: Admirable. That is exactly what I hoped you would say. That is just the quality in the British that we Germans have always saluted, that infinite capacity for holding true to an idea. We, too, believe utterly and completely, individually and collectively in our idea. We believe that it is our destiny to rule the world and by doing so make it a better place. We have always believed that and that is why – at last it is coming true. We are also, Mr. Shattock, a great deal more intelligent than your countrymen gave us credit for. You, for instance, I am sure were convinced that when we invaded you and conquered you, we should immediately embark on a considered programme of organised murder, rape, pillage and destruction. Is not that so?

FRED: Yes.

ALBRECHT: Have we done so?

FRED: Not yet.

ALBRECHT: And why do you suppose we have been so restrained?

FRED: I should think you were waiting to see which way the wind blows.

ALBRECHT: Not at all. We know that already. Our policy in this country – contrary to all expectations – is essentially a friendly one. In that lies the genius of Hitler; the psychological intuition which enables him not only to dominate the human mind but to understand the human heart as well. Believe me the Führer is fully aware of the inherent greatness of this nation.

NORA: Very nice of him, I'm sure.

FRED: Nora!

ALBRECHT: The Führer believes that the spirit of this country is indestructible. He believes – in spite of what you said just now, Mr. Shattock – that ultimately, in so many years, Great Britain will become reconciled to the inevitable, not through any weakening of her spirit but through the strengthening of her innate wisdom and common sense. As soon as that innate wisdom and common sense reasserts itself, as soon as you are willing to renounce your imperialistic convictions and cut your losses sensibly and courageously, then we can stand firmly together – your country and mine who have so much in common – and combine to drive the evil forces of Jewry and Communism from the face of the earth.

GEORGE: That was a very excellent speech, Mr. Richter.

FRED: Do you believe it, Mr. Bourne?

GEORGE: The important point is, Fred, that Mr. Richter believes it.

CHORLEY: It's rather a shock, isn't it, Fred, to be made to realise that we in England haven't got the monopoly of ideals?

FRED: Do you think that what the gentleman said just now represented an ideal?

CHORLEY: It's an intelligent and consistent policy for the future of civilisation.

FRED: There are lots of Jews in England, Mr. Richter, and lots of Communists too – what's going to happen to them?

ALBRECHT (*sharply*): The former will be liquidated or deported. The latter will change their views.

FRED: Liquidated?

ALBRECHT: A certain amount of ruthlessness is unavoidable when the end justifies the means.

FRED (*turning away*): I knew there was a catch in it. Last orders, please.

ALBRECHT (*briskly*): Good-night, Mr. Shattock.

FRED: Good-night, Mr. Richter.

DORIS (*pointing over her shoulder with her thumb*): The chain gang's still standing to attention in the 'Public', Mr. Richter. You can go through the kitchen or round by the street door, whichever you like.

ALBRECHT: Thank you, Miss Shattock. Good-night.

DORIS: Sleepy tighty.

ALBRECHT (*to the others*): Good-night.

> He makes a sign to the two uniformed men and they follow him out through the street door.
>
> There is silence for a moment.

CHORLEY: Come on, Bobby. I think, Fred, that your attitude was a little unwise.

FRED: You are at liberty to think anything you choose, Mr. Bannister. (*He glances up at the clock.*) Time, gentlemen, please.

> There is a general buzz of conversation.
>
> The HUBERMANS go. ALFIE BLAKE exits. The German soldier goes out, rather unsteadily, with GLADYS MOTT. He turns at the door.

GERMAN SOLDIER: Heil Hitler!

FRED (*affably*): Heil my foot!

CHORLEY (*to* GEORGE): I shall ring you up in the morning, George, and remind you about Grant Madison. (CHORLEY *and* BOBBY *go out.*)

FRED: Have they finished the round up in the 'Public', Doris?

DORIS (*looking through the serving window*): Yes – everybody's gone.

FRED: Shut down then and do the till.

DORIS: Righto, Dad. (*She shuts the window and proceeds to empty the till and begins to count it.*)

GEORGE: Come on, Lyia – before Fred throws us out.

FRED: Would you like a nightcap, Mr. Bourne?

GEORGE: No, I think we'd better go really – Lyia's got to run through her new numbers and she's on at eleven.

FRED (*holding up a bottle of Gordon's gin*): Just one – I keep this put by for Special Customers.

LYIA: You wily old hypocrite, Fred.

GEORGE (*holding up his hand*): Heil Gordon

NORA: Nice thing if his nibs comes back and catches us red-handed. I'd better lock the door. You don't mind going out by the mews, do you?

LYIA: Of course not.

> *Just as* NORA *reaches the door it bursts open and* BILLY GRAINGER *staggers in. He is a young man in the twenties. His head is bandaged and his clothes are dirty and bedraggled. He looks exhausted.*

NORA (*giving a little cry*): Oh!

BILLY (*breathing heavily*): Excuse me.

NORA (*quickly*): I'm afraid you're too late – it's after hours.

BILLY (*moving uncertainly over to the bar*): Please – please – can you tell me where I can find Mr. and Mrs. Grainger – I've been to their flat – they're not there—

FRED: Who are you?

BILLY: I'm their son – I've escaped – escaped from the camp— (*His voice dies and he falls down in a dead faint.*)

NORA: Good heavens!

FRED: Lock the door, Nora – quick.

> NORA *locks and bolts the door and draws the curtain over the windows.* GEORGE *kneels down by* BILLY *and lifts his head on to his knee.* FRED *quickly pours out a large tot of rum and comes round the bar with it.* DORIS *leaves the till and comes round too.*

FRED: Here – give him this.

NORA: What are we to do?

GEORGE: He's out like a light. (*To* FRED.) Here – give it to me. (*He takes the rum from* FRED *and forces a little between the boy's lips.*)

LYIA: Let me loosen his collar. (*She kneels down and loosens* BILLY'*s collar.*)

DORIS: I wonder if anyone saw him come in. (*She goes over to the window and peers cautiously through the curtains.*) There's nobody about.

FRED: He probably waited until the coast was clear. You'd better fetch Dr. Venning – Doris – it won't take a minute – go by the back way.

LYIA: Where does he live – Dr. Venning?

FRED: Just at the bottom of the mews.

NORA: Fred – we must be careful.

FRED: Dr. Venning's all right – go on, Doris – hop it.

DORIS: All right, Dad.

> *She runs out – upstage.*

GEORGE: There's more wrong with him than just a faint – look at his wrists – he's starved and exhausted.

NORA: I don't like this, Fred – really I don't. It's dangerous.

FRED: We can't turn him out, Nora – you know we can't.

LYIA: I think he's coming round.

BILLY (*opening his eyes and trying to speak*): I – I—

FRED: It's all right, son – take it easy.

GEORGE: Let's lift him up – help me, Fred.

> GEORGE *and* FRED *lift* BILLY *gently into a chair.*

FRED: That's better.

GEORGE (*giving* BILLY *the rum*): Here – sip some more of this.

BILLY (*weakly*): Thanks. (*He drinks some rum and splutters a bit.*)

NORA: I'll run and put the kettle on – a cup of tea will do him more good than that stuff.

> *She goes off to the kitchen.*

BILLY: Mr. and Mrs. Grainger – where are they?

FRED: They've probably gone to the pictures – they'll be home later on. Did anyone see you come in?

BILLY: No – I hid in a doorway opposite – it was quite dark – nobody saw me.

FRED: Good.

GEORGE: What the hell are we going to do with him?

FRED: We'll have to let the Graingers know somehow or other.

GEORGE: It'll be a bit tricky for them, won't it?

FRED: We'll think of something.

> NORA *comes back carrying a plate.*

NORA: I've put the kettle on. Here's some bread and butter and a bit of sausage—

GEORGE: I shouldn't give him anything to eat until the doctor comes.

BILLY (*trying to get to his feet*): Doctor! – I don't want to see no doctor!

FRED (*holding him down*): Relax, son—

BILLY (*almost frantic*): No really – don't let a doctor see me – he might – he might— (*He puts his hand to his bandaged head.*)

FRED: Is your head paining you?

BILLY: No – that is – oh please – I don't want to see no doctor.

FRED: Shut up, now, there's a good boy, and just do what you're told. The doctor's all right, he's a friend – nobody's going to give you away.

> DORIS *comes quietly in from the door at the back followed by* DOCTOR VENNING. *He is a middle-aged, solid-looking man. He carries a small doctor's bag.*

Good evening, Doctor Venning.

DR. VENNING: Good evening, Fred – Hallo, Nora.

FRED: This is Mr. Bourne and Miss Vivian.

DR. VENNING: How do you do? (*He goes over to* BILLY.) Well, my boy – feeling better?

BILLY: Yes, thank you, sir.

DR. VENNING (*indicating his bandage*): What's this?

BILLY: Nothing, sir – that is nothing much – I just fell off a motor-bike and grazed my face.

DR. VENNING: I'd better have a look at it.

BILLY (*obviously frightened*): It's nothing, sir – really it isn't.

DR. VENNING: Would you rather I didn't look at it?

BILLY (*in a whisper*): Yes, sir – if you don't mind, sir.

DR. VENNING: Very well – we'll leave it for the moment and have a look at the rest of you. Do you think you can stand up?

BILLY: Yes, sir. (*He stands up rather unsteadily.*)

The DOCTOR *puts his arm round his shoulder, and, with his other hand, moves his face gently from right to left.*

DR. VENNING: Walk over to the bar and back, will you?

BILLY: Yes, sir. (*He does so – with an effort.*)

DR. VENNING: Good boy. Now sit down again.

     BILLY *does so, wearily.*

When did you last eat?

BILLY: Yesterday morning.

DR. VENNING (*smiling*): Would you like a cup of tea?

BILLY: Yes, sir.

NORA: I'll go and get it, doctor – the kettle's on.

     NORA *goes out.*

DR. VENNING: Good, Nora. (*Seeing the plate.*) Eat a bit of bread. (*He hands it to* BILLY.)

BILLY (*taking it*): Thank you, sir. (*He eats it ravenously.*)

DR. VENNING: Go easy – you can have some more presently.

     There is silence while he eats. GEORGE *breaks it.*

GEORGE: How about that drink you promised us, Fred?

FRED: Righto – I forgot. (*He goes behind the bar.*) Would you like one, Doctor?

DR. VENNING (*who is still watching* BILLY): No, thanks.

FRED (*pouring out the gin – to* LYIA): Anything with it?

LYIA: Good God, no – it would be sacrilege!

     NORA *comes back with a cup of tea and gives it to* BILLY.

NORA: Here – there's some saccharine in the saucer if you fancy it.

BILLY: Thanks – thanks very much.

DR. VENNING (*gently*): I don't think there's much wrong with you, you know, beyond exhaustion and malnutrition, but I can't say for certain until you let me see what's under that bandage.

BILLY: I'm all right, sir – really I am! (*He takes a sip of tea.*)

DR. VENNING: I think you'd better tell us what happened – you can trust us – nobody will give you away.

BILLY (*looking down – almost inaudibly*): I – I escaped—

DR. VENNING: When?

BILLY: Three days ago.

DR. VENNING: Where from – which camp?

BILLY: Stalag 23 – the Isle of Wight – the one between Ryde and Cowes.

DR. VENNING: What did they put you in for?

BILLY: I was in the R.A.F. ground staff. At the beginning when we were all interned at Beaconsfield, I tried to escape. I had three tries but each time they caught me. Then instead of drafting me into a job like the others, they moved me to the Isle of Wight.

DR. VENNING: Have they beaten you, ill-treated you in any way?

BILLY: Not lately – not since Easter, really.

DR. VENNING: What did they do to you then?

BILLY: I tried to escape, and they caught me.

DR. VENNING: What did they do to you?

BILLY: They hurt my feet – and they hurt my hands – and they – and they— (*He stops because his voice chokes and he is almost crying.*)

DR. VENNING: Well, never mind about that for the moment. How did you get away this time?

BILLY (*with an effort*): A pal of mine and I started it together – we were in one of the end huts and just outside it there was a weak place in the wire. Three nights ago we got out on our stomachs and crawled nearly a mile and a half down to the beach. There was a broken bit of telegraph pole lying high up in the grass and we managed to roll it down into the water. We pushed it out and swam – shoving it in front of us – then when we got tired we hung on to it and rested. Then when we was halfway across – my pal – (*He hesitates.*) – my pal – gave up— (*He stops.*)

DR. VENNING: You mean he hadn't the strength to go farther.

BILLY: Yes – I was a better swimmer than he was, really – I tried to help him, but it wasn't any good – he – he—

DR. VENNING (*sharply*): Skip that bit. Where did you fetch up?

BILLY: Lee-on-the-Solent. I got ashore and crawled inland. After a bit I got up and walked for a couple of miles – then it was getting light and I hid in a farmyard, then I got caught by the lady that owned the farm – it was her that gave me the bandage for my head— (*He stops.*)

DR. VENNING: What about the motor-bike?

BILLY: There wasn't any motor-bike, sir.

DR. VENNING: All right – go on.

BILLY: She gave me some food and took me in a farm cart – hidden under some sacking – for a long way – then she dropped me off – somewhere near Fareham, I think it was – and I walked.

DR. VENNING: You said you ate yesterday morning – where was that?

BILLY: Near Guildford, sir. I met a clergyman – he gave me some cold meat and potato and five shillings.

DR. VENNING: And then— ?

BILLY: Then I got so tired that I couldn't walk any further, so I got a bus as far as Kingston. Then I walked again – and it got dark – and I knew about this place because of Mum and Dad having written to me about how they came here a lot. When I got home they weren't there – so I came here and waited outside until I saw it was closing up.

DR. VENNING: Now then – off with that bandage.

BILLY (after a quick look round): All right, sir.

Helped by DR. VENNING, *he slowly unwinds the bandage from his head, disclosing two large letters 'K.G.' branded on to his forehead. The scars are red but quite dry.*

NORA: My God!

DORIS: Poor kid.

DR. VENNING: Is this what they did to you last Easter?

BILLY: Yes, sir.

NORA: K.G. – K.G. – what does it mean?

GEORGE: Kriegs Gefangener – prisoner of war.

DR. VENNING (examining it): Difficult to cover.

GEORGE: I should have said impossible.

DR. VENNING: The bandage will serve temporarily, but not for long. It's too dangerous.

FRED: What are we to do, Doctor?

DR. VENNING: He'll be all right for to-night, providing they haven't traced him. (Looking at GEORGE and LYIA.) I think that the fewer people concerned with whatever happens from now on, the safer it will be for all of us.

LYIA (*finishing her gin*): You're quite right, Doctor – we'd better go, George.

GEORGE: All right. (*To* DR. VENNING.) I have a feeling that we have met before, Doctor.

DR. VENNING: Really? I wonder where it could have been?

GEORGE: Were you by any chance with the B.E.F. in the early months of the war?

DR. VENNING: No – I was with the R.A.F. Here in England.

GEORGE (*lightly*): Then it couldn't have been Dunkirk, could it?

DR. VENNING (*giving him a sharp look*): Dunkirk?

GEORGE: Yes. It's quite a distinction not to have been at Dunkirk really – the beaches were crowded with people one knew.

LYIA: What are you talking about, darling? You weren't anywhere near Dunkirk.

GEORGE (*smiling*): I might have been.

DR. VENNING (*turning away*): Yes – we both might have been.

GEORGE: Good-night, Doctor – I hope we shall meet again. I should like to be able to help over this business – so if there is anything I can do, let me know. My number is in the book and the name is Bourne – George Bourne.

DR. VENNING: Thank you – I'll remember.

GEORGE: Doris – will you let us out of the back door?

DORIS: All right – this way.

LYIA: Good-night, Nora – good-night, Fred – thanks for that wonderful gin! (*To* BILLY.) Good luck.

BILLY: Thank you, miss.

GEORGE (*to* BILLY): Chin up!

BILLY: You bet, sir.

> GEORGE *and* LYIA *follow* DORIS *out into the passage.*

DR. VENNING: Now then – on with the bandage again. Help me, will you, Nora?

> *He proceeds to rebandage* BILLY's *head, assisted by* NORA. DORIS *comes back.*

DORIS: Now what?

DR. VENNING: Nobody else saw him, did they – apart from Mr. Bourne and Miss Vivian?

DORIS: No – they're all right.

DR. VENNING: Good. (*He and* NORA *finish the bandage.*) Now then –
what's your name?

BILLY: Billy Grainger.

DR. VENNING: Have you any identification papers of any sort?

BILLY: No, sir. They stripped us clean when we was put behind
the wire.

DR. VENNING: Any other marks or scars anywhere?

BILLY: No, sir.

DR. VENNING: Now, if you put yourself in my hands completely,
I can help you. But you must promise to do exactly what I tell
you.

BILLY: Yes, sir.

DR. VENNING: To begin with, you must give up all idea of
getting in touch with your mother and father. They mustn't
know anything about this, anything at all. You are going to
stay with me for tonight. To-morrow morning I am going to
drive you to the other side of London to a clinic. There you
will have an operation on your face. They'll probably do a bit
of grafting from your backside. You have been badly burnt
when some petrol caught fire in Swaine's Garage, where you
work – is that clear? Swaine's Garage.

BILLY: Yes, sir.

DR. VENNING: You will stay in the clinic for several weeks. We
will think of another name for you. You must remember to
talk as little as possible – even to the nurses. Do you agree to
all this?

BILLY: Oh, yes, sir. Thank you, sir.

FRED: It's very good of you, Doctor.

DR. VENNING: Are you ready to come now?

NORA: Oughtn't he to have a bit more to eat, Doctor? I could
cook him something hot.

DR. VENNING: No, Nora . . . I'll see to that. I want to get him out
of here as soon as possible. Come on, Billy. Doris – pop up to
the corner and see if the coast's clear.

DORIS: All right – I've got to take Nipper out, anyway.

        BILLY *rises.*

FRED (*shaking hands with* BILLY): Good-night, son – I think you did
bloody well. Good luck to you!

NORA: Good-night, Billy – take care of yourself.

BILLY: Thanks— (*His voice breaks a little.*) Thanks ever so much for doing all this for me – I really—

FRED: Go on – we'll see you again some day.

DR. VENNING (*putting his arm round* BILLY'S *shoulder*): Come along. (*To* FRED *and* NORA.) I'll let you know from time to time how things go, but please never telephone me or ask questions. Good-night, both of you. Lead on, Doris.

    DR. VENNING *and* BILLY *follow* DORIS *out.*

NORA (*sinking into a chair and bursting into tears*): Oh, my God!

FRED (*coming to her*): Come off it, Nora – there isn't anything to cry about.

NORA: I can't help it . . . the poor boy . . .

FRED (*giving her his handkerchief*): Here – dry up – there's no sense in upsetting yourself. He'll be all right – thanks to Dr. Venning.

NORA: He'd be about the same age as Stevie, wouldn't he – if Stevie hadn't been shot down, he might have been . . .

FRED (*putting his arm round her*): There, there, dear – don't start off about Stevie now . . .

NORA (*with sudden violence*): I'm glad Stevie was killed, see? I'm glad! If he hadn't been, he might have been tortured like this boy was, branded with hot irons—

FRED (*sharply*): Shut up, Nora! What's the use of thinking of things like that . . .

NORA (*dabbing her eyes*): I'll be all right – it's been an evening of upsets.

FRED: Want a nip of Gordon's?

NORA: No, dear – I'm okay.

FRED: That's good – there's no law against me having a nip myself. (*He pours himself out a gin and puts the bottle away behind the bar.*)

NORA (*coming over to the bar*): I wouldn't mind a cigarette if you've got one.

FRED: Righto – here. (*He gives her one and lights it for her over the bar.*)

NORA: All the same – I meant what I said just now.

FRED: What about?

NORA: About Stevie.

FRED: Now then, Nora . . .

NORA: I am glad he was killed – really I am. If I knew he was alive – in this country – I'd never have a moment's peace. I think I'd go barmy . . .

FRED: Maybe you're right. I'm not arguing about it – but do try and put the thought of him out of your mind. It only makes you miserable.

NORA: Not always it doesn't. Sometimes it makes me happy to think of him.

FRED: All right – have it your own way. Go on up to bed, there's a dear. I'll finish the till and wait for Doris – we'll be up in a few minutes.

NORA (*listlessly*): All right. (*Goes behind bar and collects handbag from shelf, and goes out through arch.*)

    FRED, *left alone, stands behind the bar staring into space thoughtfully for a moment. He sighs.*

FRED (*with glistening eyes – suddenly holding up his glass*): Here's to you, son. (*He drinks.*)

    The lights fade on the scene.

Scene IV

February, 1942. Just before closing time. About 9.30 p.m.

    The GRAINGERS *are at their usual table under the window.* ALFIE BLAKE'*s wife,* LILY, *a desiccated-looking woman, is at the downstage table.*

    Behind the bar are FRED, NORA *and* DORIS.

    The street door opens, and DR. VENNING *comes in. He goes over to the bar.*

DR. VENNING: Good evening, Fred. Hallo, Nora.

NORA: Good evening, Dr. Venning.

FRED: What'll it be, Doctor?

DR. VENNING: Any beer left?

FRED: In a manner of speaking, yes – but it's terrible stuff, I warn you.

DR. VENNING: Never mind – it's wet.

DORIS (*turning from the serving window*): Oh, hello, Dr. Venning! I didn't see you come in.

Enter BEN. *Crosses to bar, stands upstage of* DR. VENNING.

DR. VENNING: I've got some news for you, Doris – for all three of you, as a matter of fact.

BEN: Half of mild, please.

DR. VENNING: You remember that young friend of mine who got burnt in a garage fire?

DORIS: Yes – but I can't think of his name. What is his name?

DR. VENNING: Fawcett – John Fawcett.

DORIS: Of course – Johnny Fawcett! I remember now. How is he?

DR. VENNING: Fine. He had an operation, you know, but he's out of hospital now. He's got a job driving a truck – so don't be surprised if he should come popping in one of these fine days.

NORA: I'm glad he's all right – we often wondered how he got on.

DR. VENNING (*raising his glass*): I thought I'd just let you know.

DORIS: Thanks, Doctor.

DR. VENNING: He quite lost touch with those friends of his, you know – Mr. and Mrs. Grainger.

NORA: Sssh!

DR. VENNING: Apparently they moved, or something. Anyhow, he can't find them. I think he'd like them to know that he is all right.

DORIS: I'll see that they know, Doctor.

BEN: Excuse me, are you Dr. Venning?

DR. VENNING: Yes.

BEN: I have a message for you. (*Gives him a note.*)

DR. VENNING: Thanks.

BEN *goes out after finishing his drink.*

FRED: They've been in a bad way – five times they've been had up for questioning – five times in two weeks.

NORA: Don't talk about it now, Fred.

FRED: All right – all right—

DR. VENNING (*to* DORIS): Don't say any more than you need. Just let them know. I must be off. (*He pays* FRED *for his beer.*) Goodnight.

NORA: Come in again soon.

DR. VENNING: George Bourne hasn't been in to-day, has he?

DORIS: No. He's away – in Brighton.

DR. VENNING: Yes, I know – I got him the health permit to go. But he's due back to-day or to-morrow. Tell him to call me if he should come in.

FRED: Righto.

> DR. VENNING *goes out.*
>> ALFIE BLAKE *comes in from up left, followed by* MR. WILLIAMS, *a superior business friend.*

ALFIE (*belligerently*): I'm not afraid of the bloody Germans!

MRS. BLAKE: Of course you are, dear – don't talk so silly. (*Rising and sitting him down at their table.*)

ALFIE: If little old 'Itler come in here this very minute, d'you know what I'd do?

MRS. BLAKE: Yes, dear – exactly what I'd do, run like hell! Would you care for anything more, Mr. Williams?

WILLIAMS: No, thanks.

ALFIE: And you call yourself an Englishwoman . . .

MRS. BLAKE: Be quiet, Alfie, there's a dear! Whatever will Mr. Williams think?

ALFIE: Who cares what Mr. Williams thinks? Who does Mr. Williams think he is?

MRS. BLAKE: Mr. Williams, dear, I expect. (*To* WILLIAMS.) Don't pay any attention to him, he gets like this sometimes.

ALFIE: Gets like what?

MRS. BLAKE: Now you put a sock in it, Alfie, see? Or else I shall forget I'm a lady and lose my temper.

ALFIE: So you'd run away from 'Itler, would you?

MRS. BLAKE: Yes – as fast as me legs could carry me.

ALFIE: Call yourself an Englishwoman . . .

MRS. BLAKE (*rising*): Come along, Mr. Williams. This is where we came in.

ALFIE (*meeting* MR. GRAINGER *who is crossing to the bar*): Call yourself an Englishwoman!

> MRS. BLAKE *and* MR. WILLIAMS *go out with dignity.* ALFIE *follows them, mumbling angrily.*
>> MR. GRAINGER *goes over to the bar.*

MR. GRAINGER: That'll be all, thanks, Fred.

FRED: Want me to charge it?

MR. GRAINGER: No, I'd better pay – I owe you about a week's worth.

FRED: Righto – I've got it written down – half a mo'.

DORIS: Had any more trouble lately, Mr. Grainger?

MR. GRAINGER: No. They've left us alone since Monday.

DORIS: You haven't heard nothing – from him?

MR. GRAINGER: No. I have a sort of feeling that he's all right – I have had all along, as a matter of fact – but Vi's terribly upset – she thinks he's dead.

DORIS (*leaning across the bar*): He isn't dead, Mr. Grainger. He's well and he's safe. He wants you to know that much, but not any more. You're not to know any more.

MR. GRAINGER (*agitated*): What do you mean, Doris? How do you—

DORIS: Don't get excited – what I said is true – absolutely true. Don't ask any questions. Don't tell Mrs. Grainger – in here. Tell her quietly when you've got home.

MR. GRAINGER: But – I don't understand—

DORIS: You understand plain English, don't you? That's all – no more – napoo – fini!

FRED (*handing* MR. GRAINGER *a bit of paper*): Here you are, Mr. Grainger.

MR. GRAINGER (*pulling himself together*): Oh – thanks, Fred— (*He fumbles in his wallet, produces pound note.*) Here . . .

FRED: Thanks. (*He pays it into the till.*)

NORA: It's been a lovely day considering, hasn't it?

MR. GRAINGER: Yes.

NORA: Did you see the procession?

MR. GRAINGER: (*still bewildered*): No, I – er – didn't.

NORA (*gently*): It really is all right, Mr. Grainger – don't worry.

MR. GRAINGER: But all I want to know is, who said ·so? I mean, how did Doris come to know?

DORIS: I was given a message for you – I can't tell you how or where or who it was gave it to me. There now – that's plain enough, isn't it? Don't ask any more questions and keep quiet.

MR. GRAINGER: All right. Thanks, Doris – thanks a lot. (*He returns to his table.*) Ready, Mother?

MRS. GRAINGER (*rising*): Yes, dear.

MR. GRAINGER (*over his shoulder*): Good-night, Fred – good-night, Nora – good-night, Doris.

MRS. GRAINGER: Good-night.

FRED: Good-night.

> *They go out, amid 'good-nights' from* FRED, DORIS *and* NORA.
> DORIS *collects some money and two mugs from the serving window.* FRED *comes round the bar, locks and bolts the street door, and collects some glasses from the tables.* DORIS *says 'good-night' through the serving window and shuts it down.*

NORA: That Nipper's out in the mews barking his head off. You might let him in, Dorrie.

DORIS: All right, Mum. I'll go round and shut up the 'Public' first.

> DORIS *goes out, humming a tune.*

FRED: I think I'll leave the till until after supper. (*Crossing and locking the main door.*)

NORA: Fred—

FRED: Yes, dear?

NORA: How do you suppose he did all that without being found out?

FRED: Who?

NORA: Dr. Venning.

FRED: I don't know. I expect he's got a few friends here and there with a bit of influence on the side ...

NORA: He's risking his life, isn't he?

FRED: Lots of people are doing that, I expect.

NORA: We're not.

FRED: Now then, Nora – what's biting you?

NORA: I wish we were sometimes, and that's a fact.

FRED: Were what?

NORA: Doing a bit more—

FRED: Don't be so silly – what could we do? There's no sense in asking for trouble.

NORA: Dr. Venning's asking for trouble.

FRED: Well, that's his look-out.

NORA: I can't get that boy out of my mind – ever since it happened, over seven weeks ago, I've been wondering—

FRED: What have you been wondering?

NORA: Well, there must be lots of people doing what Dr. Venning's doing, mustn't there? Hiding escaped prisoners, getting them new identity papers, starting them off in jobs right under the Jerries' noses . . .

DORIS (*coming back*): I'll go and fetch Nipper in now . . .

FRED: That's right, Doris.

DORIS: What are you two looking so solemn about?

FRED: Your mother's getting ideas . . .

NORA: Now then, Fred!

DORIS: What sort of ideas?

FRED (*quietly*): I don't know – not really. I don't think she does, either. All I do know is that we've got to be careful – careful what we do, careful what we say – even careful what we think . . .

NORA: What for?

FRED: Because we might just as well go on living as not.

NORA: Stevie didn't go on living.

FRED: What's Stevie got to do with it?

NORA (*with heat*): Everything! If he were here now he wouldn't be just sitting down and being careful, would he? He'd be up to something – like Dr. Venning is – like I expect a lot of people are. We can't go on like this for ever, just doing what we're told and being frightened to speak our minds. We must . . .

   A bell peals. She stops talking abruptly.

FRED: That's the back door!

DORIS: Who'd be ringing the back door bell at this time of night?

FRED: Might be Dr. Venning – might be anybody—

NORA (*rigid – as though she were listening for something*): Go and see who it is, Dorrie.

DORIS: Righto, Mum. (*Looking at her.*) What's the matter?

NORA (*quietly*): I don't know. Go and see who it is.

    DORIS *runs out into the passage.*

FRED (*anxiously*): Are you feeling all right?

NORA (*staring straight in front of her*): Yes – I'm feeling all right.

FRED (*coming round the bar*): Nora – Nora, old girl – what's the matter? What is it?

NORA: I tell you I don't know.

FRED: What are you staring like that for, Nora?

NORA: I'm not staring. I'm listening.

FRED: If it isn't Dr. Venning, it's probably only Mrs. Capper wanting to borrow some tea or something—

NORA: Be quiet a minute, Fred. Dorrie's coming back.

    DORIS *comes in slowly. She is white and trembling, but obviously making a staunch effort to control herself.*

DORIS (*in rather a stifled voice*): Mum . . .

NORA: Yes, dear?

DORIS: You've got to be calm, Mum – you mustn't get into a state or upset yourself. Sit down, Mum. Please be a dear and sit down. . . . (*She drags a chair from one of the tables.*) Here you are . . .

FRED: What the hell's going on?

NORA: I don't want to sit down, Dorrie – I'm quite all right standing.

DORIS: Mum – oh, Mum – you've got to be prepared for a shock, dear – a great shock.

FRED: What do you mean? What are you talking about?

DORIS: I'm trying to break it to you as calmly as I can. You see . . .

NORA (*quietly*): Go on, Dorrie – say what you have to say.

DORIS: It's . . . it's Stevie, Mum.

NORA (*with sudden sharpness*): Yes – go on – go on!

DORIS (*with a rush*): He wasn't killed at all. He's here.

NORA (*closing her eyes and gripping her hands tightly together*): Yes – I thought that was who it was.

DORIS (*going to the door*): Stevie – you'd better come in now. (*She goes back to* NORA.) He's all right – he's not wounded or anything – he looks fine . . .

STEPHEN *comes in. He is a nice-looking young man of about twenty-seven. His clothes are nondescript. He looks healthy enough, but a little strained. He goes straight to* NORA *and takes her in his arms. She buries her head against his shoulder.*

STEVIE (*over* NORA's *head*): Hello, Dad!

FRED (*struggling for words*): We thought – we thought you were dead . . . we thought you'd been shot down and killed. We thought . . .

STEVIE: Yes – I know.

FRED *comes over to him, making a heroic effort not to cry. He puts his arms round him.*

Give way, Mum. You're all tightened up and shaking. Give way and have a good cry, it'll make you feel better.

NORA: I can't . . . I . . . I . . . oh, Stevie, my son – my son . . . (*She breaks down.*)

STEVIE (*helping her into a chair*): That's the stuff! Poor old Mum! I didn't want to give you quite such a shock, but it couldn't be helped. There wasn't any way of warning you – not any way that was safe. . . .

FRED (*brokenly*): Stevie – for Christ's sake – what does it all mean? Where have you come from? How did you get here? It's too much to believe – all in a minute . . .

STEVIE: It's all right, Dad – everything's under control—

DORIS (*sniffing*): For God's sake don't you start crying too, Dad – you'll have us all at it!

NORA (*muffled – into her handkerchief*): I knew it! I knew it when I heard Nipper barking . . .

FRED: Don't talk so silly, Nora! How could you have known it?

NORA: I did, I tell you – I did. Something inside me knew. He's been getting closer to me – all these weeks. I've been waiting, not knowing what it was that I was waiting for, but knowing all the time that it was something – something to do with Stevie . . .

FRED: I had better go and lock the back door.

DORIS: It's all right, Dad, it's locked and bolted.

NORA (*sobbing uncontrollably*): Stevie . . .

STEVIE: You'd better go and put the kettle on, Dorrie. This situation seems to be getting out of hand.

DORIS: Okay. Stevie! (*She suddenly flings her arms round him.*) Oh, God, it's so wonderful to see you – I can't believe it yet – truly I can't! I shan't be a minute. Please don't say anything until I come back – please, please don't say a word . . .

She runs out.

STEVIE: Come on, Mum – don't overdo it, there's a dear – I haven't seen your face properly yet. Let's have a look. (*He lifts her head and stands looking down at her, smiling.*) That's better.

NORA: You're thinner than you were when – when you went away.

STEVIE: I'm Sandow compared to what I was when I left the prison camp.

FRED: Prison camp? What prison camp? Where?

STEVIE: France – near Lyons – a long time ago – eleven months, to be exact.

FRED: But since then, where have you been? How did you get here?

STEVIE: Don't rush me, Dad. Let's have a cigarette and relax for a minute. This is a bit upsetting for me too, you know. I've been wondering for weeks if I'd find you all right. I wasn't even sure you were alive – anything might have happened to you.

FRED (*giving him a cigarette*): Here you are, son. Would you like a drink of something? I've got some Gordon's.

STEVIE: No – I'd rather wait and have a cup of tea.

DORIS *comes in with a tray with cups and saucers, etc., and a plate of biscuits.*

DORIS: The kettle's on – it won't be more than a minute or two.

NORA: Sit down, son – you must be tired.

STEVIE (*drawing up a chair next to hers*): You bet your life I'm tired! I feel as if I could sleep for a month! Whew! (*He sits down.*) There, Mum – I can't get any closer, can I, without sitting on your lap? (*He takes her hand.*)

NORA: You'll start me off again if you're not careful.

STEVIE: You know that Nipper remembered me, don't you? I thought he'd wake up the whole neighbourhood, barking and jumping up. He wasn't much more than a puppy when he last saw me, was he?

146

NORA (*dully*): September the 3rd, 1940.

STEVIE (*slipping his arm round her – she leans her head against him*): Don't think back, Mum – you'll start crying again, and there's no sense in that – there isn't much time, either – I can't stay long—

NORA (*with a cry*): Stevie!

FRED: Can't stay long – what do you mean?

STEVIE: It's all right – don't get into a state – I'm not going away again – not for long, anyway – but I certainly can't stay here . . .

DORIS: Papers . . . what papers have you got?

STEVIE: My papers are all right. But my name's different – my surname, that is. That had to be changed – but you can still call me Stevie if you play your cards right.

DORIS: Stevie what?

STEVIE: Stephen Sheldon. You'll be interested to hear that I was born in 1920, Mum, of quite respectable parents – just outside Birmingham. They popped off – my poor old Mum and Dad – when I was still a child, and I was brought up by my Aunt Mona in Southport. As a matter of fact, I've just left Aunt Mona – she sent you all her love.

NORA: What are you talking about, dear? What does it all mean?

STEVIE: It means a hell of a lot, Mum – but I can't explain it too thoroughly.

DORIS: Don't explain anything that is not strictly necessary – not even to us.

STEVIE (*raising his eyebrows*): That was quite a sharp tone, Dorrie!

DORIS: We've had to learn to be sharp lately, Stevie – you'd be surprised! I'll go and make the tea.

    She goes out.

STEVIE: Dorrie's changed, hasn't she?

FRED: I expect we've all changed a bit.

STEVIE: Is she working?

FRED: Yes – but she lives here with us and helps in her off-time.

STEVIE: Where does she work?

NORA: At the Savoy Hotel. She's a receptionist.

STEVIE: That's requisitioned for high-ranking German officers and V.I.P.s, isn't it?

FRED: Yes. She's been there since November, 1940.

STEVIE (*thoughtfully*): I see.

NORA: What's the matter, Stevie?

STEVIE: Nothing's the matter.

NORA: You're thinking something, Stevie – what is it?

STEVIE: When did she get that job?

FRED: Just after we were invaded – just after they got here. You remember she was Mr. Rawlsdon's secretary at the beginning of the war—

STEVIE: Yes.

FRED: Well – when the balloon went up, Mr. Rawlsdon got her into the Savoy through a cousin of his who was one of the assistant managers.

STEVIE: Where's Rawlsdon now?

FRED: Damned if I know. I haven't heard of him for ages.

STEVIE: Has Dorrie?

FRED: What is all this? You'd better ask her.

> DORIS *comes back with the teapot.*

DORIS: Here's the tea.

STEVIE: What happened to your old boss, Dorrie – Mr. Rawlsdon?

DORIS: He was killed—

NORA: Dorrie! You never said a word about it!

DORIS: At Dunkirk.

STEVIE: Dunkirk!

FRED: Don't talk so soft, Dorrie – he wasn't even in the army.

DORIS: Well, that's the story I heard – Dunkirk. Take it or leave it.

STEVIE: I take it.

DORIS: Okay.

FRED: Have you both gone off your blinking rockers?

NORA: Fred!

DORIS (*quickly*): Listen, Stevie – Mum and Dad don't know anything about this at all. I never said a word – I don't even know how much you know – but you must know something otherwise you couldn't have got here. It's all muddled up, and there isn't any real organisation – not yet. Nothing much has happened and nothing much has been done beyond a few

individual jobs here and there. I didn't want Mum and Dad to
know anything about it at all – not until things were more
definite – because I didn't want them to be involved. I know
people have been coming into the country for the last six
months – I know—

FRED: What is all this, Dorrie? What have you been up to?

DORIS: Nothing, Dad – nothing of importance – not yet.

NORA: Be quiet, Fred. (*To* DORIS.) It doesn't matter, Dorrie, what
your Dad and me know or don't know – but there's one thing
you ought to know, and it's this – that you should be ashamed
of yourself for not trusting us – for shutting us out.

DORIS: No, Mum – it was nothing to do with not trusting you. I
swore on my sacred oath not to let anybody know anything
unless it was absolutely necessary. I realised that sooner or
later you'd be bound to find out – but until that moment I
didn't want you to be in danger.

NORA: What have we got to fear more than you have?

FRED (*quietly, but very firmly*): I want to get this straight, Dorrie,
please. What's been happening? What have you been doing
that you didn't want your Mum and me to know about?

DORIS: What Stevie's come over here to do – what hundreds of
people all over the country are doing – fighting the bloody
Germans! Fighting them in every possible way we can. We
haven't been able to do much yet – just little things – upsetting
them, irritating them, making them feel uneasy – but it's all
growing. We're getting more organised . . .

NORA: It's risking your life, isn't it? Every minute of the day and
night. Risking more than your life, really – risking being
tortured and branded with hot irons and . . . (*She breaks off and
covers her face with her hands.*)

STEVIE: Yes, Mum – it's risking all that.

NORA: Now there won't be a minute's peace in my mind, not an
hour of any day or any night that I shan't be frightened sick
for you – worrying my heart out – both my children in danger
– horrible danger – all the time! I don't think I can stand it –
not at my age – I'm too old . . .

FRED (*putting his arm round her – gently*): Don't talk like that,
Mother – you don't mean it, you know.

NORA: Oh yes, I do!

STEVIE: Listen, Mum – you'll have to stand it, see? You've got to see how important it is – more important than you or me or Dorrie or Dad and what happens to us – we're only one little family. This affects the whole country – millions and millions of families. Living or dying doesn't matter all that much – there's certainly no sense in living if you can't live the way you want. We've got to fight – all of us – to the last ditch.

FRED: Stevie's right, Nora.

NORA: Yes, I know.

FRED: You were the one that was saying only a little while ago that we ought to be doing more – you said it yourself.

NORA: That was before I saw him again – before I knew he was alive.

STEVIE: Mum, please – don't take it so hard – please!

NORA: I'll be all right – I'll get used to it – one gets used to anything. You'd better pour out that tea, Dorrie, it'll be coal black by now, I should think.

> DORIS *pours out the tea and hands round the cups in silence.*

STEVIE (*glancing at his wrist-watch*): I'll have to be going in a minute.

NORA: You couldn't stay here – just for one night?

STEVIE: It would be too risky. I might be seen – someone might recognise me. That reminds me – there aren't any photographs of me about, are there?

NORA: There are two in our room. Dorrie's got one, that snap you had taken just before you went to Biggin Hill.

STEVIE: You'd better burn them . . .

NORA: Oh, Stevie . . .

STEVIE: Burn the lot. Don't even hide them – burn them.

FRED: All right, son.

NORA: I suppose I shall wake up in a minute – I wish I could.

DORIS: Here's the tea.

FRED: What happened to you, son? There's so much we want to know. You haven't told me a thing.

STEVIE: There isn't much time . . .

FRED: Are you in the Secret Service, or something?

NORA: How did you get here?

STEVIE: Oh, Mum – darling Mum – I know it's hard for you. Listen – here's the outline – quickly. I was shot down – just near Boulogne. They caught me, and I was sent to a prison camp at Lyons . . . I was there, in the camp, until March, 1941 – then I managed to escape with three other chaps – that's a story in itself. Anyway, I was smuggled to Gibraltar in a fishing-smack. I've been there ever since – training.

FRED: Training?

STEVIE: The R.A.F. Intelligence chaps on the Rock, knowing of course that I'd been a W.T. operator and all that, put me to work on special stuff. There are factories being built secretly all over England – did you know that? Factories for the manufacture of receiving and transmitting sets – some of them so small that you can carry them in your handbag. It's wonderful – you'd never believe it. A month ago they sent me with five others in a submarine. We were landed on the Western Isles. From there we worked our different ways down south. Already there are resistance groups working underground in all the big cities. I was passed from Thursoe to Edinburgh – then Carlisle – then I was sent to Southport to contact my new relatives – that's Aunt Mona and dear old Uncle Frank! You'd love my Uncle Frank – he's wizard. From there I went to Manchester and Birmingham, and finally I arrived in London this morning – in a lorry!

NORA: I don't understand.

STEVIE: It's for the Invasion, Mum.

FRED (*sharply*): The Invasion?

STEVIE: It's all being laid on now – it may be a year, or two or three years before it actually happens – but it's being planned – minutely planned down to the last detail – in America, Canada, Africa, Iceland, Greenland, all over the world the preparations are going ahead hour by hour, day by day. That's all the hope – don't you see? The hope that we're all working for and living for. One day – one tremendous day that this country is invaded and set free again. That's what I've been sent here for, what hundreds of others are being sent here for – to organise communications – to prepare the ground—

FRED: Is it really true, son – all this? Really true?

STEVIE: Yes – it's the Beginning. The Beginning for us, and the Beginning of the End for them.

NORA (*rising to her feet*): Even if it's the Beginning of the End for us. Good luck, my son! (*She puts her arms round him as—*)

THE CURTAIN FALLS

ACT II: Scene I

January, 1945. About nine o'clock in the evening.

There are certain changes noticeable in the scene. The most obvious of which is that the old window curtains that were there before have been replaced by heavy black-out material.

There are also differences apparent in people's appearances. Everyone in one way and another betrays inner weariness and strain. FRED *and* NORA *have aged more than a normal two years would warrant,* DORIS *looks pale and taut as though she were constantly controlling her nerves.*

Customers in the bar also show signs of wear and tear. Their clothes are threadbare and shabby, many of them wear thick wooden-soled shoes as leather is unobtainable.

When the curtain rises MR. *and* MRS. GRAINGER *are at their usual table.* ALFIE *and* MRS. BLAKE *are at the downstage table.* ALMA *is at the bar.* FRED, NORA *and* DORIS *are behind it. They are all listening to the end of the nine o'clock news.*

RADIO ANNOUNCER: ... as announced in a previous bulletin, the attempted invasion by British, American and French forces of Southern France and the Bay of Biscay area has been repelled with enormous Allied land losses. In the course of a naval action to-day off the coast of Corsica between British and American destroyers and three German cruisers, no less than seven of the enemy – I beg your pardon – the Allied vessels were sunk. The German cruisers suffered only slight damage and returned safely to their bases. That is the end of to-night's communiqué. A statement issued earlier this evening by the Governor of Occupied Britain points out that these sensational victories of the Third Reich should disprove once and for all the lying propaganda originated in certain misguided, pro-Allied circles here. The false rumours spread by these subversive elements which are designed to undermine confidence in the security of the Third Reich and to encourage resistance towards the Occupation authorities must be treated with contempt. Because these rumour mongers are acting against the best interests of the British people they will be dealt with summarily and without mercy. The United Europe of the Third Reich will not tolerate traitors. That is the end of the news. Listeners are once again reminded that the penalty for tuning into any except officially sanctioned broadcasts is death. Good-night.

> *There is a slight pause.* NORA *switches off the radio.*

MRS. BLAKE: Well, there's nothing like the B.B.C. for sending us home cheerful and happy, is there?

FRED: Anyone in the 'Public', Dorrie?

DORIS (*looking through the window*): Only Mr. Lawrence and that friend of his who drives a truck.

FRED: Ask them to come in here – and go and lock up.

DORIS: Okay.

> DORIS *runs out upstage.*

ALMA: I wonder how it feels to talk to your own countrymen like that over the air?

FRED: I don't suppose he minds, otherwise he'd never have done it in the first place.

ALMA: They probably forced him to.

MR. GRAINGER (*coming over to the bar*): Is your clock right, Fred?

FRED: Yes – we've got about five minutes to go.

MR. GRAINGER (*adjusting his watch*): Thanks.

ALFIE: What about another Stubbs Special, Fred?

FRED: Righto.

MRS. BLAKE: You'll be sick again if you drink any more of that stuff – don't forget last Tuesday.

ALFIE: Fat chance you give me of forgetting anything.

> DORIS *comes back with* MR. LAWRENCE *and his friend* ARCHIE JENKINS. *They are both middle-aged men.* ALFIE BLAKE *goes over to the bar.*

MR. LAWRENCE: Good evening all.

NORA: Good evening, Mr. Lawrence.

> ARCHIE JENKINS *mutters 'Good evening'.*

ALFIE (*expansively to* ALMA): God bless him! That's all I have to say.

ALMA: God bless who?

ALFIE: Little old Mr. Stubbs of course. There's a man for you! He suddenly wakes up one morning and says to himself, 'No more beer, no more whisky, no more gin – something's got to be done,' he says, and so – being a man of action as you might say – out he goes and collects potatoes, swedes, turnip roots, horse manure and God knows what all and boils the whole lot down, ferments it and mixes in a little methylated spirit to taste and before we know where we are we're all knocking back 'Stubbs' Specials' as though they were mother's milk.

MRS. BLAKE: You and your mother's milk!

ALFIE: I've ordered you one too so stop narking.

ALMA (*laughing*): I must say it is fairly filthy, but it's effective.

The street door opens and JANET *comes in. She looks sunburned and well.*

FRED (*surprised*): Why, Mrs. Braid!

ALMA: Janet! – What a surprise – I thought you were in Cornwall.

JANET: So I was – until this morning – I've been evacuated.

ALMA: Evacuated! What on earth for?

JANET: I don't know. There were no reasons given. We were all ordered to pack up and go yesterday – at twenty-four hours' notice.

MRS. BLAKE: Well I never.

MR. LAWRENCE: They're getting panicky – you mark my words.

JANET: The air's been full of rumours for days – about the landings in France.

ALMA: That's nothing but wicked, wicked Allied propaganda, Janet. I'm surprised at you for spreading such naughty lies. Would you like a 'Stubbs'?

JANET: Certainly. My stomach is quite hardened now. Mr. Stubbs has invaded Cornwall too.

ALMA: Two 'Stubbs', please, Fred.

FRED: Righto.

NORA: It's nice to see you back again, Mrs. Braid. Looking so well too.

JANET: Thanks, Nora.

DORIS: It's time now, Dad. Do you want to stand by the window or shall I?

NORA: I will, dear. You're better at understanding what's going on than I am.

DORIS: Okay. Gather round everybody.

> NORA *comes out from behind the bar and goes over to the window.*
> *She slips behind the black-out curtains without allowing any light to*
> *escape.*

NORA (*behind the curtain*): All right – coast's clear.

> DORIS *fiddles for a moment with the radio, turning the indicating*
> *needle as far as it will go over to the right.* MR. *and* MRS. GRAINGER
> *get up and join the others round the bar.* FRED *glances through the*
> *service window and then closes it down. There is a little crackling*
> *and buzzing for a moment, then the sound begins to come through.*

FRED: It's a bit loud, Dorrie – turn it down.

> DORIS *turns it down until the voice speaking is only just audible.*

VOICE: ... Marseilles and Toulon have been liberated and our armour is making rapid advances up the Rhone valley. Local enemy resistance is weak and disorganised. In the Bordeaux area mopping up operations continue and Allied forces have penetrated a further twenty-eight miles inland since yesterday evening. Farther north, strong armoured units, supported by fighter-bombers, have advanced on a wide front past Poitiers and are approaching the line of the river Loire. Enemy formations, including two S.S. divisions, are fighting back fiercely. In the Mediterranean theatre German naval forces yesterday suffered a severe loss in the course of an action in which five American and eight British destroyers engaged three enemy light cruisers. Two of the cruisers were sunk, while the third escaped at nightfall after suffering considerable damage. One British destroyer was sunk, but most of her crew were picked up afterwards. You are listening to the Spokesman of the Supreme Allied Commander. ... The situation in Northern Italy ...

NORA (*urgently*): Shut down – somebody's coming!

> DORIS *quickly switches on to the Home Service programme. A blast*

of Wagner assaults the ears. She tones it down a little. The BLAKES
and the GRAINGERS *return to their table.* MR. LAWRENCE *and*
ARCHIE JENKINS *go back through the upstage alcove into the*
'Public'. FRED *opens up the service window.* NORA *comes swiftly out*
from behind the curtains and goes back behind the bar.

FRED: Quick, Dorrie – go and open the door of the 'Public' –
Talk everybody, please . . .

> *There is a buzz of conversation. The street door opens and* CHORLEY
> BANNISTER *comes in with a very good-looking young man,* KURT
> FORSTER.

CHORLEY: This is the place, Kurt. Good evening, Fred – Hallo,
Nora.

FRED: Good evening, Mr. Bannister.

CHORLEY: Why, Janet – I thought you were writing a ferocious
patriotic novel in the wilds of Cornwall.

JANET: It's finished, Chorley. I promise that you shall be the first
to see the proofs – but you must be careful not to read them
in public – the theme is dreadfully subversive and I should
hate you to get into trouble.

CHORLEY: How sweet of you to mind. Good evening, Mrs.
Boughton.

ALMA: Good evening.

CHORLEY: Fred – I've brought you a new client— (*He turns.*) I
won't say customer, it sounds so dreadfully commercial,
doesn't it? He has one grave defect in that he happens to be a
genius – Janet, Mrs. Boughton, Nora, Fred – this is Mr. Kurt
Forster. You can rise above those two tiresome little dots over
the 'o' if you like and just say 'Forster'. He is not a German.
He is an Austrian.

JANET: That makes the whole difference, doesn't it?

FRED (*unsmilingly*): Good evening, sir.

KURT: Good evening.

ALMA: I know your name well, Mr. Forster – your new décor for
Rosenkavalier was remarkable.

CHORLEY: 'Remarkable' comes under the heading of faint praise,
Mrs. Boughton. It was superb.

ALMA: I bow to your superior knowledge, Mr. Bannister.

JANET: We all do.

CHORLEY (*ignoring her*): We want a drink, please, Fred. Not one of Mr. Thing's Specials for God's sake – we don't want to singe the lining of Mr. Forster's stomach, do we? After all he is a guest in our country.

JANET: One might almost say a gate-crasher.

CHORLEY (*beaming*): Dear Janet – how comforting to find that the balmy air of the Cornish Riviera has in no way blunted your tiresomeness. (*To* FRED.) Just give us two bottles of your delightful ersatz ginger ale, Fred; nowadays I always take the precaution of carrying my own liquor with me. (*He produces a bottle from his pocket.*) Will you join us, Janet – Mrs. Boughton? It's pure Canadian whisky – I can't think how I got it.

ALMA: I think I'll stick to Mr. Stubbs, thank you – I've got sort of used to him.

JANET: Thank you, Chorley. If it's really expensive and genuine Black Market I should love some.

CHORLEY: Three then please, Fred.

> FRED *produces glasses and three little bottles of bright yellow liquid.* CHORLEY *proceeds to pour out his whisky and mix the drinks.*

JANET: Mr. Forster, are you doing any other productions for us?

KURT: There will be a ballet season starting in November – that I will do. There will be the visit of the Berlin Stadt Opera Company – that also I will do.

ALMA: Very interesting.

KURT: No – here in England it is not interesting – just routine.

JANET: How disappointing for you.

KURT: No, no – I was quite prepared – the English do not understand new ideas – that is a well-known fact, is it not? Here at your Covent Garden everything is old-fashioned, there is no life. Perhaps in time they will learn.

JANET (*with great effusiveness*): I think it's absolutely sweet of you to take the trouble to teach us. We've been trying for centuries to acquire a little 'kultur' without the slightest success. It is so discouraging.

KURT (*oblivious of irony*): The German occupation of your country cannot fail to make an influence on those sad circumstances. That will be good, will it not?

JANET: Absolutely splendid. That was why we were so delighted with the invasion. 'Thank God,' we said to ourselves, 'at last we shall really be able to enjoy the Opera!'

CHORLEY (*handing* JANET *a glass*): Here is your drink, Janet. (*To* KURT.) Mrs. Braid is renowned for her caustic irony. You must take it in your stride.

KURT: What is that?

JANET: A secret weapon, Mr. Forster. Laced with humour and hatred it can sometimes be quite effective.

KURT: I do not understand.

JANET: That is why. (*She lifts her glass.*) 'Happy landings!'

KURT (*sharply – raising his glass*): Heil Hitler!

> ALMA *makes a quick movement with her handbag and knocks his arm just as he is about to drink, upsetting the entire contents of his glass over his suit. He makes an angry exclamation in German.*

ALMA: Oh, I'm so frightfully sorry – how very clumsy of me.

CHORLEY: Really, Mrs. Boughton!

ALMA (*to* KURT): I'm always doing stupid things like that – please forgive me.

KURT (*controlling himself*): It is no matter. (*He dabs at his tie with his handkerchief.*)

CHORLEY: Some hot water, Fred.

FRED: There's some in the Gents. Here's a cloth.

CHORLEY: Thank you! (*Snatching it.*) Kurt, come with me, I apologise for my friend. (*He shoots an angry glance at* ALMA *and*)—

> Goes off through the door upstage with KURT.

JANET: Nice work, Alma.

ALMA (*smiling*): I can't think *what* you mean, Janet. It was the purest accident.

JANET: Mix the little beast another drink, Fred. Mr. Bannister's left his whisky here.

DORIS: Mix some 'Stubbs' with it, Dad – that'll fix him.

NORA (*protesting*): Oh Fred!

FRED: Not a bad idea at that. But I've got a better one.

NORA: Oh dear – there'll be a scene, you know – we don't want a scene.

FRED (*belligerently*): I'll teach him to bring his bloody Black Market Canadian whisky into my pub.

He takes CHORLEY's *whisky bottle, empties more than half of it into a glass, and fills up the bottle with 'Stubbs'.*

NORA: Fred – that's dishonest, you know.

FRED: He can go and complain to whoever he got it from. (*He puts the glass with the pure whisky in it out of sight under the bar.*) We can all have a nip of this later.

NORA: Oh dear!

FRED (*holding the whisky bottle up to the light*): It hasn't gone cloudy, thank God.

JANET (*lifting her glass*): Heil Stubbs.

The street door opens and STEVIE *comes in with* BILLY GRAINGER. BILLY's *forehead looks a little strange, but there is no sign of the scar.*

STEVIE (*coming over to the bar*): Good evening, Mr. Shattock . . . Mrs. Shattock.

FRED: Good evening, Mr. Sheldon.

BILLY: Good evening, Doris.

DORIS: Who are you Doris-ing, Mr. Fawcett?

BILLY (*cheerfully*): Sorry – I thought we was old friends.

STEVIE: Johnny wants to use your phone – he's left his truck in the middle of Eaton Square – no more juice.

NORA: Up in the alcove, Mr. Fawcett – you know the way.

BILLY: Anyone got any coppers?

STEVIE: Here you are. (*He gives him some coppers.*)

FRED: What'll you have, sir?

BILLY *goes off upstage in the alcove.*

STEVIE: What have you got?

FRED: Same as usual – root beer or 'Stubbs'.

STEVIE: Beer will do.

FRED (*nodding his head in the direction of the alcove*): Same for him?

STEVIE: Yes, please.

FRED *draws two draughts of pale-looking beer.*

FRED: Two and fourpence, please.

CHORLEY *and* KURT *return from upstage door. They go to the bar.*

ALMA: I hope your suit isn't stained, Mr. Forster?

KURT (*sullenly*): Thank you – it is very well.

ALMA: I can't apologise enough for having been so clumsy.

KURT: It is no matter.

CHORLEY: We'd better have another bottle of that filthy ginger ale, Fred.

FRED: Righto.

CHORLEY: Do you want some more, Janet?

JANET: No, thank you.

> FRED *having produced another bottle of ginger ale,* CHORLEY *proceeds to mix a fresh drink for* KURT *and one for himself.*

MR. GRAINGER (*coming to the bar with* MRS. GRAINGER): We're going now, Fred – will you charge it?

NORA: I'll mark it down, Mr. Grainger – I served you.

MR. GRAINGER: Oh yes, of course.

NORA: What a day it's been, hasn't it? Just like mid-summer.

MRS. GRAINGER: We went to Kew this afternoon on the Underground – it was lovely.

> BILLY *comes back from telephoning.*

STEVIE: Get through all right?

BILLY: Yes – Bob's coming down with a can – I'd better get back to the truck.

STEVIE: Here's your beer.

BILLY: Thanks.

> He takes the glass – *catches* MR. *and* MRS. GRAINGER's *eye – they betray no sign of recognition. He lifts the glass.*

Here's hoping! (*He drains the glass.*) Good-night all.

NORA: Good-night, Mr. Fawcett.

BILLY: See you later, Steve – good-night, Doris.

DORIS: I'll give you 'Doris'.

> BILLY *goes out whistling.*

MRS. GRAINGER: Billy!

MR. GRAINGER: Come on, Mother, time we went home.

NORA: How's the new flat?

MRS. GRAINGER: It isn't really a flat. Only one room and a kitchenette. But it's quiet once you've got up all the stairs. And it's nice for Leslie because it's nearer the works.

MR. GRAINGER: It'll be a great day in my life when they put the buses on again, I give you my word.

MRS. GRAINGER: Come along, dear.

MR. GRAINGER: Good-night all.

They go out.

CHORLEY (*lifting his glass*): Kurt – I drink to your *Rosenkavalier!*

KURT (*raising his glass*): Heil Hitler! (*He drinks the entire glass defiantly at one go, and makes a very wry face.*)

CHORLEY (*spluttering*): Oh ... it must be that damned ginger ale! (*He drinks some more.*) It really has a most peculiar taste.

JANET (*amiably*): It isn't very nice, is it? Whoever you got it from can't be very reliable, Chorley.

CHORLEY (*opening the bottle and sniffing it*): They swore it was genuine. (*He hands the bottle to* FRED.) Smell that, Fred ...

FRED (*solemnly sniffing the bottle*): Not very good – but I don't like Canadian whisky anyhow.

JANET: It could be something to do with the bottling, couldn't it, Fred?

FRED: It certainly could.

CHORLEY: I shall treat it like medicine! (*He gives a little laugh, shuts his eyes and drains his glass.*)

JANET: What a pity there isn't a chocolate to give you for being such a brave boy.

CHORLEY: The second taste was better – Kurt – would you like another?

KURT: No, thank you – I have to go.

CHORLEY: Stay and see Bobby – he might come at any minute – he'll be so sorry to miss you.

KURT: I am sad – but I cannot. There is a meeting of the Directors after the performance to-night. I must be there.

CHORLEY: We must have another pub crawl another night. (*To* JANET *and the others.*) I really do feel that he should see how Londoners enjoy themselves.

JANET: He doesn't know the half of it, does he?

KURT (*bowing stiffly*): Good-night – good-night.

ALMA: Good-night.

The OTHERS *murmur a few polite 'good-nights',* CHORLEY *accompanies him to the door.*

Exit KURT.

CHORLEY (*comes back to the bar – to* ALMA): I suppose you did that on purpose, Mrs. Boughton.

ALMA: I haven't the faintest idea what you mean.

CHORLEY: Kurt Forster is an artist – a very fine artist, and art is international – your discourtesy to him was utterly pointless.

JANET: Why did you bring him here, Chorley? This is a very exclusive pub – almost a club. If you like to be friends with the Germans and take them out socially that is entirely your affair – but that is no reason for you to bring them here.

CHORLEY: We've been through all this before.

JANET: In any case – as far as your Kurt is concerned – his manner is even more offensive than his nationality.

STEVIE: Can I make a phone call too, Miss Shattock?

DORIS (*off hand*): Yes – you know the way – in the alcove.

STEVIE: Thanks.

He goes off upstage left.

CHORLEY: He didn't mean to be offensive, it's just that his English isn't very good.

JANET: There are moments, Chorley, when I almost envy you your capacity for rationalisation.

CHORLEY: I don't know what you mean.

JANET: You've quite enjoyed these years, haven't you? Finding new friends, new interests – adjusting yourself?

CHORLEY: I have tried to make the best of the situation. You would probably be much happier and less embittered if you had had the sense to do likewise.

JANET: You mustn't confuse bitterness with contempt, Chorley – they are not at all the same.

CHORLEY: Really, Janet, you're quite impossible.

JANET: What are your convictions, your true beliefs? You must have some somewhere.

CHORLEY: My convictions and beliefs are entirely my own business. But one of them is that I consider you to be a militant bore and I always have done. I also resent your very aggressive assumption of superiority. As far as I can see there is very little you have done before the occupation or since to justify it. You took up an attitude of bellicose patriotism during the Munich crisis – thereby making a cracking fool of yourself – and you have resolutely maintained it ever since. I should like to know, as a matter of academic interest, what you think you have achieved by it?

JANET: I can tell you in two words – 'Self respect!'

CHORLEY: Upon what is it based, this all important self respect of yours?

JANET: Love of my country and hatred of its enemies.

CHORLEY: A simple and uplifting phrase, my dear, that a little critical analysis would reduce to rubbish.

JANET: A little critical analysis of your motives, Chorley, would be even less edifying.

CHORLEY: Motives – what do you mean?

JANET: The motives that prompt your uneasy squirmings at the feet of your conquerors.

CHORLEY: How dare you insult me like that?

JANET: Dare? Really, Chorley – I do assure you that it takes very little courage to insult you.

CHORLEY: Don't be too sure, Janet – it may be more dangerous than you bargain for.

JANET: Is that a threat?

CHORLEY: It most emphatically is – I have powerful friends.

JANET: Powerful enemies too – you had better be careful.

CHORLEY: Women like you are both mischievous and obstructive.

JANET: Obstructive to what?

CHORLEY: To reason and logic and intelligent living.

JANET: Do you consider Nazi ideology the key to intelligent living?

CHORLEY: Within its limits, yes. It is certainly efficient, which is more than can be said for the half-baked democratic ideals that have led the world to the verge of chaos.

JANET: You are an apt pupil, Chorley – your powerful friends must be proud of you.

CHORLEY: I prefer to see life as it is rather than as it should be. Being a realist I have adapted myself to the circumstances around me. It is just that considered and reasonable acceptance of inescapable facts that offends febrile emotionalists like you. You base your view of life upon a series of outworn slogans – 'God and the Right', 'King and Country', 'The Sun Never Sets . . .' etc. Jingoistic platitudes whose long-drawn out death rattle began in nineteen fourteen. The world is changing swiftly,

Janet. And to cope with its changes you need better equipment than a confused jumble of High School heroics. (*He moves.*) Good-night.

JANET: Chorley!

CHORLEY: What?

JANET: There's another slogan upon which I base my High School philosophy. 'This blessed plot, this earth, this realm, this England – This land of such dear souls, this dear dear land'.

CHORLEY: I would be the first to agree that Shakespeare was second to none in commercialising patriotism.

JANET: That, oddly enough, has made me angrier than anything you've said yet.

CHORLEY: Yes – I thought it would.

JANET: As these are the last words I ever intend to address to you, Chorley, I want you to remember them. First of all I despise you from the bottom of my soul. You and your kind pride yourselves on being intellectuals, don't you? You babble a lot of snobbish nonsense about art and letters and beauty. You consider yourselves to be far above such primitive emotions as love and hate and devotion to a cause. You run your little highbrow magazines and change your politics with every wind that blows.

CHORLEY: What on earth do you think...

JANET: In the years before the war you were squealing for disarmament at a moment when to be fully armed was vitally necessary for our survival. You were all Pacifists then.

CHORLEY: What utter nonsense you talk, Janet.

JANET: Later, a very little later, having listened obediently to a few foreign agitators, you were launching virulent attacks on British Imperialism. That was when you were all bright little Communists. Now of course your intellectual ardours are devoted exclusively to Fascism – an easy transition. Where are you going next – you clever ones? What will your attitude be when England is free again, when your German friends are blasted to hell and driven into oblivion? You had better make your plans quickly – there is hardly any time to be lost. Get ready for a lightning change of views, Chorley – make it snappy, you drivelling little rat.

CHORLEY: I will not stand here to be insulted.

JANET: And when you are arranging with your friends to have me put into a concentration camp, remember to tell them exactly what I said. I said 'Down with Hitler!' And I hope he rots in Hell with all the strutting, yelping jackals round him! Down with the Third Bloody Reich and down into the lowest depths with every Englishman who gave our enemies lip service and fawned on them and by so doing flung his country's pride into the dust!

> JANET *gives* CHORLEY *two ringing slaps on the face which send him staggering against the bar, and walks out.*
>
> *There is dead silence.* CHORLEY *recovers himself with an effort and pours out a half tumbler of neat whisky from his bottle. He gulps it down and stands, swaying a little, against the bar.*

ALMA: Good-night, Fred – good-night, Nora – I shall probably be in to-morrow.

FRED: Good-night, Mrs. Boughton.

> ALMA, *without looking at* CHORLEY, *goes out.*

NORA: I'll be in the kitchen, Fred, if you want me.

FRED: All right.

> NORA, *also without looking at* CHORLEY, *goes out upstage left.*

DORIS (*looking through the service window*): There's nobody in the 'Public', Dad.

FRED: You'd better go and lock up, then.

DORIS: Okay.

> *She goes out upstage left.*

FRED: Last call before closing, Alfie – d'you want any more mother's milk?

ALFIE: How about it, Lil?

MRS. BLAKE (*absently, staring into space*): How about what?

ALFIE: How about another?

MRS. BLAKE: How about another what?

ALFIE: Another drink of course – come out of your trance, fathead – Fred hasn't got all night.

MRS. BLAKE: Who are you calling 'fathead'?

ALFIE: No more, thanks, Fred – it looks as though I'm going to have trouble getting her home as it is. (*With exaggerated gentleness.*) Come along, love – we're going home, see! I'll make you a nice cup of grey coffee made of oak apples!

MRS. BLAKE (*ironically*): Don't make me laugh any more, there's a dear – my ribs are aching.

The telephone rings in the alcove.

FRED (*grimly – to* CHORLEY): Closing time, Mr. Bannister.

> FRED *goes out into the alcove. His voice can be heard at the telephone.*
>
> ALFIE *and* LILY *go out by the street door.*
>
> CHORLEY, *left alone, puts the cork in his whisky bottle and shoves it into his pocket. He starts across to the street door, staggering slightly, then he stops, obviously feeling very sick. He pauses uncertainly for a moment and then hurriedly goes out through the door upstage right which leads to the passage and the lavatory.*
>
> *After a moment* DORIS *comes back. She sees the bar is empty and goes over to the street door and locks it.* FRED *comes back. He sees the bar is empty and calls off through the alcove.*

FRED: It's all right, Nora.

DORIS: Who was that on the telephone?

FRED: Mr. Bourne – he'll be round in a minute with Dr. Venning.

> NORA *comes in – followed after a moment by* STEVIE *and* BEN.

NORA: Has he gone?

FRED: Yes – everybody's gone.

NORA: I wish Mrs. Braid hadn't done that – I do wish she hadn't.

DORIS: He had it coming to him and he got it.

NORA: He might get her into terrible trouble.

FRED: He might – but I don't somehow think he will – there were too many of us listening – I don't think he'd dare.

NORA: If he reported her for saying what she did it would be enough for them to put her away.

FRED: It was a personal argument – we were all witnesses. All she said was 'Down with Hitler'. They know perfectly well that millions of people say that every day of their lives. There wouldn't be room in their bloody camps if they arrested all of them.

DORIS: It might make them suspicious, Dad – we don't want that.

FRED: They're suspicious of everybody anyway.

DORIS: It might start them watching her. They might search her flat . . .

STEVIE: It wouldn't matter if they did, they wouldn't find anything. She writes all her stuff in Cornwall.

DORIS: She's been evacuated from Cornwall. That's why she came to London to-day.

BEN: Well, we'll have to send her somewhere else.

NORA: She should never have done it – she should never have lost her temper like that – it's dangerous for all of us.

STEVIE: Well, it's done now, isn't it. There's no sense in going on about it. We'll see what the Boss has to say.

FRED: You'd better go and stand by the back door, Dorrie – they'll be here at any minute.

> DORIS *goes off through the door into the passage, shutting it after her.*

NORA: Do you want a cup of tea, Stevie? – Fred?

STEVIE: No thanks, Mum – not now. You and your tea. (*He gives her a kiss.*)

NORA (*resigned*): Do you want me for anything?

FRED: No, dear. We'll go down into the cellar and start work the moment they come.

NORA: I'll be in the kitchen.

STEVIE: Good-night, Mum.

NORA: Shall I see you to-morrow?

STEVIE: No, dear – I'm going to Ashford to-morrow with the truck. I'll be away until Tuesday.

NORA: I thought Billy had the truck.

STEVIE: He'll be back before morning – all being well.

NORA: All being well!

STEVIE: Chin up, Mum – we're living in stirring times, you know.

NORA: It's really true what they said on the radio? About the landings in France?

STEVIE: Yes, dear – it's really true – things are coming to the boil.

NORA (*looking at him*): I've had two extra years anyway, haven't I?

STEVIE: How do you mean?

NORA (*with a sigh*): Nothing – I was just thinking.

> NORA *goes out. There is the sound of voices in the passage.*

STEVIE (*looking after* NORA): Poor old Mum – all this is pretty tough on her, isn't it?

FRED: She'll be all right, son – don't worry about her.

STEVIE (*smiling*): Okay, Dad.

> GEORGE BOURNE, DR. VENNING *and* LYIA *come in, followed by* DORIS.

DORIS: We're all here.

DR. VENNING: Good evening, Fred. Hello, Stevie.

LYIA: Good evening, Fred. How are you?

FRED: Fine thanks

LYIA: If there isn't a drink in that cellar, Fred, I shall shoot to kill.

> *Exeunt* DR. VENNING *and* LYIA.

GEORGE: Did Billy get away all right with the truck?

STEVIE: Yes, he brought me here from Highgate. He parked it round the corner in Eaton Square while we nipped in here and phoned Bob.

GEORGE: Who stayed with it?

STEVIE: Our old friend P.C. Maltby. I thought it wiser to keep Billy with me until we knew Bob was on the way with the stuff.

GEORGE: Have you talked to Bob since?

STEVIE: Yes – everything was okay.

GEORGE: Good. Everything ready downstairs?

STEVIE: Yes. Ben's down there – he's been there since two o'clock.

GEORGE: Who's with him?

STEVIE: Scottie and Peter and old Bert.

GEORGE: We'd better get going. Lyia's had one of her intimate little lunches with Richter to-day – there's a good deal to discuss.

FRED: Righto.

STEVIE: Come one . . .

> *They all go out via the alcove.* FRED *waits behind and switches off the lights in the bar leaving a dim one on in the alcove.*

After a few moments' pause the door into the passage opens slowly and CHORLEY *comes cautiously in. He tiptoes over to the alcove and listens for a minute, then tiptoes across the bar towards the street door.* NORA *comes in and switches on the light. She gives a little gasp.* CHORLEY *gives her one look, rushes to the door, unlocks it, wrenches it open and disappears into the night.* NORA *comes over, shuts the door, locks it again, then suddenly she runs to the alcove.*

NORA (*calling*): Fred! – Stevie! – Come quickly – come quickly . . .

CURTAIN

Scene II

February 1945.
     Between five-thirty and six p.m.
     NORA *is tidying up the tables.* FRED *is behind the bar polishing glasses and getting everything straight for opening time.*
     PHYLLIS MERE *comes in from the alcove.*

PHYLLIS: I've done the 'Public', Mrs. Shattock.
NORA: That's right, Phyllis.
PHYLLIS: Shall I wait until Doris comes, or can I go now?
FRED: What's the hurry? It isn't six yet.
PHYLLIS: The big picture starts at ten-past and I've got to pick up Sylvia.
FRED: You and that Sylvia ought to be given medals for what you do for the cinema business. Don't you ever think of anything else but pictures?
PHYLLIS: There isn't much else to think about, is there?
NORA: Don't talk so silly, Phyllis.
FRED: Well, to begin with there's what's happening all round you. There's the fact that there are German policemen and soldiers at every street corner spying on all of us every minute of the day and night. There's the fact that if you're careless enough to say a word out of turn you're liable to be run in by the Gestapo and bullied and cross-questioned until you're so dizzy that you can't remember your own name. There's the

fact that there are people being arrested here, there and everywhere for no reason at all and shoved into concentration camps and tortured and killed, and there's the fact that any day, any week, any month now, things are going to happen in this country that have never happened before in all its history. Sooner or later, and probably sooner, the Free British and the Americans and the Free French are going to invade this island with landing craft and guns and tanks and planes, and there'll be fighting on the beaches and in the streets and even in the Odeon too, I shouldn't wonder.

NORA (*warningly*): Fred!

FRED: I should think all that was more to think about than Donald Duck.

PHYLLIS: I haven't seen a Donald Duck for years.

FRED: You don't see anything at the pictures anyway but German propaganda.

PHYLLIS: It's a new British picture to-night – Grant Madison's in it. It's all about the Irish revolution and the Black and Tans, and . . .

FRED: I'll bet it is, with Mr. Grant Madison running about saving everybody and dying for freedom.

PHYLLIS: How did you know? You haven't seen it, have you?

FRED: Go on – have a good cry and enjoy yourself!

NORA: Fred – I won't have you talking like that.

PHYLLIS (*tossing her head*): Thanks very much, I'm sure! Good-night, all!

> PHYLLIS *takes her hat off a peg and goes off through the door upstage.*

NORA: What do you want to go nagging at the girl like that for? What does it matter to you how she amuses herself in her spare time?

FRED: It matters because there are too many like her. A few years more of the Germans being here and her and her lot wouldn't know the difference. They believe all they see – that's why it's dangerous. All the sentimental muck, all the lying propaganda, they take it all as gospel. It was bad enough before the war when we only had Hollywood to contend with

– now we've got our own people mixed up with the Germans and that's a damned sight worse.

NORA: They've got to live, haven't they, the film people? You couldn't expect the whole industry to shut down – it would throw thousands out of work.

FRED: All right, all right – we've had all this before.

NORA: We must try to be fair.

FRED: Skip it, Nora – I know what I'm talking about, and so do you.

NORA: It's the back door – I'll go.

> *She goes out of the upstage door.*
>
>   FRED *arranges some bottles of ginger ale on the bar. There is the sound of voices in the passage.* LYIA *comes in, followed by* NORA. LYIA*'s arm is in a sling.*

LYIA: Hallo, Fred – I've got a message for Doris. Nora says she isn't home yet.

FRED: She ought to be here any minute now.

NORA: Why did you come by the back?

LYIA: They're probably watching the front and George told me not to be seen if I could help it.

FRED: If they're watching the front they'll be watching the mews, too.

LYIA: It's all right – I went to see Dr. Venning. Look – I've got a sprained wrist! (*She takes her right arm out of the sling and waves it.*) I came through his yard and out of the side door – you can't see the entrance to the mews from there, it's round the corner.

FRED: What's the message?

LYIA: The message is that Billy – I beg your pardon, Johnny Fawcett, got to headquarters all right with the report. And that Doris is being followed home. She probably knows that, anyhow.

NORA: What report?

LYIA: That's all I know. I'll probably come in later in a nonchalant manner when the dear doctor has rebandaged me. I'll tell you here and now I'm mad about Dr.Venning. I've tried everything from womanly understanding to vintage coquetry, but he's got a dreary wife stuck in the Cotswolds somewhere and there's no future in it. (*She puts her arm back in the sling.*) I must go back. It's all right, Nora, I can let myself out.

She waves gaily to them and goes out the way she came in.

NORA: She seemed nervous to me, Fred – sort of strung up. Something's happening.

FRED (*drily*): Something's always happening.

NORA: They'd never have risked sending her here through Dr. Venning's yard and the back way and everything unless it was important. I wish Doris would come home – I'm worried.

FRED (*coming out from behind the bar*): It's no use being worried, dear – the only thing to do is sit tight and hope for the best.

NORA: She said Doris was being followed home.

FRED: Well, that's nothing. We're all followed every time we go out – we're all on the suspect list ever since that little rat gave us away – ever since the raid.

NORA: We haven't any proof that he gave us away.

FRED: Proof! Who else could it have been? You saw him with your own eyes, sneaking out – if you hadn't, we should be behind the barbed wire by now – or dead. But the fact that they didn't find anything that time doesn't mean that they've given up. They'll go on watching us now until Kingdom Come.

NORA: It's Doris I'm worried about. She might have done something foolish.

FRED: Don't fuss, Mother – she's got her head screwed on all right.

NORA: I knew Mrs. Braid oughtn't to have lost her temper that night – it all started then – with you trying to be funny and mixing his drinks and making him sick ...

FRED: I wish it had been prussic acid instead of dear old 'Stubbs'!

NORA: I've got a feeling that something's gone wrong ...

FRED: You've had that feeling every day and night for over two years ... ever since Stevie came back.

NORA: It's different now – they suspect us – they know we're up to something, otherwise they wouldn't have come that night and ransacked the house and the cellar ...

FRED: They didn't find anything. Everything was cleared, and everybody was gone an hour before they got here. And they can't find anything now – not if they search till they're black in the face. We're out of commission.

NORA: I know all that, but – but—

FRED: But what?

NORA: We ought to go away, Fred – you and me and Dorrie – somewhere in the country.

FRED: How could we, without a permit?

NORA: We could go to Ethel at St. Albans – she's going to have a baby anyhow and she *is* a relative.

FRED: It would be a nice job convincing the authorities that the whole lot of us have to shut up shop and go to St. Albans just because your cousin twice removed is going to have a baby! Besides, what about Stevie?

NORA: We're no use to Stevie any more – we're more a danger to him than a help – we haven't even seen him for three weeks.

FRED (*stubbornly*): This pub's our livelihood – it's stayed open all through the bad times – and it's going on staying open. You and Dorrie can go if you like, though I doubt if you'll persuade her to – but I'm staying here.

NORA: Don't be unkind, Fred. You know I wouldn't leave you.

FRED (*putting his arm round her*): Listen, love – I know it's awful for you – I know the strain of never knowing what's going to happen from one minute to the next is getting you down – I know you're eating your heart out with anxiety and worry and that you're frightened out of your wits – not for yourself, but for all of us. But I know, and you know too inside, that we can't run out now – not now just when things are coming out right at last. It may only be a question of a few weeks before the day comes, before we're set free again. We can't *not* be here to see it happen. This is where we belong. We've stuck it out through all the nightmare years of shame and defeat – we can't *not* be here for the victory!

NORA (*lifting her hand and patting his face*): Very well, dear. Have it your own way. (*She glances up at the clock.*) It's just on six – we'd better open up. (*She moves over to unlock the street door.*)

DORIS *comes in through the upstage door. She is obviously strained and excited.*

DORIS: Dad, don't open up for a minute – I've got some news.

NORA (*apprehensively*): What is it?

DORIS: There's going to be a round-up of all Resistance groups – not only in London, but all over the country.

FRED: How do you know?

DORIS: The whole Savoy has been in a state for three days – we all knew something was up – the entire third floor has been shut off – there's been a lot of furniture moving and cleaning, and one of the river suites has had a wall knocked down so that it can be made into a conference room. We knew it couldn't be Goering or Goebbels because they're both at Carlton House Terrace. I found out to-day who it is from Mickey. He got hold of a decoded copy of a telegram. It's Himmler. He's arriving to-night. (*She hangs her hat and coat on a peg.*)

NORA: That's bad news, isn't it?

DORIS: No, Mum – good news. It means that they're scared – really scared. It may mean that the invasion will come sooner than we thought it would.

FRED: It mightn't mean that at all, Dorrie. After all, he's been here before often enough.

DORIS: This time he's bringing a staff of forty – they'll be picked men – he hasn't done that before. It's obvious what they're going to do. They're going to clamp down on all danger spots, on all suspects. I had to let Avenue Road know at once – that's why I took the risk.

NORA: What risk?

DORIS: Don't worry – it wasn't all that of a risk really – and I got away with it. I didn't dare to phone H.Q. so I tried old Bert, but there wasn't any answer. Then I got through to the Finchley number and got Johnny Fawcett. I told him to meet me by the pelicans in St. James's Park at four-thirty. Then I went back to the desk and fainted – it was a beautiful faint – and the hotel doctor gave me sal volatile and I got permission to come home early.

NORA: You were followed, though – you know you were followed!

DORIS: Yes, I know – but it couldn't be helped. I tried to dodge him in Trafalgar Square, but it was no good. Anyhow, I got Billy all right – I pretended to ask him for a match. I told him the whole thing while he was fiddling about lighting my cigarette – thank God I had one – and I told him to let Avenue Road know at all costs. Then I left him and went for a walk in Hyde Park. I only hope my following friend's feet are as tired as mine are. The only thing that's worrying me now is whether Billy got the report back all right.

FRED: He did. Lyia Vivian's been here. She told us to tell you that H.Q. had got the report.

DORIS: Good, that's a weight off my mind.

NORA: I wish it was a weight off mine.

FRED: Now then, Nora!

DORIS: Don't you think it would be a good idea if you and Mum closed down and went away somewhere in the country for the next few weeks? After all, this place has probably been black-listed, since the raid – and you never know what they mightn't do.

NORA: What about you?

DORIS: I can't go. I'll have to stay. I'll be all right.

FRED: So will we. They can't prove anything. This place is not used any more. It's not a danger spot.

DORIS: That's exactly what I mean. You're not doing any good by staying here.

FRED: We're earning our living, aren't we? We're keeping the pub open so that our friends will have somewhere to come and talk and have a drink or two – even if it is only 'Stubbs' and watery beer.

DORIS: I'd rather you went – I think Stevie would, too.

NORA: Did he say so?

DORIS: No – not exactly – but—

NORA: Your father wants to keep open, Dorrie, and I do, too. If we could all go it would be different, but you don't suppose we could stand being buried somewhere in the country with everything going on here and you and Stevie in the thick of it, do you?

DORIS: All right – all right – it was only an idea.

FRED: Open up, Mother!

> NORA *unlocks the street door.*

NORA: Go and get yourself a cup of tea, Dorrie, before you start work. I'll deal with the 'Public'. The kettle's on.

DORIS: All right – thanks, Mum.

> DORIS *goes off through the alcove.*

NORA: Shan't be a minute, dear.

FRED: Righto.

> NORA *follows* DORIS *off through the alcove.*
>
> FRED *leans on the bar, thoughtfully gazing into space. The street door opens, and* MR. *and* MRS. GRAINGER *come in. They are carrying a rather bulky parcel.*

MR. GRAINGER: Good evening, Fred.

FRED: Well, you are early birds!

MRS. GRAINGER: Good evening, Fred.

FRED: Good evening, Mrs. Grainger.

MRS. GRAINGER: We came early on purpose. We wanted to talk to you and Nora for a minute.

FRED: Nora's gone to open up the 'Public' – I'll call her. (*He opens the serving window.*) Mr. and Mrs. Grainger are here, Nora – they want to talk to you.

NORA (*off*): All right – I'm coming.

MR. GRAINGER: Is Doris back yet?

FRED: Yes – she's having a cup of tea in the kitchen.

MR. GRAINGER: How's the beer to-day, Fred?

FRED: Same as usual – bloody awful!

> NORA *comes back and goes behind the bar.*

MR. GRAINGER: Give us two mild, then, will you?

FRED: It's all mild, really – that's what's the matter with it. (*He proceeds to draw two glasses of beer.*)

MR. GRAINGER: We're worn out. We've had a day of it, and no mistake.

MRS. GRAINGER: Get on with it, dear.

MR. GRAINGER: We wanted to say 'thank you' for all you've done for us.

FRED: Why, we haven't done anything, Mr. Grainger – not more than anybody else would have done.

MR. GRAINGER: You only just happened to save our son's life – that's all you did.

MRS. GRAINGER: If it hadn't been for you – he probably wouldn't be alive to-day.

NORA (*smiling*): We couldn't very well have turned him out, could we?

MRS. GRAINGER: I know some as would have, at that.

> DORIS *comes in, carrying her cup of tea. She goes behind the bar.*

MR. GRAINGER: Hallo, Doris!

DORIS: Good evening, Mr. Grainger.

MR. GRAINGER: We want to say 'thank you' to Doris, too – it's through her that we've been able to see Billy as often as we have during the last two years. We haven't asked Billy any questions – but we do know that him and Doris have been working together, and he thinks she's the bravest girl he's ever known, and . . .

DORIS: Don't talk like that, Mr. Grainger – please don't!

MRS. GRAINGER: We've brought you a present – it's for the bar. Go on, Les, give it to them.

MR. GRAINGER (*pushing the package across to* NORA): This is with our love, Mrs. Shattock – and with our gratitude – all our lives.

NORA: You really shouldn't have – I don't know what to say – really I don't.

FRED: Go on, Nora – undo it.

MRS. GRAINGER: You could use it here – or in your sitting-room.

MR. GRAINGER: You could change it if you don't like it.

> NORA *undoes the paper and discloses a really lovely Staffordshire jug.*

NORA: Oh, Mr. Grainger, it's beautiful!

FRED: Thanks ever so much, Mrs. Grainger – thank you both ever so much!

> DORIS *puts down her cup and runs round from behind the bar. She kisses* MRS. GRAINGER *first, and then* MR. GRAINGER.

DORIS: It was wonderful of you to think of it. We shall treasure it always . . .

NORA: I don't know how to thank you enough . . .

MR. GRAINGER (*with a rush*): It's for us to thank you – really it is. You see, this place has been a second home to us. This is where we always came and had a drink or two and sat quietly – watching the people come in and out and it's given us an interest – something to take our minds off our troubles, something to look forward to. That's what we want to thank you for. Come on, Mother – let's have our beer.

NORA: Good luck to you both – always. (*She dabs her eyes.*)

FRED: Now then, Nora – none of that.

> MR. *and* MRS. GRAINGER *go over to their usual table*, MR. GRAINGER *carefully carrying the glasses of beer.*
>
> DORIS *goes back behind the bar.* MR. LAWRENCE *pokes his head through the serving window.*

MR. LAWRENCE: Anybody home?

NORA: Why, Mr. Lawrence – what a fright you gave me!

MR. LAWRENCE: Guilty conscience, I shouldn't wonder. What-ho, Doris!

DORIS: What-ho yourself.

MR. LAWRENCE: Two of the usual for me and Archie – our throats are quite parched from spreading rumours.

DORIS: Two halves of mild.

> FRED *proceeds to draw two beers.*
>
> ALMA BOUGHTON *comes in from the street, accompanied by an elderly lady,* MRS. MASSITER. MRS. MASSITER *has a faint air of eccentricity about her. She wears sturdy country clothes, boots and a rather large hat.* ALMA *guides her to the bar.*

ALMA: Good evening, Fred – hallo, Nora!

FRED: Good evening, Mrs. Boughton.

NORA: You're quite a stranger.

ALMA: I've been away. I've brought my mother to visit you. We've come up from the country to-day. Mother, this is Fred and Nora Shattock – I've told you all about them.

MRS. MASSITER: How do you do?

> FRED *and* NORA *shake hands over the bar.*

NORA: Pleased to meet you, I'm sure.

FRED: Welcome to 'The Shy Gazelle', ma'am!

ALMA: Doris! This is my mother, Mrs. Massiter.

DORIS: How do you do?

ALMA: Now take a good look round, Mother – you've always envied me my wicked London night life. This is it.

MRS. MASSITER: It feels like Paradise to me. (*To* FRED.) I've been gardening for seven years, and I'm sick to death of it. I never thought I'd live to be grateful to the Germans, but I am. They've turned me out of my house bag and baggage. I've been chained to it like a slave to the galleys since 1938. Now I'm free and I should like something very strong to drink.

ALMA: Two 'Stubbs', Fred. It's kill or cure.

MRS. MASSITER: We mix it with rum in Kent – it gives it more of a kick.

NORA: Well, I never!

DORIS: Where is your house, Mrs. Massiter?

MRS. MASSITER: Five miles from Maidstone – it's hideous.

NORA: I should think you'd feel lost being suddenly uprooted like that!

MRS MASSITER: Not in the least. I was rather worried about the dogs, that's all.

DORIS: How many have you?

MRS MASSITER: Nine. I've left them with the Vicar – they're very fond of him.

> FRED *hands them two drinks.*

FRED: Here are your drinks, Mrs. Boughton – I'm sorry we haven't any rum to go with them.

MRS. MASSITER: Please don't think I was boasting – about the rum, I mean. It isn't real rum – we make it in the village.

FRED: What from?

MRS. MASSITER: I really don't know – all sorts of things – each new lot tastes of something different.

NORA: Have you many Germans in your village?

MRS. MASSITER: Yes, quite a lot – but they don't interfere with us much – as a matter of fact the farmers have found them quite useful on the land. They're mostly from Silesia and Prussia – so much nicer than those horrid sentimental Bavarians. We keep them in order fairly well. I'm the head of the local Resistance Group.

ALMA: Mother! Do be careful what you say!

MRS. MASSITER: Nonsense, dear – everybody knows that. (*She lifts her glass.*) Down with Hitler!

NORA (*agitated*): Oh dear!

ALMA: You mustn't say things like that in public – Mother – you really mustn't. You'll get everyone into trouble.

ALFIE *and* LILY BLAKE *come in from the street.*

ALFIE (*at the bar*): Give us a couple of mild, Fred. We've just been thrown out of the 'Regal'.

FRED: What for?

MRS. BLAKE: The whole audience was thrown out you've never seen such a fuss! I nearly died laughing.

NORA: What happened?

MRS. BLAKE: It was a news reel, see? It began with the usual stuff – you know – pictures of mines being put on the beaches, and guns and tanks lined up on the cliffs, and the man's voice telling us the old baloney about Allied armies trying to land being driven back and bashed to blazes. Then suddenly there was a close-up of little old 'Itler 'imself puffing 'imself out like he always does, and suddenly when he opens his mouth to speak it's not his voice at all, see? It's a child's voice singing 'Who's afraid of the big bad wolf'! You should have heard the laugh that went up! People fell about and cheered and screamed – then all the lights were put up and a whole lot of Germans come in and started knocking people about – a real old free-for-all. Everybody was turned out – Alfie and me got through one of the side doors. Oh dear, I haven't laughed so much since father's funeral!

Enter GLADYS MOTT *and* YOUNG SOLDIER.

FRED (*giving the* BLAKES *their beer*): Nice work – very nice work indeed!

LADY (*in public bar*): A small port, please.

FRED: There's a lady in the 'Public' asking for a port, Dad.

FRED: Well, she's out of luck, isn't she?

DORIS (*at serving window*): Sorry, there isn't any.

A murmur from the other side.

Okay, Dad. She'll settle for some of that Peppermint Cordial.

FRED: Well, that's her look-out, isn't it?

> NORA *takes down a bottle of Peppermint Cordial and gives it to* DORIS.
>> GEORGE BOURNE *and* LYIA *come in from the street.* LYIA's *arm is still in a sling.*

GEORGE: Hello, Fred – hello, Nora!

FRED: Good evening, Mr. Bourne.

NORA: Why, whatever have you done to your arm, Miss Vivian?

LYIA: I was practising waving a Union Jack and I sprained my wrist.

GLADYS: Good evening, Mr. Shattock.

FRED (*coldly*): Good evening. (*Laconically.*) What's yours?

SOLDIER: *Bitte!*

FRED: We're out of bitter – you can have brown, or mild.

GLADYS (*vivaciously*): '*Bitte*' means 'please' in German.

FRED: Well, you ought to know.

GLADYS (*sharply*): Give us two mild, then. You can't blame him for not speaking English very well – he's only been here three weeks.

FRED: What a pity! He won't have much time to learn now, will he?

GLADYS: How do you mean?

FRED: Skip it. (*He gives them two beers.*)

> The GERMAN SOLDIER *produces a purse.* GLADYS *finds the right money for him and plonks it down on the bar.*

GERMAN SOLDIER: *Feuer bitte.* (*To* MRS. BLAKE.)

MRS. MASSITER (*as they go over to the downstage table*): He looks almost too young to travel, doesn't he?

> The street door opens, and ALBRECHT RICHTER *comes in, followed by two S.S. Guards.*

ALBRECHT (*coming over to the bar*): Good evening, Mr. Shattock. I am sorry to inconvenience you. This is merely a routine matter. Good evening, Mrs. Shattock.

NORA: Good evening.

The uniformed men proceed round the bar asking questions in low tones and demanding identity cards.

ALBRECHT: Can I have some of your curious ginger ale, Mr. Shattock? (*He produces a flask from his pocket.*) I have brought my own liquor. I find that your 'Stubbs' mixture doesn't agree with me very well.

SOLDIER (*to uniformed men*): Heil Hitler!

FRED: That's quite all right. (*He opens a bottle of ginger ale and passes it across.*)

ALBRECHT: George – I haven't seen you for a long time. Lyia – I hope you are both well.

GEORGE: In the pink, Albrecht. The Brighton air, you know – such a pity we were not allowed to stay there.

ALBRECHT: Can I offer you some whisky?

GEORGE: Thanks – you most certainly can.

ALBRECHT: Lyia?

LYIA: I'd take the flask too at the drop of a hat – just to be able to sniff it before I go to sleep at night.

ALBRECHT (*to* FRED): Two more, please, Mr. Shattock.

LYIA: No, no, Fred – I'll take it straight.

GEORGE: Me, too.

ALMA: It's all right, Mother, it's only routine.

MRS. MASSITER: I'm quite used to it dear, they do it all the time at the 'Langley Arms'.

> ALBRECHT *pours out whisky into three glasses;* GEORGE *adds water.* ALBRECHT *hands one to* LYIA *and one to* GEORGE.

GEORGE: Thanks! (*He raises his glass.*) Cheers!

ALBRECHT (*raising his glass*): Heil Hitler!

LYIA (*raising hers*): Hail and farewell.

ALBRECHT (*smiling*): Amusing Lyia – if a little previous.

> *The uniformed men arrive at the table at which* ALMA *and* MRS. MASSITER *are sitting.*

MRS. MASSITER (*to the* GUARD): I hasten to remind you, young man, that that is the *number* of my card, not my age.

> *The* SOLDIERS *bow stiffly and hand it back to her.*

ALBRECHT: I never see Mrs. Braid nowadays – she seems to have completely disappeared.

GEORGE: She's in Wales, I believe – isn't she, Fred?

FRED: Yes – we had a card from her a couple of weeks ago.

ALBRECHT: Still writing successfully, I hope?

GEORGE: Janet is extremely diligent.

ALBRECHT (*to* DORIS): Good evening, Miss Shattock.

DORIS (*turning from the serving window*): Good evening.

ALBRECHT: I hope you have quite recovered?

DORIS (*after an infinitesimal pause*): Oh yes, quite, thanks! I feel fine.

NORA (*quickly*): Recovered? What do you mean? What's the matter?

ALBRECHT: Your daughter was taken ill this afternoon, Mrs. Shattock. She left the Savoy at four instead of five-thirty.

DORIS (*casually*): Yes – I don't know what came over me – I suddenly felt all sick and dizzy and I fainted. The manager was awfully kind and let me come home early. It must have been something I ate.

ALBRECHT: It was very wise of you to take a walk in the park. Fresh air and exercise are always beneficial.

DORIS: You know you're getting me into trouble, don't you?

FRED: What is all this? What's up?

DORIS: I've been caught out – that's what's up. Just my luck.

GEORGE: It seems to me, Albrecht, that you have been tactless in the extreme.

ALBRECHT (*smiling*): I am so sorry.

DORIS: Who does he think he is – Sexton Blake?

ALBRECHT: Who is Sexton Blake?

GEORGE: A famous gimlet-eyed detective – entirely fictional, of course – about the same period as Epp's Cocoa.

ALBRECHT: I see. I thought it might be the name of the young gentleman Miss Shattock met by the pond in St. James's Park.

DORIS: Well, it wasn't, so there.

ALBRECHT: What was his name, then, Miss Shattock?

FRED: There's no law against a girl meeting a boy friend in the park if she wants to, is there?

ALBRECHT: That depends.

DORIS: It's all right, Dad – don't interfere – I'll explain.

FRED: There's no call for you to explain anything you don't want to.

ALBRECHT: I'm afraid there is.

DORIS (*bitterly*): Mr. Nosey Parker.

ALBRECHT (*imperturbably*): Who is Mr. Nosey Parker?

GEORGE: Another fictional character – idiomatic.

ALBRECHT: Very interesting – thank you. (*He puts down his glass sharply.*) I am afraid I must ask you to come with me.

DORIS: Come with you – where?

ALBRECHT: I am not entirely satisfied with your story, Miss Shattock. There are some questions I should like to ask you at my office. Will you please get your hat and coat?

DORIS: Now? You want me to come now?

ALBRECHT (*steely*): Immediately. I fear I have no more time to waste.

GEORGE: Look here, Albrecht . . .

ALBRECHT: No more time to waste, Mr. Bourne – no more time at all.

DORIS: Don't worry, Mum – I'll be all right.

> *There is dead silence in the bar as* DORIS *takes her hat and coat from the peg and puts them on.* ALBRECHT *barks an order to his two* GUARDS. *They close in on either side of* DORIS. *She smiles uncertainly, and waves to* FRED *and* NORA.

Don't worry – please don't worry. (*She looks round the bar.*) Goodnight, all.

> DORIS *goes out with the* GUARDS.
>
>   ALBRECHT *bows stiffly to* FRED *and* NORA, *and* GEORGE *and* LYIA, *and putting his flask back into his pocket he follows her.*

CURTAIN

Scene III

Three days later. It is about two-thirty in the afternoon.

   There is nobody in the saloon except ALFIE *and* LILY BLAKE *and* PHYLLIS, *who is behind the bar.*

   ALFIE, *sitting on one of the stools at the bar, is explaining the Allied strategy with the help of some beer mugs and ash trays.*

ALFIE: ... This is the French coast, see? And this is the English coast – here.

MRS. BLAKE: Where's Belgium?

ALFIE: That's where Phyllis's elbow is. Now it stands to reason that all our invasion craft would start from here and here and here ...

MRS. BLAKE: Where would they get them from?

ALFIE: Where would they get what from?

MRS. BLAKE: The invasion craft – them flat-bottomed boats you've been going on about?

ALFIE: Never you mind where they'd get 'em, they've got 'em.

PHYLLIS: How do you know?

ALFIE (*patiently*): Shut up a minute, will you, Phyllis? It's bad enough trying to get high-powered military strategy into Lily's thick head without you asking silly questions.

PHYLLIS: I only said 'How d'you know'?

MRS. BLAKE: Fat lot you know about high-powered military strategy.

ALFIE: All right, all right – we'll go back to the beginning again. This is the French coast, see—

MRS. BLAKE (*to* PHYLLIS, *who has moved*): Put Belgium back, Phyllis, there's a dear – I'm muddled enough as it is.

PHYLLIS (*replacing her elbow*): Pardon me.

ALFIE: Now it stands to reason, doesn't it, that before they actually start the invasion the Allied Command will send over aircraft to soften up the Jerries' coast defences here and here and here and here and here.

MRS. BLAKE: By dropping bombs on them?

ALFIE (*irascibly*): What do you think they'd drop – liquorice allsorts?

MRS. BLAKE: You know the trouble with you, Alfie Blake, is that you can't never explain anything without losing your temper.

PHYLLIS: Let him go on, Mrs. Blake, it's ever so interesting.

MRS. BLAKE: Let him go on! Try and stop him! He knows everything, he does, and nobody else knows nothing.

ALFIE (*heatedly*): Now look here, stupid ...

MRS. BLAKE: Don't you 'stupid' me – I've had this damned invasion rammed down my throat morning, noon and night for the last six months, and I'm sick to death of it – Life hasn't been worth living since you took up high-powered military strategy. (*She takes up her mug of beer.*) I'm taking my bit of the English coast over to the table to have a little peace and quiet. And if and when the invasion does come, you know what you can do with it.

ALFIE (*with irony*): It's our wedding anniversary to-morrow – we're just working up for it – fifteen years of married bliss, and never a cross word – you'd never believe it, would you? (*He takes his mug and goes to join* LILY.) And you'd be right.

     BILLY GRAINGER *comes in from the street down left.*

BILLY: Hullo!

ALFIE: Hullo, son!

BILLT (*crossing to bar. To* PHYLLIS): Hullo, glorious!

PHYLLIS: Good afternoon, Mr. Fawcett. You're quite a stranger.

BILLY: Where's Doris?

PHYLLIS (*her face changing*): Doris?

BILLY: Yes – it's Saturday – she isn't at the Savoy, is she?

PHYLLIS: No, she isn't at the Savoy.

BILLY: What's the matter?

PHYLLIS (*coming out from behind the bar*): Mrs. Shattock's upstairs. I'll call her.

BILLY: What is all this?

PHYLLIS (*calling*): Mrs. Shattock! Mrs. Shattock!

NORA (*off*): What is it?

BILLY: Something's happened, what is it? Something's happened to Doris. (*He grips* PHYLLIS'*s arm.*) Where is she?

PHYLLIS: They took her away.

BILLY: Who took her away?

PHYLLIS: Mr. Richter – the Gestapo . . .

BILLY: When?

PHYLLIS: You're hurting my arm.

BILLY (*he lets her go*): When did they take her away?

PHYLLIS: Three days ago. Mrs. Shattock's in an awful state – so is Mr. Shattock. He's been over to Gestapo headquarters every day – but they won't let him in.

     NORA *comes down the stairs. She is obviously strained and miserable.*

NORA: What's the matter, Phyllis?

PHYLLIS: It's Mr. Fawcett. He . . .

BILLY: Is it true – what Phyllis said about Doris being taken?

NORA: Yes, Billy – Mr. Fawcett. Get back behind the bar, Phyllis.
(*To* BILLY.) You'd better come upstairs in case somebody
comes in. Is there anybody in the 'Public'?

PHYLLIS (*looking through the hatch*): No.

NORA: You'd better shut down the window, anyway. It's nearly
closing time.

PHYLLIS: Yes, Mrs. Shattock. (*She does so.*)

FRED *comes in from the street. He looks leaden and hopeless.*

NORA (*appealing*): Fred . . .

FRED: Nothing. The guards wouldn't even let me in at the door.

BILLY: When did they take her? I was sent out of London –
nobody told me – I've only just come back.

NORA: Wednesday – the day you met her in the park – that same
afternoon.

FRED (*with a warning look towards the* BLAKES): Nora . . .

NORA: It's all right – Mr. and Mrs. Blake were here – they saw
them take her. Fred's been trying ever since to see Mr.
Richter, but they won't let him in. Yesterday they gave him a
message – from Mr. Richter. It said they'd send her back –
when she had answered their questions satisfactorily.

BILLY: That was all?

FRED (*wearily, turning away and hanging up his hat*): Yes – that was
all.

NORA: You've been gone a long time, Fred. You said they
wouldn't let you in – I was getting worried. Where have you
been?

FRED: Just walking about.

There is the sound of a car drawing up outside.

NORA: What's that?

*Two S.S. Guards walk in. They are carrying between them the inert
body of* DORIS.

    NORA *gives a cry. One of the Guards gives an order to the other
one. They both fling the body at* NORA's *feet.*

    They then salute, shoot out their arms, say 'Heil Hitler!' *and go
out, slamming the door behind them.*

> NORA *runs to* DORIS, *and, kneeling down, takes her head tenderly on her lap.* DORIS *makes a slight movement, and groans. Her face is almost unrecognisable, her hair is dank and matted with sweat, and her hands are covered with blood.*

NORA (*in a whisper*): Dorrie – my Dorrie – my little girl!

DORIS (*opening her eyes – with a despairing effort*): I didn't say anything . . . I didn't . . . (*Her head drops back – she gives a little choke, and dies.*)

FRED: Christ! They've tortured her! They've tortured her to death!

NORA (*with sudden frenzy*): Dorrie! Dorrie!

> NORA *gathers* DORIS'*s huddled body into her arms. She begins to scream, a high-pitched, toneless scream.*

CURTAIN

Scene IV

May 1945. Early afternoon. It is just before closing time.

> FRED *and* PHYLLIS MERE *are behind the bar. At the bar are* ALMA, MRS. MASSITER, ALFIE, LILY *and* MR. LAWRENCE. *Everyone is listening intently to the sound of distant firing, intermixing with sharp explosions.*

ALFIE: There – that sounds like grenades.

ALMA: It's quite near.

FRED: Round about Sloane Street I should think.

ALMA: It's getting more general, isn't it – the fighting?

FRED: All over London – and the suburbs – ever since last night.

ALMA: I'm so dreadfully afraid that they may have started too soon – the Resistance men – so many of them might be killed unnecessarily – they said on the wireless that our troops couldn't get here for two or three days at least—

FRED: They must have had the O.K. from the Allied Command—

> *Planes are heard going over.*

189

There's another lot going over.

ALFIE: Sounds like fighter bombers.

MRS. BLAKE: What else would they sound like?

ALFIE: Now look here, Lily . . .

MRS. BLAKE: Well, they wouldn't be likely to send over sewing machines, would they?

> GLADYS MOTT *comes in from down left.*

GLADYS: Give me a drink, please – anything will do.

FRED: Sorry, we haven't got anything left.

GLADYS: What are they drinking, then?

FRED: That's their business.

GLADYS: I'm dry – I've been running – there was firing in the Pimlico Road – I want a drink.

FRED: You'll have to go somewhere else.

GLADYS: It isn't after hours – this is a licensed house – what right have you got to say I can't have a drink when I want one.

FRED: I'm not serving you, Miss Mott – not to-day or any other day. That's clear enough, isn't it?

GLADYS: You've got a bloody nerve, talking to me like that! Who do you think you are?

FRED: Nothing doing, Miss Mott. Get cracking.

GLADYS: I've been here regular for years.

FRED: You've brought your German boy friends here often enough and I've had to serve you because I hadn't the right to refuse. But things have changed now. You don't get another drink in this house as long as you live. Get out and stay out!

GLADYS: I'll report you for this . . .

FRED: Who to?

GLADYS: Never you mind who to . . . (*Becoming a little maudlin.*) You haven't any right to insult me – I've had to earn my living, haven't I, the same as everybody else?

FRED: Not quite the same as everybody else.

ALFIE: Better hop it, lady – you're annoying Mr. Shattock.

GLADYS (*slamming down some money on the bar*): There's my money, and I want a drink.

FRED (*picking up the money and throwing it on the floor*): Pick up that money and get out before I throw you out. And you'd better get this into your head here and now. It isn't because you're a tart that I'm refusing to serve you – it's because you've been selling yourself to the enemy – that's quite enough for me. Get out, and never show your face round that door again.

In silence GLADYS MOTT *picks up her money from the floor and – goes out.*

Sorry, Mrs. Massiter – I've been promising myself that for a long time.

MRS. MASSITER: The vicar wrote me that one of the girls in our village did what she did last week. They shaved her head – the Germans didn't seem to mind a bit.

There is the sound of planes flying over.

MR. LAWRENCE: There they go again! Up the R.A.F.

ALFIE: They're after them ammunition dumps at Hendon.

MRS. BLAKE: How d'you know?

ALFIE: It stands to reason, don't it?

MRS. BLAKE: I thought they might have sent you a post-card!

ALFIE: You think you're very funny, don't you?

The street door opens and JANET BRAID *comes in.*

ALMA (*turning*): Janet! I haven't seen you for ages.

JANET: I suddenly felt that I couldn't bear not to be here, so up I came.

FRED: Hullo, Mrs. Braid.

JANET: Hullo, Fred, how's Nora?

FRED: She's all right, thank you – as well as can be expected, that is. We liked getting your letter. It was good of you to write.

ALMA: Janet – this is my mother.

JANET: (*shaking hands*): How do you do?

MRS. MASSITER: Have a drink with us – we're celebrating.

JANET: The whole of England will soon be celebrating.

FRED: The drinks are on the house to-day, Mrs. Braid.

JANET: Is everyone else all right – apart from – you know what I mean?

FRED: Yes, Mrs. Braid, everyone else is okay. We're still watched and searched every now and then, but not so much as we were. They've got a good deal to keep them occupied at the moment.

ALFIE: A day or two more – three at the outside, I should think –
and it'll be all over bar the shouting.

ALMA: It's all incredible, isn't it? One can scarcely believe it.

JANET: What about that drink, Fred? (*She turns to* ALMA.) What
are you all having?

FRED: That's my little surprise – don't let those thick glasses fool
you. This is what we're having! (*He produces a bottle of
champagne.*)

JANET: Fred! How wonderful!

FRED: I've had it hidden since 1939. I've still got a few put by for
the day we're actually liberated. But I thought we'd make a
start now – just to get ourselves into the mood. (*He pours a
glassful.*) Here you are, Mrs. Braid.

JANET (*lifting her glass*): Thank you, Fred. I drink to you and yours
with affection and gratitude – so very much affection and
gratitude.

ALMA: Hear, hear!

ALFIE: Good old Fred!

 The others all murmur 'Hear, hear'.

JANET: You see, we have known – all of us in our different ways
– that your age-old character, your kindness and firmness and
stubborn humour could never let us down, never fail us for a
moment. That is why we are proud – so very proud – to wish
you well.

ALL: Hear, hear!

FRED (*with difficulty*): Thank you, Mrs. Braid. I'll tell Nora – I'll
tell Nora what you said . . .

 FRED *goes hurriedly out through the alcove.*

MRS. BLAKE: Lend us your handkerchief, Alfie. We don't want
any of them advance British spearheads to come marching in
and find us with tears running down our faces.

ALFIE: Don't talk so soft! They couldn't get here for days.

PHYLLIS: Anyone want another drop before closing? There's still
some left in the bottle.

ALMA: You have it, Phyllis.

PHYLLIS: I don't mind if I do. (*She pours the remains of the
champagne.*) Here's how!

MRS. BLAKE: Come on, Alfie – we'd better be pushing off.

Mother and Aunt Alice will be having a fit if we leave them in that flat alone all day.

ALFIE: Nobody asked them to stay in the flat all day.

MRS. BLAKE: They're old! You couldn't expect them to go rushing about the streets waving flags at their age. Besides, think of Mother's feet!

ALFIE: I've been thinking of your mother's feet for fifteen years. I'd like to think about something else now.

ALMA: We'd better go too, Mother ... it's after closing time.

MRS. BLAKE: Come on, Alfie – Mr. Lawrence, are you coming our way?

MR. LAWRENCE: All right.

MRS. BLAKE (*to* ALMA): I like having a couple of men with me in case anything happens.

MRS. MASSITER: I believe there are several historical precedents for that.

MRS. BLAKE: Good-bye all.

    MRS. BLAKE, ALFIE *and* MR. LAWRENCE *go out.*
    FRED *comes back.*

FRED: Nora would like to see you for a minute, Mrs. Braid, before you go.

JANET: Shall I go through?

FRED: No. She's coming down.

ALMA: Come along, Mother. Good-bye, Janet. Come to the flat later on, if you haven't anything better to do. We still have a little hoarded tea left.

JANET: I'd love to.

ALMA: Good-bye, Fred, see you later.

MRS. MASSITER: I hope there's a post office open somewhere. I want to send a telegram to Mrs. Burrage.

ALMA: Who's she, darling?

MRS. MASSITER: My chief of staff in the Resistance Group. She's liable to lose her head in a crisis.

ALMA: She's probably lost it by now.

    ALMA *and* MRS. MASSITER *go out.*

FRED: It's all right, Phyllis – you can go now.

PHYLLIS: Thanks, Mr. Shattock.

FRED: Where are you going to spend these next few historical hours – Empire, Regal or Odeon?

PHYLLIS (*taking her hat and coat from the peg*): Metropole, Victoria. They've got a double feature. King Kong and Jeannette Macdonald.

> PHYLLIS *goes out.*

FRED: You'll notice a bit of a change in Nora, Mrs. Braid.

JANET: Yes, Fred, I'm prepared for that.

FRED: It's been bad for her – very bad – at one time I thought the shock had done for her – but she's been getting better lately—

JANET: Stevie's all right, isn't he?

FRED: Yes – that's what's kept her going, really.

> NORA *comes in from the alcove. She has changed a lot. Her face is colourless and her hair is almost white.*

JANET (*going to her*): Nora – how glad I am to see you!

NORA: Welcome back, Mrs. Braid. We've missed you.

JANET: Fred's been giving us champagne – a real celebration.

NORA: I know – he wanted me to have some, but it doesn't agree with me. You'd better lock up, Fred. It's long after three.

JANET: I must go anyhow. I've got to find somewhere to have my hair washed – it's filthy. Do you think anywhere will be open.

NORA: There's that place in the Fulham Road that Doris used to go to.

JANET: I know it. I'll try there first. See you later, Nora.

NORA: Good-bye, Mrs. Braid. Thank you for saying what you did to Fred.

JANET: I was only saying what we all feel – what we've felt all along – about you both. (*She puts her arms round* NORA *and kisses her.*) Good-bye for now, Fred, take care of yourselves.

FRED: If you hear any firing – pop into the nearest doorway.

JANET: I'll be all right, Fred.

> *She goes out.*
> *They both watch her out of the door. They shut it and come back into the room.*

FRED: Sure you wouldn't fancy a little drop of something?

NORA: No, dear – you know I never do. It's after closing time – hadn't you better lock up?

FRED: Not to-day, Nora – nor to-morrow and the next day either – Service with a smile – day and night until they come marching in – that's our motto from now onwards.

NORA: Do you think Stevie's in all this fighting?

FRED: Maybe he is – maybe he isn't – it all depends what orders he's got—

NORA: I wish we knew where he was – I wish he'd let us know.

FRED: He's all right – I know he's all right – I feel it in my bones. You had a message from him two days ago – he'll get in touch with us when he has a minute.

NORA: What will happen if our troops don't get here when the wireless said they would? What happens if it isn't to-morrow or the day after – if it's a week or a fortnight? Our boys will be killed – all of them – they'll be outnumbered – you know they can't hold out that long.

FRED: They wouldn't have started this rising unless they'd had the order to go.

NORA: Yes I know, but—

FRED: Do you remember what Stevie said to you – that night when he first came back. He said, 'Living or dying doesn't matter all that much – there's certainly no sense in living if you can't live the way you want to. We've got to fight – all of us – to the last ditch!'

NORA (*turning away*): Yes, Fred, I remember.

FRED (*putting his arm round her*): Nora, this is the last ditch, love. And we *are* in it together. That's a bit of a comfort, isn't it? Whatever happens!

NORA: Whatever happens!

FRED: I know what you're thinking. Doris has gone and maybe Stevie'll go too. Well, if he does that'll be that, won't it? We shall have to face being alone – being alone together to the end of our days. Maybe they won't be such very long days, but whichever way it goes there's nothing you or I could do to stop our boy or any of the other boys fighting for what they believe in.

NORA: Very well, Fred.

BILLY GRAINGER *comes hurriedly through the upstage door.*

BILLY: I thought you'd have locked the front door so I came by the back.

NORA: Billy!

BILLY: I've got a message for you from Mr. Bourne – it's urgent.

FRED: What is it, son?

BILLY: You're to come with me – now – at once – I've got a truck at the end of the mews.

FRED: Come with you – where to?

BILLY: Not very far – just outside London.

FRED: Why – what for?

BILLY: Please come quickly – I'll explain as we go.

NORA: Where's Stevie?

BILLY: I don't know – please come, Mrs. Shattock – it's urgent.

FRED: We're not moving from here, Billy.

NORA: Where's Stevie?

BILLY: I tell you I don't know.

NORA: Have you seen him?

BILLY: Yes – no – that is – please do what I say – both of you— Mr. Bourne sent me on ahead to get you away as quickly as possible.

NORA: Is Stevie fighting?

BILLY: Yes. We're all fighting.

NORA: Is he dead?

BILLY: No, he isn't – I swear he isn't – he's fine – but please do as I say—

FRED: Don't waste your breath, son – we're not running away from London now or any other time – not while Stevie's still here fighting—

There is a sound of a van screeching to a standstill outside.

BILLY (*in agony*): Oh please, please – it's orders – Mr. Bourne's the boss – it's orders, Mr. Shattock.

The doors are flung open and GEORGE BOURNE *comes in.*

GEORGE (*furiously*): You bloody little fool, I told you to get them away!

BEN *and* DR. VENNING *come in dragging* RICHTER, *who is semiconscious. They drop him on to the ground.*

GEORGE: Lock and bolt the door – quick. Tell Lawrence to go—

BEN (*running to door*): Okay – get. (*He shuts and bolts the door.*)

GEORGE (*as* RICHTER *gives a groan*): Tie him into a chair.

NORA: Where's my son, Mr. Bourne – where's Stevie?

GEORGE: He's all right, Nora. I want you and Fred to leave at once, please, with Billy. The truck's at the end of the mews.

FRED: We're not running away, Mr. Bourne. Not for you or anyone else.

GEORGE: I order you to go – immediately.

FRED: Sorry, Mr. Bourne – I'm too old to take orders – even from you.

GEORGE: Stay then and be damned to you – but for God's sake get Nora away. Things are going to happen – there's no time to waste.

NORA: I'm staying with Fred.

GEORGE (*angrily*): All this deathless heroism. Window, Ben.

> BEN *takes his stand by the window.* RICHTER *begins to come round – he utters a hoarse cry –* GEORGE *stuffs a handkerchief into his mouth.*

GEORGE: Gag, Venning – quickly.

DR. VENNING (*producing one*): Right. Help me, Billy.

> *He and* BILLY *gag* RICHTER *effectively.*

GEORGE: Swivel him round.

> DR. VENNING *and* BILLY *turn the chair round facing* GEORGE.

Now then. (*He takes a glass of water from the bar and dashes it in* RICHTER's *face.*) You'd better come to for a minute – I've got something to say to you. Sorry, Fred. We had to use this place. We hadn't planned to but things went wrong at the last minute.

FRED: What are you going to do?

GEORGE: You'll see. (*To* RICHTER.) This is part of a plan, Mr. Richter. A plan that was made a long time ago. We had a purpose in bringing you here – we are going to kill you.

> NORA *stiffens and stands rigidly staring at* RICHTER.

Unfortunately we have no time for the formality of a full trial. However, before 'liquidating' you we propose to read you a list of the substantiated changes against you. We should hate the thought of you leaving this life smarting under a sense of British injustice.

> RICHTER *lifts his head and stares balefully at* GEORGE.

GEORGE: First and foremost you were directly responsible for the arrest, torture and murder of Miss Doris Shattock.

> *There is a noise in the passage.*

Quick – the door.

> BEN *and* BILLY *stand by the upstage door with their guns ready.* STEVIE *bursts in. He is wearing a blood-stained bandage round his arm and he looks rather battered.*

NORA (*with a cry*): Stevie!

GEORGE: Quiet!

STEVIE: Quick – they've rumbled us – they know we've got him – they're coming now—

GEORGE: Damn – damn and blast.

STEVIE: They know we're here – Mickey got through to headquarters – they want to get us all at one go.

GEORGE: Billy – Stevie – put him in line with the door. Barricade the door with that table and the chairs.

> STEVIE, BEN, BILLY *and* DR. VENNING *do so.* NORA *stands still watching.*

Here – this is just in case of accidents. (*He tears off* STEVIE'S *Union Jack Resistance armband and ties it round* RICHTER'S *arm.*) This – I think – comes under the heading of poetic justice. Come on – it's time to go – (*He looks at* NORA *and* FRED *with a slight smile.*) All of us.

BILLY: Aren't we going to let him have it?

GEORGE: No – it's better this way.

STEVIE: He can't get free, can he?

DR. VENNING: No – he's fixed all right.

GEORGE: Go on – all of you – quickly. (*He snatches* BILLY'S *cap off and jams it on to* RICHTER'S *head.*)

STEVIE: Come on, Mum – I'll be with you – come on.

> *Just as* NORA *is about to go she comes back into the room. She walks up to* RICHTER, *looks at him intently for a moment, then she lifts her head. There is a little smile on her face.*

NORA: I'm ready, Stevie.

They all go. FRED, STEVIE *and* NORA *last.*

GEORGE *turns at the door and comes back; switches on the radio.*

GEORGE: You spoke once – a long time ago, Mr. Richter – rather contemptuously I thought – about our friends in America and our Dominions overseas. They're on their way, Mr. Richter – they're on their way. You also informed us – most graciously – that your Führer believed the spirit of this country to be indestructible.

Radio speech is now heard faintly.

GEORGE: He was quite right. It is. *Auf wiedersehn*, Mr. Richter. *Exit.*

The radio, which has been crackling and buzzing, warms up.

VOICE: If in doubt as to your proper course of action, make contact with a member of the Free British Forces, identified by a Union Jack armband, and place yourselves under his orders. Continue to listen in to this wavelength for further bulletins and instructions. Allied troops are rapidly approaching your area and you will soon be liberated. Meanwhile, keep cool, obey orders and play safe. This is the Spokesman of the Supreme Allied Commander speaking to you from Dover Castle. This is the Spokesman of the Supreme Allied Commander speaking to you from Dover Castle.

During this speech there has been the sound of cars screaming to a stop outside the pub. Then sharp orders in German, and then in English an order to open the door. This order is repeated with the threat that if it is not immediately obeyed the guards will open fire.

The radio speech comes to an end and is followed by 'God Save the King' played full out. There comes the sound of machine-gun bullets and breaking glass. RICHTER *struggles convulsively in his chair. Finally, riddled with bullets, he overturns the chair and crashes to the floor.*

CURTAIN

WE WERE DANCING

A Comedy in Two Scenes

from

TO-NIGHT AT 8.30

We Were Dancing was produced in London at the Phoenix Theatre on 9 January 1936, with the following cast:

LOUISE CHARTERIS	Miss Gertrude Lawrence
HUBERT CHARTERIS	Mr. Alan Webb
KARL SANDYS	Mr. Noël Coward
CLARA BETHEL	Miss Alison Leggatt
GEORGE DAVIES	Mr. Edward Underdown
EVA BLAKE	Miss Moya Nugent
MAJOR BLAKE	Mr. Anthony Pelissier
IPPAGA	Mr. Kenneth Carten

TWO OR THREE UNNAMED MEMBERS OF THE COUNTRY CLUB

———

Scene I. *Veranda of the Country Club at Samolo. Evening.*

Scene II. *The same. Early morning.*

TIME: The Present.

Scene I

The scene is the veranda of the Country Club at Samolo.

*On the right is a room in which dances are held every Saturday
night. For these occasions a dance-band flies up from Pendarla by
the new Imperial Inter-State Airways. The band arrives in the
afternoon, plays all night and departs early on Sunday for Abbachi
where it repeats the same procedure for the inhabitants there,
returning wearily on Mondays to the Grand Hotel, Pendarla
where, during the week, it plays for the tourists.*

*When the curtain rises the veranda is deserted. A full moon is
shining over the sea and, far away, above the chatter and music of
the dance-room, there can occasionally be heard the wailing of
native music rising up from the crowded streets by the harbour.*

*IPPAGA, a Samolan boy, crosses the veranda from right to left
carrying a tray of drinks. He is yellowish brown in colour and, like
most Samolans, comparatively tall. He wears a scarlet fez, a green,
purple and mustard-coloured sarong, black patent-leather shoes,
silver earrings and three wooden bracelets.*

*As he goes off on the left the dance music stops and there is the
sound of applause.*

*GEORGE DAVIES and EVA BLAKE come out of the dance-
room. GEORGE DAVIES is a hearty, nondescript young man
dressed in the usual white mess-jacket, black evening trousers and
cummerbund.*

*EVA, equally nondescript, is wearing a pink taffeta bunchy little
dress, pink ribbon in her hair and pink shoes and stockings which
do not quite match. She carries a diamanté evening bag and a blue
chiffon handkerchief round her wrist. She also wears a necklace of
seed pearls and a pendant.*

*The dance music starts again. EVA looks furtively over her
shoulder.*

GEORGE enters first and walks up to balcony and calls:

GEORGE: Eva! Eva!

EVA: It's all right, they're playing an encore.

GEORGE: Come on, then.

EVA: Where's the car?

GEORGE: I parked it at the end of the garden where the road turns off. My boy's looking after it.

EVA: He won't say anything, will he?

GEORGE: Of course not. He's been with me for years.

EVA: Oh, George!

GEORGE (*impatiently*): It's all right – come on—

EVA: Where are we going?

GEORGE: Mahica beach, nobody ever comes near it.

EVA: Oh, George!

GEORGE (*taking her hand*): Come on—

> *They go off right.*
>
> *The band is playing a waltz and the stage is empty for a moment.*
>
> LOUISE CHARTERIS *and* KARL SANDYS *come dancing in from the left. They are both in the thirties, soignée and well-dressed, and they dance together as though they had never been apart.*
>
> *They waltz three times round the stage finishing in the centre with a prolonged kiss. The music ends, there is the sound of applause. Two women and a man come in. They stop short on observing* LOUISE *and* KARL, *they whisper together for a moment and then go back into the dance-room.*
>
> LOUISE *and* KARL *remain clasped in each other's arms oblivious of everything.*
>
> *The music starts again.*
>
> HUBERT CHARTERIS *and* CLARA BETHEL *come out of the dance-room.* CLARA *is a nice-looking, grey-haired woman in the forties.* HUBERT *her brother, is about the same age. He has dignity and reserve and looks intelligently British.*
>
> *They both stand for a moment looking at* KARL *and* LOUISE *who, still entranced with their kiss, have not even noticed them.*

HUBERT (*quietly*): Louise.

LOUISE (*jumping*): Oh!

CLARA (*reproachfully*): Louise, really!

> LOUISE *and* KARL *step a little away from each other.*

LOUISE (*with a social manner*): This is my husband. (*She hesitates and turns to* KARL.) I'm afraid I didn't catch your name?

KARL: Karl. Karl Sandys. (*To* HUBERT *and* CLARA.) How do you do?

HUBERT (*with perfect control*): The car's here, I think we'd better go if you're ready.

LOUISE: I'm not ready.

CLARA (*going towards her*): Come along, Louise.

LOUISE: I can't go, really I can't.

HUBERT: This is most embarrassing, please don't make it worse.

LOUISE: I'm sorry, Hubert. I do see that it's all very difficult.

KARL: I fear I was partly to blame.

HUBERT (*ignoring him*): Please come home now, Louise.

LOUISE (*gently*): No, Hubert.

HUBERT: I'm afraid I must insist.

LOUISE: We have fallen in love.

KARL: Deeply in love.

HUBERT: I would prefer not to discuss the matter with you, sir.

LOUISE: That's silly, Hubert.

HUBERT (*sternly*): Please come away.

LOUISE: I've told you, I can't.

KARL: Have a drink?

HUBERT (*irritably*): Good God!

LOUISE: That is a good idea, Hubert, let's all have a drink.

KARL: We might also sit down.

CLARA: Listen, Louise, you can't behave like this, it's too idiotic.

LOUISE: It's true, can't you see? It's true.

CLARA: What's true? Don't be so foolish.

KARL: We're in love, that's what's true, really it is, Mrs. – Mrs.—

LOUISE: Bethel. This is my husband's sister, Mrs. Bethel.

KARL: How do you do?

CLARA: I appeal to you, Mr. – Mr.—

KARL: Sandys.

CLARA: Mr. Sandys – please go away. Go away at once.

KARL: That's quite impossible.

HUBERT: I detest scenes and I am finding this very unpleasant. I don't know who you are or where you come from, but if you have any sense of behaviour at all you must see that this situation is intolerable. Will you kindly leave the club immediately and never speak to my wife again in any circumstances whatever?

LOUISE: It's more important than that, Hubert, really it is.

KARL: It's the most important thing that has ever happened to me in my whole life, Mr. – Mr.—

LOUISE: Charteris.

KARL: Mr. Charteris.

HUBERT: Once more, Louise, for the last time, will you come home?

LOUISE: No – I can't.

HUBERT: Very well. Come, Clara.

He turns to go away, LOUISE *catches his arm.*

LOUISE: You can't go, either. I know you hate scenes and that you're trying to be as dignified as possible, and that I'm apparently behaving very badly, but it's true, this thing that's happened, I mean – we have fallen in love—

HUBERT: Please let go of my arm, Louise, and don't be ridiculous.

LOUISE: Look at me – look closely – I've been your wife for thirteen years. You're wise and intelligent and you know me well – look at me!

CLARA (*anxiously*): Please go, Mr. Sandys.

KARL (*shaking his head*): No.

HUBERT (*to* LOUISE): I'm looking at you.

LOUISE (*emotionally*): Well – don't you see?

HUBERT *looks quickly at* CLARA *then at* KARL *and then back to* LOUISE *again.*

HUBERT: Yes – I see.

CLARA: Hubert.

MAJOR BLAKE *comes in from the dance-room. He is a red-faced, elderly man.*

MAJOR BLAKE: I say, have you seen Eva?

HUBERT: What?

MAJOR BLAKE: I can't find Eva.

CLARA: I think she went home.

MAJOR BLAKE: She can't have, the car's there.

CLARA: She told me she was driving back with the Baileys.

MAJOR BLAKE: Oh, did she, did she really?

CLARA: She told practically everybody in the club that she was driving back with the Baileys, I'm surprised she didn't mention it to you.

MAJOR BLAKE: Oh, she's all right then – thanks – thanks awfully.

CLARA (*after a pause*): You'll be able to pick her up on the way home.

MAJOR BLAKE: It's hardly on the way, it means going all round by the Woo Ching Road.

HUBERT: Why not telephone her?

MAJOR BLAKE: They won't have got there yet, it's an hour's drive.

CLARA. Why not wait until they have got there?

MAJOR BLAKE: Yes, I suppose I'd better. Anybody feel like a Stengah?

HUBERT: No, thanks.

MAJOR BLAKE (*to* KARL): Do you, sir?

KARL: No, thank you.

MAJOR BLAKE: All right – I shall go back to the bar—

KARL: Bar.

MAJOR BLAKE: Thanks very much.

> *He goes out to right.*

KARL: Who is Eva?

CLARA: His wife.

KARL: And who are the Baileys?

CLARA (*with irritation*): Does it matter?

KARL: I don't know.

LOUISE: They live in that large reddish-looking house at the top of the hill.

KARL: I've never been to the top of the hill.

CLARA: Good-night, Mr. Sandys.

KARL: Good-night.

CLARA (*with almost overdone ordinariness*): Come along, Louise.

LOUISE: Don't be silly, Clara.

CLARA: I'm not being silly. I'm acutely uncomfortable. You're behaving abominably and putting Hubert in an insufferable position. For heaven's sake pull yourself together and be reasonable. You talk a lot of nonsense about being in love. How could you possibly be in love all in a minute like that—?

KARL: We are.

CLARA: Please be quiet and let me speak.

LOUISE: Hubert, do make Clara shut up.

CLARA: You must be insane.

HUBERT: Shut up, Clara.

CLARA: And you must be insane, too, I'm ashamed of you, Hubert.

LOUISE: It's no use railing and roaring, Clara. Hubert's much wiser than you. He's keeping calm and trying to understand and I'm deeply grateful to him—

CLARA: Grateful indeed!

LOUISE: Yes, if he behaved as you seem to think he ought to behave, it would only make everything far worse. I suppose you want him to knock Mr.— (*To* KARL.) What is your first name?

KARL: Karl.

LOUISE: Karl – in the jaw?

CLARA: I don't want anything of the sort. I want him to treat the situation as it should be treated, as nothing but a joke, a stupid joke, in extremely bad taste.

LOUISE: It's more than that, Clara, and you know it is, that's why you're scared.

CLARA: I'm not in the least scared.

HUBERT: You'd better allow me to deal with this, Clara, in my own way.

CLARA: There is such a thing as being too wise, too understanding.

LOUISE: You're usually pretty intelligent yourself, Clara. I can't think what's happened to you. This thing is here – now – between Karl and me. It's no use pretending it isn't, or trying to flip it away as a joke, nor is it any use taking up a belligerent attitude over it. God knows I'm confused enough myself – utterly bewildered, but I do know that it's real, too real to be dissipated by conventional gestures—

CLARA: What is real? What are you talking about?

KARL: Love, Mrs. Bethel, we've fallen in love.

CLARA: Rubbish!

LOUISE: It's not rubbish! It's not nonsense. Be quiet!

HUBERT (*to* LOUISE): What do you want me to do?

LOUISE (*looking at* KARL): I don't know.

KARL: May I ask you a question?

HUBERT (*stiffly*): What is it?

KARL: Are you in love with Louise?

CLARA: Well really!

HUBERT: I am devoted to Louise. We have been married for many years.

KARL: I said are you in love with her?

HUBERT: I love her.

LOUISE: Don't go on evading, Hubert, you know perfectly well what he means.

HUBERT: Of course I know what he means. (*To* KARL.) I'll answer you truly. I am not in love with Louise in the way that you imagine yourself to be in love with her—

KARL: I worship her.

HUBERT: You know nothing about her.

KARL: I know that suddenly, when we were dancing, an enchantment swept over me. An enchantment that I have never known before and shall never know again. It's obvious that you should think I'm mad and that she's mad too, our behaviour looks idiotic, cheap, anything you like, but it's true, this magic that happened, it's so true that everything else, all the ordinary ways of behaviour look shabby and unreal beside it – my heart's thumping, I'm trembling like a fool, even now when I'm trying so hard, so desperately hard to be calm and explain to you reasonably, I daren't look at her, if I did, my eyes would brim over with these silly tears and I should cry like a child—

LOUISE (*making a movement towards him*): Oh, my darling—

KARL: Don't, don't speak – let him speak, let him say what's to be done.

> KARL *leaves the three of them and goes up to the veranda rail and looks out at the sea.*

CLARA: You didn't even know his name.

LOUISE: Oh, Clara! What the hell does that matter?

CLARA (*walking about*): This is really too fantastic – it's beyond belief – it's—

LOUISE (*gently*): Listen. I know you feel dreadfully upset for Hubert and for me too, but it's no use huffing and puffing and getting yourself into a state. Here it is this thing that's happened – it's terribly real – as large as life – larger than life, and we'd all better look at it clearly and as sensibly as we can.

HUBERT: You go home, Clara, you can send the car back for me.

CLARA: I shall do no such thing.

LOUISE (*hurriedly – to* HUBERT): We'd better go away – he and I – as soon as possible.

HUBERT: Where to?

LOUISE: I don't know – anywhere—

HUBERT: For God's sake be reasonable. How can you? How can I let you?

LOUISE: How much do you mind – really?

HUBERT: That obviously has nothing to do with it.

LOUISE: I want to know.

HUBERT: I want to know, too. I can't possibly tell. You've made this up, this magic that he talked about, you've conjured it out of the air and now it's smeared over everything – over me, too – none of it seems real but it has to be treated as if it were. You ask me how much I mind – you want that as well, don't you, in addition to your new love?

LOUISE: Want what? What do you mean?

HUBERT (*almost losing control*): You want me to mind – don't you – don't you?

LOUISE: Oh, Hubert – please don't look like that—

HUBERT: You want everything – everything in the world, you always have.

LOUISE: You're pitying yourself. How beastly of you to be so weak, how contemptible of you!

CLARA: Louise!

LOUISE: I've been faithful to you all these years, we stopped being in love with each other ages ago – we became a habit – a well-ordered, useful, social habit. Have you been as faithful to me as I have to you?

KARL: That's nothing to do with us – what's the use of arguing?

He joins the group again.

LOUISE: Answer me. Have you?

HUBERT: No.

CLARA: Hubert!

LOUISE: Fair's fair.

CLARA: Hubert! Louise!

LOUISE: Do stop saying Hubert and Louise, Clara, it's maddening.

KARL: What is all this? Can't you keep to the point both of you? What does it matter whether he's been faithful to you or not, or you to him either? You're not in love with each other any more, that's clear enough, and even if you were this forked lightning that has struck Louise and me would shatter it – scorch it out of existence—

CLARA: Forked lightning indeed!

KARL: Earthquake then, tidal wave, cataclysm!

HUBERT: I've never not loved you, Louise.

LOUISE (*irritably*): I know that perfectly well. I'm deeply attached to you, too. I hated it when you had your tiresome little affairs on the side—

HUBERT: With your heart?

LOUISE: Of course not. Don't be so damned sentimental. You haven't come near my heart for years.

CLARA: If Hubert doesn't strike you in a minute, I will.

IPPAGA *comes out of the dance-room with an empty tray.*

KARL: Boy, bring four whisky-and-sodas.

IPPAGA: Yes, sir.

LOUISE: They're called Stengahs here.

KARL: Four Stengahs then.

CLARA: I'd rather have lemonade.

KARL: You seem bent on complicating everything. (*To* IPPAGA.) Four Stengahs.

IPPAGA: Yes, sir.

He goes off.

LOUISE: Karl, where were we?

HUBERT: Nowhere – nowhere at all. (*He turns away.*)

KARL (*to* HUBERT): Listen, Charteris – I know you won't believe me, or even care, but I really am dreadfully sorry, about all this – not about falling in love, that's beyond being sorry about, but that it should happen to be your wife—

HUBERT: Who are you, where do you come from?

KARL: My name is Karl Sandys. I come from Hampshire. My father is Admiral Sandys—

LOUISE: Dear darling, I wouldn't mind if he were only a bosun's mate.

KARL: I know you wouldn't, sweetheart, but I must explain to your husband—

CLARA: How you can have the impertinence to be flippant, Louise, at a moment like this—

LOUISE: There's never been a moment like this, never before in the history of the world – I'm delirious.

HUBERT (to KARL): Please go on.

KARL: I was in the Navy myself but I was axed in 1924.

LOUISE: What's axed?

KARL: Kicked out.

LOUISE: Oh dear, whatever for?

HUBERT: Never mind that, I understand, go on.

KARL: I'm now in the shipping business. I represent the I.M.C.L.

LOUISE: What in God's name is the I.M.C.L.?

HUBERT: Imperial Malayan China Line.

KARL: Passenger and Freight.

HUBERT: I know.

KARL: I've come from Singapore, I've been interviewing our agents in Pendarla—

HUBERT: Littlejohn Thurston and Company?

KARL: Littlejohn Thurston and Company.

LOUISE (to CLARA): Littlejohn Thurston and Company.

KARL: I flew up here in the morning plane because I wanted to see a little of the country before I sail on Wednesday.

LOUISE: Wednesday!

HUBERT: Are you married?

KARL: I was, but we were divorced in 1927.

LOUISE: Oh, Karl. Did you love her?

KARL: Of course I did.

LOUISE: The moment's changed – I'm not delirious any more – I can't think of you ever having loved anybody else—

HUBERT: Have you any money?

KARL: Not very much – enough.

LOUISE: What was her name?

KARL: Ayleen.

LOUISE: You mean Eileen.

KARL: I do not, I mean Ayleen – A-y-l-e-e-n.

LOUISE: Very affected.

KARL: It's you I love, more than anyone in the world, past or future—

LOUISE: Oh, Karl!

HUBERT (*sharply*): Please – just a moment – both of you.

KARL: I'm sorry. That was inconsiderate.

HUBERT: I'm trying to be as detached as possible. It isn't easy.

LOUISE: I know it isn't, it's beastly for you, I do see that.

CLARA: You're all being so charming to each other it's positively nauseating.

LOUISE: My dear Clara, just because your late husband was vaguely connected with the Indian Army, there is no reason for you to be so set on blood-letting—

CLARA: I'm not – I should like to say—

LOUISE: You're no better than a Tricoteuse.

KARL: What's a Tricoteuse?

LOUISE: One of those horrid old things in the French Revolution with knitting-needles.

HUBERT: All this is beside the point.

LOUISE: Clara's been beside the point for years.

KARL: Dearest, I want you so.

LOUISE: Oh, Karl!

CLARA: This is disgusting—

HUBERT: You'd much better go home, Clara—

CLARA: I've told you before I shall do no such thing, I'm apparently the only one present with the remotest grip on sanity. I shall stay as long as you do, Hubert.

KARL: Dear Mrs. Bethel.

CLARA: I beg your pardon?

KARL: I said, 'Dear Mrs. Bethel,' because I admire your integrity enormously and I do hope when all this has blown over that we shall be close friends.

CLARA: I think you're an insufferable cad, Mr. Sandys.

LOUISE: Blown over! Oh, Karl.

KARL: Darling, I didn't mean that part of it.

HUBERT: I have something to say to you, Louise. Will everybody please be quiet for a moment?

CLARA: Hubert, I honestly think—

LOUISE: That's exactly what you don't do.

HUBERT: This man, whom you so abruptly love, is sailing on Wednesday.

KARL: On the *Euripides*.

LOUISE: But the *Euripides* goes to Australia, I know because the MacVities are going on it.

KARL: That can't be helped, I have to interview our agents in Sydney—

LOUISE: We'll have to go on another boat, I can't travel in sin with the MacVities.

HUBERT: Do you really mean to go with him?

LOUISE: Yes, Hubert.

CLARA: You're stark staring mad all of you; Hubert, for God's sake—

HUBERT: Excuse me— (*Gently.*) Louise, how true is this to you?

LOUISE: Oh, Hubert, don't be too kind.

HUBERT: Will it be worth it?

LOUISE: Oh yes, yes, of course it will – it must!

HUBERT: What has happened exactly – how do you know so surely, so soon?

SONG: 'WE WERE DANCING'

I

If you can
Imagine my embarrassment when you politely asked me to
    explain
Man to man
I cannot help but feel conventional apologies are all in vain.

You must see
We've stepped into a dream that's set us free
Don't think we planned it
Please understand it.

REFRAIN

We were dancing
And the gods must have found it entrancing
For they smiled
On a moment undefiled
By the care and woe
That mortals know.
We were dancing
And the music and lights were enhancing
Our desire
When the World caught on fire
He and I were dancing.

2

Love lay in wait for us
Twisted our fate for us
No one warned us
Reason scorned us
Time stood still
In that first strange thrill.
Destiny knew of us
Guided the two of us
How could we
Refuse to see
That wrong seemed right
On this lyrical enchanted night
Logic supplies no laws for it
Only one cause for it.

REPEAT REFRAIN

We were dancing ... *etc.*

LOUISE: We were dancing – somebody introduced us, I can't remember who, we never heard each other's names – it was a waltz – and in the middle of it we looked at each other – he said just now that it was forked lightning, an earthquake, a tidal wave, cataclysm, but it was more than all those things – much more – my heart stopped, and with it the world stopped too – there was no more land or sea or sky, there wasn't even any more music – I saw in his eyes a strange infinity – only just him and me together for ever and ever – and – ever—

> *She faints.* KARL *catches her in his arms.*
> IPPAGA *enters with a tray of drinks.*

IPPAGA: Stengahs, sir.

KARL: Bring them here, quick.

> KARL *lowers* LOUISE *gently into a chair and kneels beside her with his arm under her head.* HUBERT *kneels on the other side of her.* CLARA *kneels in front of her and endeavours to make her swallow a little whisky. After a moment her eyelids flutter and she moves her head.*
>
> *The dance music that has been playing intermittently throughout the scene comes to an end, there is the sound of applause, then it strikes up the National Anthem.*

LOUISE (*weakly*): Good God! God Save the King!

> *She staggers to her feet supported by* KARL. *The others rise also and they all stand to attention as the lights fade on the scene.*

Scene II

> *When the lights come up on the scene,* CLARA, HUBERT, LOUISE *and* KARL *are all sitting in attitudes of extreme weariness. There is a table near them on which are the remains of bacon and eggs and sandwiches.* IPPAGA *is lying on the floor on the right, fast asleep. Dawn is breaking and the stage gets lighter and lighter as the scene progresses.* LOUISE, *in a state of drooping exhaustion, is arranging her face in the mirror from her handbag which* HUBERT *is holding up for her.*

LOUISE (*petulantly*): —But surely you could interview your agents in Sydney another time—

KARL: I can't see why I should alter the whole course of my career just because of the MacVities.

LOUISE: It isn't only the MacVities, it's Australia.

KARL: What's the matter with Australia?

LOUISE: I don't know, that's what's worrying me.

HUBERT: Haven't you got any agents anywhere else?

KARL: There's Havermeyer, Turner and Price in Johannesburg but I've seen them.

LOUISE: You could see them again, couldn't you? It's not much to ask.

KARL: If I start giving in to you now, darling, we shall never have a moment's peace together.

CLARA: Well I wish you'd make up your minds where you're going and when, it's very early and I'm tired.

LOUISE: You've been wonderfully patient, both of you – I'm tired too.

HUBERT: Would you like another sandwich, dear? There are three left.

LOUISE (*patting his hand*): No thank you, Hubert, they're filthy.

KARL: I'd like to say too how grateful I am to you, you've been understanding and direct and absolutely first-rate over the whole business.

HUBERT: I'm terribly fond of Louise, I always have been.

CLARA: Fortunately Hubert's leave is almost due so we shan't have to face too much unpleasantness in the Colony.

HUBERT: What time does your plane leave?

KARL (*glancing at his watch*): Seven-thirty – it's now a quarter to six.

LOUISE: I'll come by the night train and join you in Pendarla in the morning.

HUBERT: I shall miss you dreadfully, Louise.

LOUISE: I shall miss you, too.

KARL: I'm not sure that I shan't miss you, too.

LOUISE: Oh, dear, I do wish it didn't have to be Australia.

KARL: Now then, Louise!

CLARA: Some parts of Australia can be lovely.

LOUISE: Yes, but will they?

CLARA: And there's always New Zealand.

KARL: I haven't any agents in New Zealand.

LOUISE: I shall have to write to Mother and explain. I'm afraid it will be dreadfully muddling for her.

HUBERT: Serve her right.

LOUISE: Hubert! It's not like you to be unchivalrous about Mother.

HUBERT: Now that you're leaving me the situation has changed.

LOUISE: Yes. You're quite right. I do see that.

HUBERT: Without wishing to wound you, Louise, I should like to take this opportunity of saying that she lacks charm to a remarkable degree.

LOUISE: It's funny, isn't it, when you think how attractive Father was.

KARL: This seems an ideal moment for you to give us a detailed description of where you lived as a girl.

LOUISE: I do hope you're not going to turn out to be testy.

CLARA: Never mind, come along, Hubert, we can't stay here any longer, the Fenwicks will be arriving to play golf in a minute.

HUBERT (*to* LOUISE): Do you want to come now or stay until his plane goes?

LOUISE: I'll stay for just a little while, send the car back.

HUBERT (*to* KARL): Would you care to come to the house and have a bath?

KARL: No, thanks, I can have one here.

HUBERT: Then I shan't be seeing you again.

KARL: Not unless you come and see us off on the boat.

HUBERT: I shan't be able to on Wednesday, I have to go up-country.

KARL: Well, good-bye, then.

HUBERT: Good-bye.

> *They shake hands.*

Try to make her happy, won't you?

KARL: I'll do my best.

HUBERT: Clara—

CLARA (*to* KARL): Good-bye.

KARL: Good-bye.

CLARA: I wish my husband were alive.

KARL: Why?

CLARA: Because he'd horsewhip you and, Tricoteuse or no Tricoteuse, I should enjoy it keenly.

KARL: Thank you very much.

> CLARA *and* HUBERT *go off.*
>
> LOUISE *gets up and goes to the veranda rail, she leans on it and looks out at the sea.*

LOUISE: I feel as if I'd been run over.

KARL (*joining her*): Dearest.

LOUISE: Don't.

KARL: Don't what?

LOUISE: Don't call me dearest, just for a minute.

KARL: I love you so.

LOUISE: We ought to be able to see Sumatra really at this time of the morning.

KARL: I don't want to see Sumatra.

LOUISE: I think I will have another sandwich after all.

KARL: All right.

> *They come down from the rail and pensively take a sandwich each.*

LOUISE: Are you happy?

KARL: Wildly happy. Are you?

LOUISE: Dear Karl!

KARL: What's the matter?

LOUISE: You're doing splendidly.

KARL: Don't talk like that, my sweet, it's unkind.

LOUISE: Ayleen would be proud of you.

KARL: That was worse than unkind.

LOUISE: Where is it, our moment? What's happened to the magic?

KARL (*sadly*): I see.

LOUISE: I wonder if you do really?

KARL: Dance with me a minute.

LOUISE: Very well.

> *She hasn't quite finished her sandwich so she holds it in her left hand while they waltz solemnly round the stage.*

KARL: Of course the music makes a great difference.

LOUISE: There isn't always music.

KARL: And moonlight.

LOUISE: Moonlight doesn't last.

> *They go on dancing. The sound of a native pipe is heard a long way off in the distance.*

KARL: There's music for us.

LOUISE: It's the wrong sort.

KARL: I wish you'd finish your sandwich.

LOUISE: I have.

KARL: Kiss me.

LOUISE: My dear—

> *They kiss.*

You see!

KARL: The joke is on us.

LOUISE: It was a nice joke, while it lasted.

KARL: We've never even been lovers.

LOUISE: I don't want to now, do you?

KARL: Not much.

LOUISE: We missed our chance—

KARL: Don't talk like that, it sounds so depressing— (*They turn away from each other.*)

LOUISE: What's the name of your agents in Sydney?

KARL: Eldrich, Lincoln and Barret.

LOUISE: Give them my love.

> *She pats his face very gently and sweetly and goes quickly away. He makes a movement as if to follow her, then pauses and lights a cigarette. He hums for a moment the tune to which they were dancing and then goes up to the rail where he stands leaning against a post looking out into the morning.*
>
>   GEORGE DAVIES *and* EVA BLAKE *come quietly almost furtively on from the right; they talk in whispers.*

EVA: It's awfully light.

GEORGE: There's nobody about.

EVA: Oh, George, you're so wonderful!

GEORGE: Shhh!

> *They kiss swiftly.*

I suppose it's all right about the Baileys?

EVA: Yes, Marion promised – she'll never say a word.

GEORGE: I won't take you right up to the house, I'll just drop you off at the end of the garden—

EVA: Oh, George, you think of everything—

KARL: Excuse me, is your name Eva?

EVA: Yes.

KARL: I congratulate you!

> EVA *and* GEORGE *go off.*
>
> KARL *comes down and kicks* IPPAGA *gently.*

Wake up – wake up, it's morning—

> IPPAGA *stretches himself as the curtain falls.*

SHADOW PLAY

A Musical Fantasy

from

TO-NIGHT AT 8.30

Shadow Play was produced in London at the Phoenix Theatre on 13 January 1936, with the following cast:

VICTORIA GAYFORTH	Miss Gertrude Lawrence
SIMON GAYFORTH	Mr. Noël Coward
MARTHA CUNNINGHAM	Miss Everley Gregg
GEORGE CUNNINGHAM	Mr. Alan Webb
LENA	Miss Moya Nugent
SIBYL HESTON	Miss Alison Leggatt
MICHAEL DOYLE	Mr. Edward Underdown
A YOUNG MAN	Mr. Anthony Pelissier
HODGE, *dresser*	Mr. Kenneth Carten

———

TIME: The Present.

The scene is a well-furnished, rather luxurious bedroom in the GAYFORTHS' *house in Mayfair. There is a bed on the right with a table by the side of it on which are various bottles, books and a telephone.*

Below the bed there is a door which leads to the bathroom. On the left there is a door leading to the passage and the rest of the house. Above this is a dressing-table. At the foot of the bed there is a small sofa.

When the curtain rises LENA, VICTORIA's *maid, is bustling about the room. It is about midnight and she is laying out a dressing-gown or negligee on the bed and generally arranging the room for the night.*

VICTORIA *and* MARTHA *come in from the left.* VICTORIA *is about thirty; beautifully gowned. Her manner is bored and irritable.* MARTHA *is slightly older, also well dressed but more tranquil.*

VICKY: —It couldn't matter less whether I go to Alice's or not – in fact it would be infinitely more comfortable for everybody concerned if I didn't.

MARTHA: What nonsense!

VICKY: Alice's parties are always dreary, and I don't feel in the mood even for a good party to-night.

MARTHA: What's the matter?

VICKY: I've told you – I've got a headache.

MARTHA: I think you're unwise.

VICKY: What do you mean, darling?

MARTHA: You know perfectly well what I mean.

VICKY (*sitting down at the dressing-table*): Of course I do, but I'm getting tired of everybody being subtle and hiding behind the furniture – I know that Simon will go without me and I know that Sibyl will be there and I know that if I don't go he will leave with her and if I do go he will leave with me and wish he was leaving with her. I also know that I'm bored stiff with the whole situation – let it rip—

MARTHA: Line of least resistance.

VICKY: Exactly – I have a headache – I feel thoroughly disagreeable – all I want is sleep – no more resisting – just sleep – Lena – give me three Anytal—

LENA: Three, madame?

VICKY: Yes, three – and you can go to bed.

LENA: Yes, madame.

MARTHA: Is the extra tablet a gesture of defiance?

VICKY: Don't be tiresome, Martha.

> LENA *brings her three tablets from a bottle by the bed and a glass of water.*

MARTHA: Do you take those things every night?

VICKY (*swallowing the tablets*): No, darling, I don't. And even if I did it wouldn't matter a bit – they're perfectly harmless.

LENA: Are you sure that's all, madame?

VICKY: Yes, thank you, Lena – good-night.

LENA: Good-night, madame.

> *She goes out.*

MARTHA: I don't like seeing people unhappy.

VICKY: I'm not in the least unhappy – just tired.

MARTHA: How much do you mind?

VICKY: Mind what?

> *She takes the dressing-gown off the bed and goes into the bathroom, leaving the door open.*

MARTHA (*firmly*): About Simon and Sibyl.

VICKY: Heart-broken, dear— (*She laughs.*) You mustn't be deceived by my gay frivolity, it's really only masking agony and defeat and despair—

MARTHA (*helping herself to a cigarette*): You're extremely irritating.

VICKY: That's what you wanted, isn't it?

MARTHA: You needn't be suspicious of me, you know – I have no axe to grind – I merely wanted to help—

VICKY: You're a noble, understanding old friend, darling, that's what you are, and I must say I should like to crack you over the head with a bottle.

MARTHA: Thank you, dear.

> *The telephone rings.*

VICKY: Answer that, will you? – it's probably Michael – I'll be out in a minute—

MARTHA: All right. (*She goes to the telephone.*) Hallo – No, it's Martha – She's in the bathroom, she'll be out in a minute – No, she's not – We've been to a play and it was so good that it gave her a headache – Hold on, here she is—

> VICKY *comes in in a dressing-gown, flings herself on to the bed and takes the telephone.*

VICKY: Hallo, Michael – No, I'm not – Yes, I've doped myself to the eyes and I'm about to go off into a coma – Of course you can't, don't be so idiotic – What are you in such a state about? – I thought we'd settled all that – It's no use dropping your voice like that – Martha can hear perfectly well, she's got ears like a hawk—

MARTHA: Perhaps you'd like me to go?

VICKY (*to* MARTHA): Be quiet, darling— (*At telephone.*) —I'm tired, Michael, and I've got a headache and so will you kindly shut up – Yes, all right – tomorrow – Good God, no, I shall be sound asleep – Go away, Michael, I can't bear any more— (*She hangs up.*) It's lovely being loved, isn't it?

> *She rolls over on the bed face downwards.*

MARTHA: You'd better get into bed—

VICKY: Perhaps you'd like to fill a hot-water bottle and take my temperature?

MARTHA (*patiently*): Have you got a book to read?

VICKY: Yes, but it's unreadable.

MARTHA: Do get into bed.

VICKY: Go to hell, darling, and don't fuss—

MARTHA (*seriously*): I really wish I could do something—

VICKY (*violently*): Stop it, I tell you— I don't want your sympathy —I don't want anybody's sympathy – whatever happens, happens – let it – what does it matter—

MARTHA: Very well. (*She turns to go.*)

VICKY (*jumping off the bed and coming to her*): I'm sorry – I know I'm beastly, but you see it's no use discussing things – the Anytal will begin to work soon and I shall have a nice long sleep and feel much better in the morning – It was the play that upset me, I think – you were quite right – everybody seemed to be having such a good time, didn't they? – it's a bit tantalising to see everybody having quite such a good time – it would be so much easier, wouldn't it, if we had music when things go wrong – music and a little dancing and the certainty of 'Happy ever after' – I hope you didn't miss the ironic twist at the end when they were married – crashing chords and complete tidiness – very convenient – Go away, darling – go and collect George and Simon and go on to Alice's – I shall go to sleep in a minute – really I will—

MARTHA: All right – I'll telephone you in the morning—

She kisses her and is about to go, when SIMON *comes into the room. He is wearing a dressing-gown over his evening clothes.*

VICKY (*surprised*): Simon!

SIMON (*to* MARTHA): George is waiting for you, Martha – he's getting a bit restive.

VICKY: Aren't you going to Alice's?

SIMON: No, I didn't feel that I could face it.

VICKY: Oh, I see.

MARTHA: Do you want me to make excuses for you both, or just not say anything about it?

VICKY: Say that you haven't seen us, and why aren't we there, and is there any truth in the rumour that we're not getting on very well— (*She laughs.*)

SIMON: Don't be silly, Vicky.

VICKY: Say that I've gone to Ostend with Michael and that Simon's shot himself – but only in the leg.

SIMON (*bitterly*): Say that it's definitely true that we're not getting on very well – say that it's due to incompatibility of humour.

MARTHA: I shall say that I don't know you at all – any more.

She goes out.

VICKY (*calling after her*): Give my love to Sibyl!

SIMON: That was a bit cheap, wasn't it?

VICKY: I thought it was only kind – Sibyl can't live without love – like the woman in the play to-night – don't you remember—? (*She hums.*) 'Nobody can live without loving somebody, nobody can love without leaving somebody!'

SIMON: You mustn't forget to sing that to Michael.

VICKY: Are we going to bicker? There's nothing like a nice bicker to round off a jolly evening.

SIMON: I'm getting a little tired of bickering.

VICKY: Let's not then, let's be absolutely divine to each other – let's pretend.

SIMON: I didn't go to Alice's party on purpose—

VICKY: I didn't think it was a sudden attack of amnesia.

SIMON: I want to talk to you.

VICKY: Do you, Simon? What about?

SIMON: Lots of things.

VICKY: Name fifteen.

SIMON: Seriously.

VICKY: There you are, you see – our moods are clashing again – it really is most unfortunate.

SIMON: I failed to notice during the evening that your spirits were so abnormally high.

VICKY: A sudden change for the better, dear, let's make the most of it.

SIMON: There's something I want to say to you – I've been wanting to say it for quite a while.

VICKY: Take the plunge, my darling – we're alone in the swimming bath.

SIMON: Would you consider divorcing me?

VICKY: Oh, Simon!

SIMON: If I made everything easy—

VICKY: Naming Sibyl?

SIMON: Of course not.

VICKY: You mean you'd prefer to be implicated with a professional homebreaker as opposed to an amateur one?

SIMON: I would like, if possible, to keep this conversation impersonal.

VICKY: We might put on fancy dress for it.

SIMON: I'm serious, Vicky.

VICKY: I'm told that all really funny comedians are serious.

SIMON: You haven't answered my question yet.

VICKY: I thought perhaps I hadn't heard it quite clearly.

SIMON: I want you to divorce me.

VICKY: Yes, now I hear – it's a beastly question, isn't it?

SIMON: Not so very beastly if you analyse it – quite sensible really.

VICKY: It oughtn't to be such a shock – but somehow it is – it makes me feel a little sick.

SIMON: I'm sorry.

VICKY: Don't worry about being sorry – feeling a little sick doesn't matter that much.

SIMON: I've thought it all over very carefully.

VICKY: Oh, Simon, have you? Have you really?

SIMON: Of course I have. It's been on my mind for a long time.

VICKY: How sinister that sounds – surely not for a very long time?

SIMON: Long enough.

VICKY: You're cruelly definite.

SIMON: It's less cruel to be definite – in the long run.

VICKY: It's been an awfully short run – really.

SIMON: You haven't answered me yet.

VICKY: An amicable divorce – everything below board?

SIMON: Yes.

VICKY: Where will you go with your temporary light of love? The South of France, or just good old Brighton?

SIMON: I don't think we need discuss that.

VICKY: It's a nasty business, isn't it – a very nasty business.

SIMON: Not necessarily, if it can be arranged discreetly and without fuss.

VICKY: Do you love her so much? Sibyl, I mean.

SIMON: I'd rather not discuss that either.

VICKY: Perhaps you'd prefer to conduct the whole thing by signs – sort of Dumb Crambo.

SIMON: You're unbelievably irritating.

VICKY: When did you first begin to hate me? – When did I first begin to get on your nerves? – What did I say? – What did I do? – Was it a dress I wore – the way I laughed at somebody's joke? – Was I suddenly gay when you were sad? – Was I insensitive? – Was I dull? When did it start – tell me if you can remember – please tell me.

SIMON: Don't be so foolish.

VICKY: I won't be irritating any more, Simon – I'll try to be sensible – really I will – but I must know why – why things change – I wish to God I hadn't taken those sleeping tablets – my head's going round – I would so love to be clear, just at this moment, but nothing's clear at all.

SIMON: I didn't know you'd taken anything.

VICKY: Don't be alarmed – I'm not becoming a drug fiend – it's an amiable, gentle prescription, just to make me sleep when I have a headache, or when I'm overtired or unhappy—

SIMON: There's the overture – we shall be late.

VICKY: What did you say?

SIMON: —You really ought not to get into the habit of taking things to make you sleep – however harmless they are—

VICKY: We've only been married five years – it seems longer at moments – then it seems no time at all.

The music begins, and, after a few chords, stops again.

SIMON: There it is again – listen.

VICKY: If you really love Sibyl, deeply and truly, it's different, but I have an awful feeling that you don't – anyhow, not enough—

SIMON: 'We will wander on together—
Through the sunny summer weather—
To our cosy little château
Like a pastoral by Watteau.

TOGETHER: To our cosy little château on the Rhine.'

SIMON: —It isn't that I don't love you – I always shall love you— but this is something else – I don't know what started it, but I do know that it's terribly strong – and then there's Michael – I've been awfully angry about Michael—

VICKY: That's idiotic – Michael doesn't mean a thing to me – you know perfectly well he doesn't—

The music begins again, this time more loudly.

SIMON: There it is again – do hurry. (*He dances a few steps.*)

VICKY (*calling*): Lena – Lena – hurry up – I was miserable anyhow to-night – all the time we were in the theatre – everybody was having such a good time – and then they were married in the end – that was funny, wasn't it? – about them being married in the end. . . .

SIMON: —It isn't that I want to make you unhappy, but you

must admit we haven't been hitting it off particularly well during the last year – if we're not comfortable together surely it would be much more sensible to separate—

The scene darkens. The side flats move off and upstage away from the centre flat.

VICKY: I feel so sad inside about it – I wish I could make you understand – it was so lovely in the beginning—

SIMON: Things never stay the same – you can't expect what was lovely then to be lovely now—

VICKY (*almost crying*): Why not – why not? – Then we were happy—

SIMON: But, darling, you must see—

'THEN'

SIMON: Here in the light of this unkind familiar now
    Every gesture is clear and cold for us,
    Even yesterday's growing old for us,
      Everything changed somehow.
      If some forgotten lover's vow
    Could wake a memory in my heart again,
    Perhaps the joys that we knew would start again.
      Can't we reclaim an hour or so
      The past is not so long ago.

VICKY: Then, love was complete for us
    Then, the days were sweet for us
    Life rose to its feet for us
      And stepped aside
      Before our pride.
      Then, we knew the best of it
      Then, our hearts stood the test of it.
      Now, the magic has flown
      We face the unknown
      Apart and alone.

SIMON: Hodge – where's Hodge? – I must change – quick – we're going back.

The orchestra swells. FLORRIE (LENA) *comes hurrying in with an evening gown over her arm and a pair of shoes, a mirror, a powder-puff, etc., in her hands.* VICKY *sinks on to the bed.*

SIMON: You can't sit there – we're going back—

FLORRIE: Here, dear – here's a chair.

VICKY: I'm not sure that I want to – I'm not at all sure – maybe it won't be as lovely as I think it was—

SIMON: Don't be such a fool – grab it while you can – grab every scrap of happiness while you can – Hodge – come on—

HODGE, *a dresser, comes in with a dinner-jacket.* SIMON *takes off his dressing-gown and puts on the dinner-jacket.* VICKY *is changing on the opposite side of the stage. Meanwhile the whole scene is changing. The lights in the foreground fade except for the two spotlights on* SIMON *and* VICKY.

VICKY (*breathlessly*): Play – go on playing – we must have music—

SIMON *comes down to the footlights and begins to sing to the conductor. He sings*

'PLAY, ORCHESTRA, PLAY'

SIMON: Listen to the strain it plays once more for us,
There it is again, the past in store for us.
    Wake in memory some forgotten song
    To break the rhythm – driving us along
And make harmony again a last encore for us.

    Play, orchestra, play
    Play something light and sweet and gay
      For we must have music
      We must have music
    To drive our fears away.
While our illusions swiftly fade for us,
    Let's have an orchestra score.
In the confusions the years have made for us
    Serenade for us, just once more.
Life needn't be grey,
Although it's changing day by day,

Though a few old dreams may decay,
Play, orchestra, play.

VICKY joins him and they finish it together. Meanwhile all the lights fade entirely except for two pin-spots on the two of them. The spot on SIMON goes out and VICKY is left singing almost hysterically 'We Must Have Music'. The orchestra rises to a crescendo and there is a complete black-out.

To measured music and in a pool of light, SIBYL HESTON appears. She lights a cigarette and glances at her wrist-watch. SIMON appears from the opposite side of the stage. He stands a little apart from her. The music stops.

SIBYL: I'm waiting – I'm waiting – why don't you tell her?

SIMON: It will hurt her, you know.

SIBYL: She can weep on Michael's shoulder – it's a very attractive shoulder.

SIMON: I don't want to hurt her.

SIBYL: She'll have to know sooner or later. Nobody can live without loving somebody, nobody can love without leaving somebody.

SIMON: I saw you in the theatre to-night – you looked marvellous.

SIBYL: Sweet Simon.

SIMON: Very cool and green and wise.

SIBYL: Not wise – oh, my dear, not wise at all. I happen to love you.

SIMON: Is that so unwise?

SIBYL: Let's say – indefinite!

SIMON: It's less cruel to be indefinite in the long run.

SIBYL: Tell her the truth – you must tell her the truth.

SIMON: I have been awfully angry about Michael.

SIBYL: Why be angry, darling? It's such waste of energy.

SIMON: I don't like Vicky making a fool of herself.

SIBYL: I don't like Vicky making a fool of you.

SIMON: I didn't know she took things to make her sleep.

SIBYL: You must tell her the truth – sleep or no sleep.

The music starts again. MICHAEL walks on. He passes SIBYL and

SIMON, *stops, lights a cigarette and glances at his wrist-watch. The music stops.*

MICHAEL: I'm waiting – I'm waiting – why don't you tell her?

SIMON: I don't want to hurt her.

MICHAEL: Give her my love.

SIMON: That was a bit cheap, wasn't it?

SIBYL (*laughing*): When did she first begin to get on your nerves, Simon? What started it? Was it a dress she wore? Was it the way she laughed at somebody's joke? Was she suddenly gay when you were sad? Was she insensitive? Was she dull?

MICHAEL: Was she dull?

SIBYL: Was she dull?

SIMON: It was so lovely in the beginning.

SIBYL: Things never stay the same – you can't expect what was lovely then to be lovely now.

SIMON: We're going back all the same – it's our only chance—

SIBYL: Was she dull?

MICHAEL: Was she dull?

SIMON: Shut up – shut up both of you – we're going back—

He begins to sing and as he sings the lights fade on SIBYL *and* MICHAEL.

Life needn't be grey
Though it is changing day by day.
Though a few old dreams may decay
Play Orchestra – Play Orchestra – Play – Orchestra—
Play—

Blackout.

The lights come up on a moonlit garden. There is a stone seat on the left of the stage. VICKY *and a* YOUNG MAN *are sitting on it.*

VICKY: It's nice and cool in the garden.

YOUNG MAN: It's nice and cool in the garden.

VICKY: Country house dances can be lovely when the weather's good, can't they?

YOUNG MAN: Rather – rather – yes, of course – rather.

VICKY: I'm waiting for something.

YOUNG MAN: Country house dances can be lovely when the weather's good, can't they?

VICKY: This is where it all began.

YOUNG MAN: It's nice and cool in the garden.

VICKY: Please hurry, my darling, I can't wait to see you for the first time.

YOUNG MAN: Do you know this part of the country?

VICKY: Intimately. I'm staying here with my aunt, you know.

YOUNG MAN: Does she ride to hounds?

VICKY: Incessantly.

YOUNG MAN: That's ripping, isn't it? – I mean it really is ripping.

VICKY: Yes. She's a big woman and she kills little foxes – she's kind *au fond*, but she dearly loves killing little foxes.

YOUNG MAN: We're getting on awfully well – it's awfully nice out here – I think you're awfully pretty.

VICKY: This is waste of time – he should be here by now – walking through the trees – coming towards me.

YOUNG MAN: I think you're an absolute fizzer.

VICKY: Yes, I remember you saying that – it made me want to giggle – but I controlled myself beautifully.

YOUNG MAN: I think you know my sister – she's in pink.

VICKY: I remember her clearly – a beastly girl.

YOUNG MAN: In pink.

VICKY (*suddenly*): 'In pink – in pink—
　　　　　　　　Your sister's dressed in pink
　　　　　　　　It wasn't very wise I think
　　　　　　　　To choose that unbecoming shade
　　　　　　　　Of pink—'

YOUNG MAN: I'm so glad you like her – you must come and stay with us – my mother's an absolute fizzer – you'd love her.

VICKY: God forbid!

YOUNG MAN: That's absolutely ripping of you.

VICKY: Now – now – at last – you're walking through the trees— hurry—

　　　SIMON *comes through the trees. He is smoking a cigarette.*

VICKY: I thought you'd missed your entrance.

SIMON: Are you engaged for this dance?

VICKY: I was, but I'll cut it if you'll promise to love me always and never let anything or anybody spoil it – never—

SIMON: But of course – that's understood.

YOUNG MAN: Will you excuse me – I have to dance with Lady Dukes.

VICKY: Certainly.

YOUNG MAN: Good hunting.

VICKY: Thank you so much – it's been so boring.

YOUNG MAN: Not at all – later perhaps.

   He goes.

SIMON: Well – here we are.

VICKY: The first time – we knew at once, didn't we? Don't you remember how we discussed it afterwards?

SIMON: I saw you in the ballroom – I wondered who you were.

VICKY: My name's Victoria – Victoria Marden.

SIMON: Mine's Simon Gayforth.

VICKY: How do you do?

SIMON: Quite well, thank you.

VICKY: I suppose you came down from London for the dance?

SIMON: Yes, I'm staying with the Bursbys—

VICKY: What do you do?

SIMON: I'm in a bank.

VICKY: High up in the bank? Or just sitting in a cage totting up things?

SIMON: Oh, quite high up really – it's a very good bank.

VICKY: I'm so glad.

SIMON: How lovely you are.

VICKY: No, no, that came later – you've skipped some.

SIMON: Sorry.

VICKY: You're nice and thin – your eyes are funny – you move easily – I'm afraid you're terribly attractive—

SIMON: You never said that.

VICKY: No, but I thought it.

SIMON: Stick to the script.

VICKY: Small talk – a lot of small talk with quite different thoughts going on behind it – this garden's really beautiful – are you good at gardens?—

SIMON: No, but I'm persevering – I'm all right on the more

237

straightforward blooms – you know – Snapdragons, sweet william, cornflowers and tobacco plant – and I can tell a Dorothy Perkins a mile off.

VICKY: That hedge over there is called Cupressus Macrocapa.

SIMON: Do you swear it?

VICKY: It grows terrifically quickly but they do say that it goes a bit thin underneath in about twenty years—

SIMON: How beastly of them to say that – it's slander.

VICKY: Did you know about Valerian smelling of cats?

SIMON: You're showing off again.

VICKY: It's true.

SIMON: I can go one better than that – Lotuses smell of pineapple.

VICKY (sadly): Everything smells of something else – it's dreadfully confusing—

SIMON: Never mind, darling – I love you desperately – I knew it the first second I saw you—

VICKY: You're skipping again.

They sing a light duet: 'You Were There', after which they dance.

'YOU WERE THERE'

I

SIMON: Was it in the real world or was it in a dream?
Was it just a note from some eternal theme?
Was it accidental or accurately planned?
   How could I hesitate
   Knowing that my fate
Led me by the hand?

REFRAIN

You were there
I saw you and my heart stopped beating
You were there
And in that first enchanted meeting

Life changed its tune, the stars, the moon came
    near to me.
Dreams that I dreamed, like magic seemed to be
    clear to me, dear to me.
    You were there.
Your eyes looked into mine and faltered.
    Everywhere
The colour of the whole world altered.
    False became true
    My universe tumbled in two
The earth became heaven, for you were there.

2

VICKY: How can we explain it – the spark, and then the fire?
      How add up the total of our hearts' desire?
      Maybe some magician, a thousand years ago—
      Wove us a subtle spell – so that we could tell – so that
        we could know—
      You were there—(etc.)

*During the dance the lights fade on the scene and they finish in each
other's arms in a spotlight. The spotlight fades and in the darkness a
voice is heard singing 'Then they knew the best of it – then their
hearts stood the test of it', etc.*

   A spotlight picks up LENA *– singing, holding the tablets and a
glass of water. After song fade again.*

Then love was complete for them
Then the days were sweet for them
Life rose to its feet for them
And stepped aside
Before their pride.
Then they knew the best of it
Then their hearts stood the test of it.
Now the magic has flown
They face the unknown
Apart and alone.

The lights go up again on the interior of a limousine. MARTHA *and* GEORGE CUNNINGHAM *are sitting in it.*

GEORGE: On the whole this has been one of the most uncomfortable evenings I've ever spent.

MARTHA: There, there, dear, I know, but for heaven's sake don't go on about it.

GEORGE (*petulantly*): Why, if they had to take us to dinner and a play, should they have chosen that particular dinner and that particular play?

MARTHA: What was wrong with the dinner?

GEORGE: Gastronomically speaking it was excellent, but the atmosphere reeked with conjugal infelicity – when people are at loggerheads they should refrain from entertaining – it's bad for the digestive tract.

MARTHA: For an elderly barrister you're unduly sensitive.

GEORGE: I expected the grouse to sit up on its plate and offer me a brief.

MARTHA: Never mind, when we get to Alice's you'll be able to have a nice drink and talk to some lovely young things and feel much better.

GEORGE: And why that play? Sentimental twaddle.

MARTHA: The music was lovely.

GEORGE: That's no good to me. You know perfectly well I can't distinguish 'Abide with me' from 'God Save the King'.

MARTHA: Concentrate on 'God Save the King'.

GEORGE: I couldn't even go to sleep with those idiotic people loving each other for ever all over the stage.

MARTHA: Well we'll go to a nice soothing gangster picture to-morrow night and you can watch people killing each other all over the screen.

GEORGE: What's wrong with them, anyway?

MARTHA: Who, Simon and Vicky?

GEORGE: Yes.

MARTHA: They're unhappy.

GEORGE: Well, they oughtn't to be – they've got everything they want.

MARTHA: Sibyl Heston's got hold of Simon and Vicky's trying to pretend that she doesn't mind a bit and everything's in a dreary muddle – women like Sibyl Heston ought to be shot.

GEORGE: Sometimes they are.

MARTHA: Not often enough.

GEORGE: I suppose Vicky's got a young man hanging around, hasn't she?

MARTHA: No, not really – she's been encouraging Michael Doyle a bit but it doesn't mean anything – it's just part of the pretending.

GEORGE: Damn fools – they're all damn fools—

> VICKY *runs on from the side of the stage. She is picked up by a blue spotlight.*

VICKY: Go away, you're spoiling it all – I know what you're saying – I know what everybody's saying—

MARTHA: I was only trying to help.

VICKY: I know – I know – you're very kind – but it isn't any use—

GEORGE: People were so much more sensible twenty years ago – take my sister, for instance – look how brilliantly she managed her life – you ought to have known my sister—

VICKY: In pink.

GEORGE: In brilliant pink.

VICKY (*singing*): 'In pink – in pink
Your sister's dressed in pink,
It wasn't very wise I think
To choose that unbecoming shade
Of pink—!'

> SIMON *enters and is picked up in a blue spot.*

SIMON: This compartment is reserved – we're going back.

GEORGE: I'm most awfully sorry.

VICKY: There are probably some empty ones farther along the train.

MARTHA: But of course – we quite understand – George, help me with my dressing-case—

SIMON: Allow me—

> *He helps them to remove imaginary luggage from the rack.*

GEORGE: I suppose you don't happen to know what time we reach Milan?

SIMON: I know we arrive in Venice at about six-thirty – I think there's about four hours' difference.

VICKY: It's really charming of you to be so considerate – you see we are on our honeymoon.

MARTHA: Grab every scrap of happiness while you can.

GEORGE: We shall meet later.

SIMON: I hope so.

> MARTHA *and* GEORGE *step out of the car and walk off.*
> SIMON *and* VICKY *climb in. The spotlights follow them into the* cab.

SIMON: Well, here we are.

VICKY: My name's Victoria.

SIMON: Victoria what?

VICKY: Victoria Gayforth.

SIMON: What a silly name.

VICKY: I adore it.

SIMON: That's because you're sentimental.

VICKY: Fiercely sentimental – over-romantic too.

SIMON: Dearest darling.

VICKY: The wedding went off beautifully, didn't it?

SIMON: Brief, to the point, and not unduly musical.

VICKY: Didn't Mother look nice?

SIMON: Not particularly.

VICKY: Oh, Simon!

SIMON: It was her hat, I think – it looked as though it were in a hurry and couldn't stay very long.

VICKY: Was that man who slapped you on the back your uncle?

SIMON: Yes, dear – that was my uncle.

VICKY: I'm so sorry.

SIMON: He ran away to sea, you know, when he was very young, and then, unfortunately, he ran back again.

VICKY: Your sister looked charming.

SIMON: In pink.

VICKY: In pink – in pink—

SIMON: Stop it – stop it – you'll wake yourself up.

VICKY: It was that rhyme in the play to-night – it keeps coming into my mind.

SIMON: Do concentrate – we're on our honeymoon.

VICKY: Happy ever after.

SIMON: That's right.

VICKY: Do you think that those people we turned out of the carriage ever loved each other as much as we do?

SIMON: Nobody ever loved each other as much as we do with the possible exception of Romeo and Juliet, Héloïse and Abélard, Paolo and Francesca, Dante and Beatrice—

VICKY: I wish she hadn't been called Beatrice – it's such a smug name.

SIMON: Antony and Cleopatra, Pelléas and Mélisande—

VICKY: I've always felt that Mélisande was rather a silly girl – so vague.

SIMON: All right – wash out Mélisande.

VICKY (looking out of the window): Look at all those little houses flashing by – think of all the millions of people living in them – eating and drinking – dressing and undressing – getting up and going to bed – having babies—

SIMON: When I was a young bride I never mentioned such things on my honeymoon.

VICKY: Things never stay the same.

SIMON: It was considered immodest to do anything but weep gently and ask for glasses of water.

VICKY: I'm abandoned, darling – I can't wait to be in your arms—

SIMON: Dear heart—

He takes her in his arms.

VICKY (struggling): No no – this isn't right – my clothes are all wrong – I must go—

SIMON: Don't go.

VICKY: I must – this dressing-gown's all wrong I tell you – when we arrived in Venice I was wearing a blue tailor-made – and then later we dined – and I was in grey—

SIMON: In grey – in grey
Your dress was soft and grey
It seems a million years away

The ending of that sweet and happy day.

VICKY: Oh darling—

SIMON: Don't go—

VICKY: I must – I must—

> *She steps out of the carriage and disappears into the darkness.*
>
> SIMON *left alone, sings a reprise of 'You Were There', and the lights fade completely.*
>
> *When the lights go up* SIMON *and* VICKY *are sitting at a little table with a shaded light on it. They are just finishing dinner.*

SIMON: We can sit on the piazza for a little and then we can drift . . .

VICKY: Let's call the gondola right away and cut out the piazza – I'm a big drifting girl.

SIMON: I think the band on the piazza will be awfully disappointed.

VICKY: It's funny, isn't it, to be so frightfully in love that you feel as if you were going mad?

SIMON: Ever so funny.

VICKY: Do you think our front gondolier is nicer than our back one?

SIMON: Not altogether – he has better teeth, of course, but then he's about fifty years younger.

VICKY: Let's come here again in fifty years' time.

SIMON: All right.

VICKY: We can arrange to be carried on to the train – it will be quite simple.

SIMON: It won't be a train, darling – it will be a pointed silver bullet leaving Croydon at four and arriving here at twenty-past three.

VICKY: Oh dear!

SIMON: What's the matter?

VICKY: We haven't quarrelled yet.

SIMON: Never mind.

VICKY: We'll have a nice quarrel when we get back to London, won't we?

SIMON: I shall sulk for the first few days, anyhow – I'm the sulky type, you know.

VICKY: That's why I married you.

SIMON: Oh, darling – I'm going to be terribly serious for a
minute – will you bear with me?

VICKY: Of course.

SIMON: There's something I want to say to you – I've been
wanting to say it for quite a while—

VICKY (*with panic in her voice*): Oh, Simon, don't – what is it? What
is it?

SIMON: I love you.

VICKY (*putting her head down on the table*): You mustn't make
people cry on their honeymoons – it's not cricket.

SIMON (*tenderly*): Dearest – everything's cricket if only you have
faith.

VICKY: When did you know you loved me – the very first
minute, I mean?

SIMON: In the garden – during the dance – I saw you and my
heart stopped beating—

VICKY: It was a most enchanted meeting.

SIMON: Life changed its tune – the stars and moon came near to
me—

VICKY: Dreams that I'd dreamed, like magic seemed to be clear
to me – dear to me—

SIMON: False became true – my universe tumbled in two – the
earth became heaven – for you were there—

VICKY: Stop it – stop it – it's that damned musical comedy again
– going round and round in my head – listen – before the
dream breaks say what you said that night in Venice – say it
from your heart as you said it then – say it, please – please—

SIMON: I'm not sure that I can remember – it's a long while
ago—

VICKY: Please, Simon – please—

SIMON: It's this, darling – we're here together close as close and
it's the beginning – but we're going to be together for a long
time – probably all our lives, so we must be careful – I want to
reassure you now about later on – about any tricks the future
might play on us – I know I love you with all my heart – with
every bit of me – it's easy now, because it's summer weather
and there isn't a cloud in the sky and we're alone – but there'll
be other people presently – we can't live our whole lives on

SHADOW PLAY

this little island – other people are dangerous – they spoil true love, not consciously because they want to, but because they're themselves – out for all they can get – mischievous – you do see what I mean, don't you—?

VICKY: You mean they might make us want them one day instead of each other.

SIMON: Yes, but only a little – not like this – not all the way round—

VICKY: I can't imagine even that – I'm very single-tracked.

SIMON: Don't look sad – don't even have a flicker of unhappiness not for ages yet, anyway – but whenever you do – if I'm bad or foolish or unkind, or even unfaithful – just remember this, because this is what really matters – this lovely understanding of each other – it may be a jumping-off place for many future journeys – but however long the journey one's got to come back some time, and this is the white cliffs of Dover – hang on to the white cliffs of Dover—

VICKY: I'll try—

They hold hands for a moment across the table.
There is a burst of music which dies away on a discord. Then a dance tune starts and keeps up a steady rhythm during the ensuing scene. The light on SIMON and VICKY fades a little. They are sitting quite still gazing at each other. SIBYL HESTON and MICHAEL DOYLE dance on together out of the shadows. They are in a brilliant spotlight.

MICHAEL: We're a bit early, aren't we? They're still on their honeymoon.

SIBYL: Nonsense. The curtain will be lowered between scenes two and three to denote a lapse of four years—

The light on SIMON and VICKY goes out completely.

MICHAEL (*over his shoulder*): I'm so sorry.

SIBYL: It's impossible to dance here.

MICHAEL: They put so many tables on the floor.

SIBYL: There's no room at all.

MICHAEL: Let's go on to the Florida.

SIBYL: And the Coconut Grove.

MICHAEL: And the Four Hundred.

SIBYL: And the Blue Train.

246

SIMON *and* VICKY *dance on in another spotlight.*

SIMON: There's always the Florida.

VICKY: And the Coconut Grove.

SIMON: And the Four Hundred.

VICKY: And the Blue Train.

The rhythm gets slightly faster. The two couples circle round each other.

SIBYL: The Florida.

SIMON: The Coconut Grove.

MICHAEL: The Four Hundred.

VICKY: The Blue Train.

SIBYL: The Florida.

VICKY: The Coconut Grove.

MICHAEL: The Four Hundred.

SIMON: The Blue Train.

The music gets faster still. They change partners. SIMON *dances with* SIBYL *and* MICHAEL *with* VICKY – *then they change back to each other again* – *then once more* – *all saying together: 'The Florida', 'The Coconut Grove', 'The Four Hundred', 'The Blue Train'.* MICHAEL *and* VICKY *disappear and* SIBYL *and* SIMON *are left dancing round and round together, faster and faster. From the darkness can be heard voices shouting rhythmically: 'The Florida', 'The Coconut Grove', 'The Four Hundred', 'The Blue Train', coming to a crescendo and then a black-out.*

LENA *appears on the right-hand side of the stage with a telephone.* MARTHA *appears on the opposite side, also with a telephone. Both in spotlights.*

MARTHA: Hallo – who is it?

LENA: It's Lena, madame.

MARTHA: Oh, Lena – yes – what is it?

LENA: Mr. Gayforth asked me to telephone to you, madame—

MARTHA: Is anything wrong?

LENA: It's Mrs. Gayforth, madame – those sleeping tablets – Mr. Gayforth wants to know if you can leave the party and come at once—

MARTHA: Good heavens! Is she ill?

LENA: Yes, madame – that is – she's not exactly ill but—

MARTHA: Have you sent for a doctor?

LENA: No, madame – Mr. Gayforth didn't want to send for a doctor until he'd seen you.

MARTHA: I'll come at once.

LENA: It was that extra Anytal tablet, madame – I knew she shouldn't have taken it—

MARTHA: I'll be there in a few minutes – in the meantime – give her some strong black coffee—

The lights fade.
In the darkness VICKY's *voice is heard.*

VICKY: Simon, Simon – where are you? – I'm lonely – I'm frightened – don't go away from me yet – in spite of what they say there is still time if only we're careful—

SIMON: There's something I want to say to you – I've been wanting to say it for quite a while—

VICKY: Don't say it – don't say it yet.

SIMON: I would like if possible to keep this conversation impersonal.

VICKY: I would so love to be clear at this moment. But nothing's clear at all—

SIMON: I didn't know you had taken anything—

VICKY: It was only to make me sleep – whenever I'm tired or unhappy, oh, Simon – Simon – come back – the White Cliffs of Dover – I'm trying so hard – I'm trying to hold on – don't leave me – don't leave me—

SIMON: Give her a little more, Lena.

LENA: Yes, sir.

SIMON: You don't think we ought to send for a doctor?

MARTHA: No, she'll be all right.

SIMON: It was awfully sweet of you to come back, Martha – I got in a panic – you were the only one I could think of—

VICKY: I shall be sick if I have any more of that damned coffee.

SIMON: That's a very good idea – be sick.

VICKY: No, no – I hate being sick – it's mortifying – I'm perfectly all right now – really I am.

The lights slowly go up on the bedroom.
VICKY *is sitting on the edge of the bed.* SIMON *is sitting by her side with one arm round her, holding a cup of coffee in his other*

hand. MARTHA *is kneeling on the floor at her feet.* LENA *is standing anxiously at the foot of the bed holding a coffee pot.*

SIMON: There, darling – won't you lie down a bit?

VICKY: Don't fuss.

SIMON: You ought to be ashamed of yourself.

VICKY: What are you rolling about on the floor for, Martha? It looks very silly.

MARTHA (*rising*): You may well ask.

VICKY: I think I should like a cigarette.

SIMON: Then you will be sick.

VICKY: No, it's passed off.

LENA (*handing her a cigarette*): Here, madame.

VICKY: Thank you, Lena. Match, please.

SIMON: Here, Martha, take this cup, will you?

He gives MARTHA *the coffee and lights* VICKY's *cigarette.*

VICKY: That's lovely. (*She puffs.*)

SIMON: It's all right, Lena – you can go to bed again.

LENA: Are you sure, sir?

SIMON: Yes, thank you, Lena.

LENA: Good-night, sir.

SIMON: Good-night.

LENA *goes out.*

VICKY: Now perhaps somebody will explain. What happened to me?

SIMON: You just went mad, that's all – raving.

VICKY (*interested*): Did I froth at the mouth?

SIMON: I don't know – I was too agitated to notice.

MARTHA: I think I'd better go back to Alice's.

VICKY: Alice's! Oh yes, of course. Oh, Simon – I remember now.

SIMON: Don't think of anything – just relax.

MARTHA (*kissing her*): Good-night, darling.

VICKY (*absently – her thoughts a long way away*): Good-night.

MARTHA: Good-night, Simon.

SIMON: Thanks awfully, Martha.

MARTHA *goes out.*

VICKY: I'm so sorry, Simon – I'm feeling quite tranquil now – let's talk about the divorce in the morning.

SIMON: Divorce? What do you mean?

VICKY: You asked me to divorce you, didn't you?

SIMON: Certainly not.

VICKY: Are you trying to make me believe that that was part of the dream?

SIMON: I don't know what you're talking about.

VICKY: It's sweet of you to lie – but it won't wash.

SIMON *sits on the bed again and puts his arms round her.*

SIMON: Please forgive me.

VICKY (*sleepily*): We'll talk it all over calmly – to-morrow.

SIMON: All right.

VICKY (*resting her head on his shoulder*): If you really love her all that much I'll try not to be beastly about it—

SIMON: I don't love anybody that much.

VICKY: What did I do when I went mad? I'm so interested.

SIMON: You talked a lot – I thought it was nonsense at first and then I realised that it was true – then you began dancing about the room – then you really did go mad – and I got very frightened and told Lena to ring up Martha—

VICKY: It was certainly a very strange feeling—

She closes her eyes and the music starts again very softly.

SIMON: It will be all right now – it really will – I promise.

VICKY: The music's beginning again.

The music swells. SIMON lifts her gently on to the bed and covers her over with the counterpane. Then he kisses her, disentangles her cigarette from her fingers, tiptoes across the room and switches off the lights, all but a little lamp by the bed, and stretches himself on the sofa at her feet.

The music reaches a crescendo as—

THE CURTAIN FALLS

FAMILY ALBUM

A Victorian Comedy with Music

from

TO-NIGHT AT 8.30

Family Album was produced in London at the Phoenix Theatre on 9 January 1936, with the following cast:

JASPER FEATHERWAYS	Mr. Noël Coward
JANE, *his wife*	Miss Gertrude Lawrence
LAVINIA FEATHERWAYS	Miss Alison Leggatt
RICHARD FEATHERWAYS	Mr. Edward Underdown
HARRIET WINTER	Miss Everley Gregg
CHARLES WINTER	Mr. Anthony Pelissier
EMILY VALANCE	Miss Moya Nugent
EDWARD VALANCE	Mr. Kenneth Carten
BURROWS	Mr. Alan Webb

———

The action of the play passes in the drawing-room of the Featherways' house in Kent on an Autumn evening in the year 1860.

The scene is the drawing-room of the FEATHERWAYS' *house in Kent not very far from London.*

It is an Autumn evening in the year 1860.

When the curtain rises the entire family is assembled. They are all in deep mourning. The music plays softly; an undercurrent to grief. The family group would be static were it not for an occasional slight movement from one or other of them. Apart from the music there is silence for quite a while. EMILY, *who is by the window, breaks it.*

EMILY. It has stopped raining.

RICHARD (*moving to the window*): Not quite, Emily, but it is certainly clearing.

LAVINIA: It was fitting that it rained to-day. It has been a sad day and rain became it.

JASPER: True, very true.

JANE: A little sunshine would have been much pleasanter nevertheless.

JASPER: Lavinia has a tidy mind. She likes life to be as neat as her handkerchief drawer.

HARRIET: I hope Mr. Lubbock reached London safely.

JANE: Dear Mr. Lubbock.

LAVINIA: Really Jane!

JANE: I think he's a sweet man. He read the will with such sympathy.

HARRIET: He coughed a great deal, I thought. I wanted to give him one of my pastilles.

CHARLES: I'm glad you didn't, my dear, they have an alarming flavour and he was already considerably nervous.

HARRIET: They're very efficacious.

EMILY (*pensively – at the window*): I wonder if he knew.

EDWARD: What was that, my love?

EMILY: Papa – I wonder if he knew it was raining?

LAVINIA: Perhaps he was watching – from somewhere above the trees.

HARRIET: Oh! Do you suppose he was!

LAVINIA: I like to think it.

JANE: Do you, Lavinia?

LAVINIA: Of course.

JANE: When I die I hope I shall go swiftly and not linger above familiar trees. It must be painful to watch those you have left, in black and weeping.

EMILY: Oh, don't, Jane, don't! (*She weeps.*)

EDWARD (*comforting her*): There, there, my dear.

HARRIET: Poor Papa.

EMILY: Poor dear Papa.

> *The door opens quietly and* BURROWS, *a very aged butler, enters staggering under the weight of a heavy tray on which is a decanter containing Madeira, and the requisite number of glasses.*
>
> RICHARD *goes quickly and relieves him of it.*

RICHARD: Oh, Burrows, you should have let Martin carry the tray, it's too heavy for you.

BURROWS (*cupping his hear with his hand*): Pardon, Master Richard?

JASPER (*bending down to him and speaking clearly*): You should have let Martin carry the tray, Burrows, it's too heavy for you.

BURROWS: Martin is young, Mr. Jasper. He would have been out of tune with the evening's melancholy. His very bearing would have been an intrusion.

LAVINIA: Thank you, Burrows, that was very considerate of you.

BURROWS: I beg your pardon, Miss Lavvy?

LAVINIA (*loudly*): I said thank you, Burrows, that was very considerate of you.

BURROWS: Your servant to the grave, Miss Lavvy.

JANE: Oh, Burrows!

BURROWS: I beg your pardon, ma'am?

JANE (*loudly*): I only said 'Oh, Burrows', Burrows.

BURROWS: Very good, ma'am.

> BURROWS *goes out.*

HARRIET: Poor Burrows looks very depressed.

JASPER: Burrows has looked depressed for at least thirty years.

JANE: One could scarcely expect him to be hilarious now.

LAVINIA: Hilarious! Really, Jane.

HARRIET: I think sorrow has increased his deafness.

JASPER: He was just as deaf last Christmas really, and that was a gay occasion.

JANE (*with meaning*): Gay!

JASPER (*reprovingly*): Hush, Jane.

HARRIET: A bereavement in the house must affect the servants profoundly, although I must admit I heard Sarah singing in the pantry this morning.

EMILY (*horrified*): This morning!

HARRIET: It was quite early.

LAVINIA: Disgraceful.

HARRIET: She was singing very softly, and it *was* a hymn.

LAVINIA: Nevertheless, I hope you scolded her.

HARRIET: I hadn't the heart, she has such a pretty voice.

CHARLES: What hymn was it?

HARRIET: 'For Those In Peril On The Sea'.

LAVINIA: Most inappropriate.

JASPER: Sarah's young man is a sailor, you know, he's on the *Brilliant*.

CHARLES (*with interest*): That's a Three Decker.

EDWARD: She carries 114 thirty-two pounders, 2 sixty-eight pounders and 4 eighteen pounders.

EMILY: Oh, Edward, how clever of you to know.

RICHARD: A fine ship, I have seen her at anchor.

CHARLES: Surely not a hundred and twenty guns?

EDWARD: Yes, she is the same class as the *Britannic* and the *Prince Regent*.

RICHARD: Cast-iron muzzle loaders, I presume?

EDWARD (*enthusiastically*): Yes, their recoil is checked by stout rope breechings.

CHARLES: How are they elevated?

EDWARD: Quoins – and trained by handspikes.

RICHARD: Oh – handspikes.

JANE (*with slight mockery*): Handspikes, Lavinia – do you hear that? – they're trained by handspikes!

LAVINIA: I declare I'm more at sea than Sarah's young man.

JANE: Oh, Lavvy – a joke – how sweet!

EMILY (*hugging her*): Darling Lavvy!

LAVINIA: Behave, Emily – let me alone.

JASPER: It seems odd that the solemnity of this particular family reunion should be dissipated by gunnery.

LAVINIA: Such irrelevance, on such a day.

EDWARD: It was my fault, I apologise.

JANE: With so much to be done, so much to be decided.

LAVINIA (*raising her handkerchief to her eyes*): Oh, dear!

JASPER: Steel yourself, Lavinia – be brave.

LAVINIA: I'll try.

HARRIET: We must all try.

> CHARLES *and* RICHARD *go to the table on which* RICHARD *has placed the tray.*

CHARLES: Jane – a little wine?

JANE: Thank you, Charles.

CHARLES: Harriet?

HARRIET: Thank you, Charles.

RICHARD: A little Madeira, Emily?

EMILY: Just a drop, please.

RICHARD: Lavinia?

LAVINIA: No, thank you.

HARRIET: Oh, Lavvy, a little sip would warm you.

LAVINIA: I am not cold.

JASPER (*brusquely*): Come, Lavvy, don't be annoying.

LAVINIA: How can you, Jasper—

JASPER: I insist – here— (*He gives her a glass.*)

JANE: We should drink a toast.

LAVINIA: You should be ashamed.

JANE: Don't be alarmed, I meant quite a gentle toast.

RICHARD: An excellent idea.

CHARLES: Why not?

LAVINIA: As though this were a moment for celebrating.

CHARLES: Again – why not?

JASPER (*sternly*): Charles – behave yourself!

JANE: Charles is right. Why not indeed!

LAVINIA: I am at a loss to understand your behaviour this evening, Jane.

JANE: A billiard room – I heard Charles and Harriet discussing it – they're going to have a billiard room—

HARRIET: It's an extravagance – I told Charles it was an extravagance.

JANE: Never mind, you can afford it now.

CHARLES: That's what I say.

JANE: Isn't it splendid! – Isn't it absolutely splendid?

LAVINIA (*immeasurably shocked*): What!

JANE: About Charles and Harriet being able to afford a billiard room, about Emily and Edward being able to send John and Curly to Eton, about you, Lavinia, being able to buy a little house anywhere you like, about Jasper and me living here—

RICHARD: What about me?

JASPER: I think Crockford's should be congratulated – that's where all your money goes.

RICHARD: Touché, Jasper – a new black fleece, though, for the blackest of black-sheep.

EMILY: Where will you go, Lavvy?

LAVINIA: I feel this conversation to be abominably out of place.

JANE: Darling, don't be stuffy.

LAVINIA: It is my father who has passed away, remember.

JANE: Jasper's too, and Emily's and Richard's and Harriet's.

JASPER: Leave Lavinia her decorum, Jane, polite grief should be respected.

LAVINIA: Polite! Oh, Jasper!

JASPER: I am your brother, dear, I know your heart.

JANE: Smile, Lavinia – just once.

EMILY: Yes, Lavvy, just one smile.

LAVINIA: You are disgraceful, all of you – all of you – unfeeling and disgraceful – I am ashamed of you.

JASPER: Smile, then, and you can be ashamed of yourself as well.

HARRIET: Please, Lavvy.

RICHARD: Come along, Lavvy.

JASPER: Think, Lavvy – a little house in some gay country – France or Italy – you've always loved foreigners – a little villa in the sun – you can paint your pictures – blue seas and cypresses – you could take tabby with you, she's an insular cat but I doubt whether French or Italian mice taste so very different—

JANE: We'll all come and stay with you, Lavinia.

RICHARD: Hurrah, Lavinia – smile and say Hurrah!

LAVINIA (*struggling*): No – no—

EMILY (*flinging her arms round her*): Yes – yes—

LAVINIA: Be still, Emily – for shame!

HARRIET: Her mouth twitched – I saw it.

JASPER (*tickling the back of her neck*): Come along, Lavvy—

LAVINIA (*slapping his hand away*): How dare you, Jasper!

JANE: Think of Mrs. Hodgson's bonnet at the funeral – do you remember? – I nudged you—

LAVINIA (*breaking at last into laughter*): Oh, dear – how horrid you all are – I hate you – it was the most ridiculous bonnet I ever saw – like a little black pie – oh, dear—

JASPER: Are your glasses charged?

LAVINIA: No, Jasper, no – I don't approve—

JASPER (*raising his glass*): To Mrs. Hodgson's little black pie!

ALL (*raising their glasses*): Mrs. Hodgson's little black pie!

JASPER (*triumphantly, as* LAVINIA *drinks*): There!

> LAVINIA *chokes – everyone gathers round her and pats her on the back.*

Some more – quickly, Richard—

> RICHARD, CHARLES, EDWARD *and* JASPER *refill all the glasses.*

LAVINIA: This is so wrong – so dreadfully wrong—

JASPER: Another toast – be prepared—

LAVINIA: Please, stop, Jasper – the servants will hear.

JASPER (*raising his glass*): To ourselves – a closely united family and the dear strangers who have joined us – I allude to you, Jane, darling, and Charles and Edward—

CHARLES: Does that mean that we three may not drink?

JASPER: Certainly not – drink to yourselves – to each other – and the happiness of us all.

CHARLES: Good!

HARRIET: Do be quiet, Charles.

JASPER: Where was I?

JANE: The happiness of us all, my dear.

> JASPER *sings a short toast to each of them – everybody joins in. The tempo becomes more gay and there is much laughter as each individual is commented upon.*

The gaiety is interrupted by the clock on the mantelpiece striking ten.

The music drops to the minor. Everyone puts down his glass.

LAVINIA: Papa's eight-day clock – he would never allow anyone to wind it but himself – who will wind it now?

She bows her head. EMILY, JASPER, HARRIET *and* RICHARD *all sing sadly together.*

EMILY
JASPER   'Ah, who will wind it now – alack-a-day – who
HARRIET   will wind it now!'
RICHARD

JANE: Jasper, of course – don't be so silly.

JASPER: Richard, be so kind as to ring for Burrows.

RICHARD: Now?

JASPER: Yes, now.

LAVINIA: The box?

JASPER: The box.

RICHARD: Very well.

He pulls the bell-rope by the fireplace.

EMILY: Oh, dear!

There is a gloomy silence for a moment. EDWARD *breaks it.*

EDWARD (*at the window*): Look – there's a squirrel!

CHARLES (*eagerly*): Where?

EDWARD: There – by the steps.

RICHARD (*joining them*): How can you tell – it's so dark.

EMILY: There's only a little moon but enough to see by, look – there he goes – back into the wood.

LAVINIA: Poor Papa – poor dear Papa – he'll never see a squirrel again.

HARRIET: Don't, Lavinia.

JANE: Do you think he would wish to? – I mean – not to see any more squirrels is surely one of the lesser disadvantages of dying.

LAVINIA (*coldly*): You take me too literally, Jane.

EMILY (*coming away from the window*): Oh, it's all so dreadful – death is so frightening.

LAVINIA: So lonely.

JASPER: Lonelier even than life.

JANE (*hurt*): Jasper!

JASPER: Forgive me, my love – it was a generalisation.

BURROWS *enters.*

BURROWS: You rang, Mr. Jasper?

JASPER: We are ready for the box now, Burrows.

BURROWS: Every one of them, Mr. Jasper – regulated to the minute – I did them myself.

JASPER: Not the clocks, Burrows, the box.

BURROWS: I had a mort of trouble with the one in the library – it struck fifteen three times – but I fixed it. (*He gives a slight cackle and then controls himself.*)

JASPER: The box, Burrows – we want the box – I told you to have it brought down from the attic this morning.

BURROWS: Oh, the trunk! Very well, Mr. Jasper.

He goes off.

LAVINIA: It seems callous somehow – so soon to pry upon Papa's secrets.

JASPER: Callous perhaps, but certainly necessary.

JANE: I observed one of his more open secrets at the back of the church this morning.

LAVINIA: What do you mean, Jane?

JANE: Mrs. Wynant.

HARRIET: That creature.

JASPER: Hush, Harriet – we cannot resent her grieving, too – in her own way.

HARRIET: Nevertheless, I do resent it.

LAVINIA: She should not have come.

EMILY: Poor Mrs. Wynant.

LAVINIA: Really, Emily – poor Mrs. Wynant indeed!

EMILY: I was thinking of the will.

RICHARD: It was perfectly just – she had no claim.

JASPER: No legal claim at any rate.

LAVINIA: Jasper!

JASPER: It would be unchristian to deny her a certain moral right.

CHARLES: Moral is hardly the word I should have chosen.

JASPER: Spoken like a soldier, Charles – and also, I'm afraid, like a gentleman.

BURROWS *enters.*

BURROWS: The box is outside, Mr. Jasper – if you and Mr. Richard – I would rather Martin did not enter—

JANE: Why, Burrows, it really wouldn't matter.

BURROWS: It isn't the clatter, ma'am, it's his face, it's so very hot and red – in this pale room – you understand?

JASPER: Very well, Burrows – come along, Richard.

RICHARD *and* JASPER *go out.*

BURROWS: Will there be any tea required, ma'am?

JANE: Yes, please, Burrows – a little later.

BURROWS (*cupping his ear with his hand*): I beg your pardon, ma'am?

JANE (*shouting*): A little later, Burrows.

BURROWS (*respectfully*): Oh, no, ma'am – certainly not – not for the world, ma'am.

BURROWS *goes out.*

JANE: What could he have thought I said?

CHARLES: I fear that we shall never know.

RICHARD *and* JASPER *return with a very dusty little trunk. They put it down.*

JASPER: Sarah has done her best with a duster, but I fear it needs scrubbing.

RICHARD: Never mind.

LAVINIA: The box.

HARRIET: Oh, dear – the box.

JASPER: Yes, there it sits – reproaching us – almost frowning at us.

JANE: That little strap makes it look even more disagreeable than it really is.

JASPER: You have the key, Lavinia. You took it from Father's chain.

LAVINIA: Yes, it's here. (*She hands it to* JASPER.) You're the eldest.

JASPER: Before opening it – before unearthing our dear Father's secrets – I must most earnestly enjoin – complete discretion.

CHARLES: Of course.

JASPER: You, Charles, and Edward, and my dear Jane—

JANE: Open it, Jasper, and don't be silly.

JASPER: You cut me short, Jane, in the most frivolous way.

JANE: Never mind.

CHARLES: We understand, Jasper – complete discretion.

JANE (*impatiently*): Open it!

JASPER (*on his knees*): Poor Papa! (*He wrestles with the lock.*) The key doesn't fit – (*He lifts the lid.*) It's already open – (*He puts his hand into the box and produces a gilt paper crown.*) It's the wrong box!

LAVINIA: Oh, how stupid of Burrows!

EMILY: A paper crown.

HARRIET: I remember it.

RICHARD: Where's the sceptre – there should be a sceptre, too – I made it myself from Uncle William's walking-stick— (*He searches in the box.*)

EMILY: He was very angry.

RICHARD (*finding it*): Here it is.

LAVINIA: There was a scarf with beads on it from India – I wore it when I was the Queen— (*She goes on her knees too, and searches in the box.*)

HARRIET: And there were four swords – flat ones – but one was broken—

> She joins LAVINIA *and searches in the box.*

EMILY (*rushing to the box*): Princes and Princesses – oh, how lovely!

JANE: What on earth are you talking about?

JASPER (*smiling*): Princes and Princesses – it was a dressing-up game – we played it when we were children—

HARRIET: On Sundays – only on Sundays—

> *They sing a foolish little tune: 'Princes and Princesses'. They act a little too, fragments of the game they remember.* LAVINIA *is crowned with the paper crown.* JASPER *and* RICHARD *fight a brisk duel with the swords. At the end* LAVINIA *tears off her crown and throws it on to the floor.*

LAVINIA: This is wicked – wicked – I shall never forgive myself to the end of my days—

> *She sinks on to a sofa, in tears. The others look at her mutely.*

RICHARD rises from the floor where he has been lying since being killed in the duel and dusts himself down.

JASPER: Don't cry, Lavvy – please don't.

LAVINIA (*tearfully*): —God must surely punish us for this heartlessness, dancing and singing and playing, with Father not yet cold in his grave.

JASPER: That is an emotional statement, my dear, understandable in the circumstances, but hardly accurate.

EMILY: The cemetery really is very exposed, Lavinia.

LAVINIA: Forgive us, Papa, forgive us—

RICHARD: A little more Madeira, Charles, our sister is becoming hysterical.

CHARLES pours out some Madeira and hands it to RICHARD, who takes it to LAVINIA.

Here, my dear.

LAVINIA: No, no – I don't want it.

JASPER: Drink it, Lavinia, it will calm you.

JANE: I think I should like a little more, too.

CHARLES (*pouring it for her*): Very well – Harriet?

HARRIET: Yes, please.

JASPER (*to LAVINIA*): Come along, dear.

LAVINIA (*sipping the wine*): How shameful – oh, how shameful!

CHARLES: Emily, some more wine?

EMILY: May I, Edward?

EDWARD: Yes, my love, but only a little.

CHARLES: There is only a little left.

RICHARD: We had better ring for some more.

LAVINIA: No, Richard, no – I forbid it.

RICHARD: As you say, Lavvy, but my throat is cruelly dry.

CHARLES: Mine too – Jasper?

JASPER: Dry as dust.

LAVINIA (*bursting into tears again*): Dust! Oh, Jasper!

The door opens discreetly and BURROWS enters bearing another decanter of Madeira. Everyone looks at him in silence as he places it ceremoniously on the tray. He looks enquiringly at CHARLES who is holding the empty decanter. CHARLES gives it to him. He bows politely and goes to the door. He turns and regards them all lovingly for a moment then, from his cuff, he produces a large white handkerchief with which he wipes his eyes, but it is difficult to tell whether he is laughing or weeping.

He goes out, closing the door behind him.

JASPER: With every advancing year Burrows grows wiser.

HARRIET: And kinder.

RICHARD: And more understanding.

JASPER: Surely, among ourselves, a little private toast to Burrows would not be entirely without grace?

CHARLES: Hear, hear!

EMILY: I think Papa would have wished it.

EDWARD: Well spoken my love.

LAVINIA: Papa would not have approved at all – Jasper – I appeal to you—

HARRIET: Oh, Lavvy, I know he would—

RICHARD: Tinge your grief with tolerance, Lavinia.

CHARLES: What harm is there, Lavinia?

JANE: Don't be silly, Lavinia.

JASPER: The 'Ayes' have it – charge your glasses.

Everybody refills their glasses.

(*Raising his glass.*) To Burrows – our first friend – don't you remember, Lavinia? He made us toys in the woodshed. He read us stories when we were ill; he gave us forbidden sweets from the pantry. He loved us all – you particularly, Lavinia – have you forgotten his tenderness when Mother died? Have you forgotten his welcoming smile when we came home from school? Surely this small gesture of affection to him can only be a pale sin in the eyes of heaven. To Burrows, Lavinia.

LAVINIA (*rising to her feet*): To Burrows! (*She drinks.*)

ALL: To Burrows! (*They drink.*)

CHARLES: That was delicious.

RICHARD: I think it must have come from Papa's special cellar.

EMILY: I believe I should like a little more.

EDWARD: No, Emily.

EMILY (*gaily*): Spoilsport – I defy you!

She quickly pours herself out another glassful and drinks it before anyone can stop her.

HARRIET: Emily!

LAVINIA: Behave, Emily.

JASPER: You shock me appallingly, Emily – I'm almost sure you do.

EMILY: Nonsense!

EDWARD: I apologise – I apologise to you all. Come to bed, Emily.

EMILY: Papa liked wine – he liked it to excess – I expect this is hereditary. (*She giggles.*)

EDWARD: Come to bed immediately.

EMILY: I shall do no such thing, my love, so there! I want to see what more there is in the box— (*She kneels on the floor beside it and begins to rummage about in it.*)

JANE: Poor Edward, I fear the grape has robbed you of your marital authority.

RICHARD: Vanquished, Edward – be a man and admit it.

LAVINIA: I feel a little faint – the heat, I think, and everyone behaving so strangely—

HARRIET (*going to her*): My dear—

JANE: Would you like me to take you upstairs?

LAVINIA: No, no, it will pass – it's nothing.

RICHARD: Some salts – some vinegar?

LAVINIA: No, no – I think perhaps a thimbleful more of that wine—

CHARLES (*pouring her out some*): Here, my dear—

LAVINIA: Thank you, Charles – how kind. (*She accepts it weakly.*)

JANE: I feel very curious myself.

JASPER: Beloved!

HARRIET: Open the window.

JANE: No – the air is damp – it would be dangerous—

RICHARD: Some wine?

JANE: Perhaps – perhaps that would revive me.

CHARLES (*pouring her out some*): Here, my dear.

JANE (*smiling gaily*): Thank you, Charles.

> *They all casually take a little more wine.*

EMILY (*at the box*): Oh, look – look—!

JASPER: What is it?

EMILY: The musical box – don't you remember?

RICHARD: I thought it had dropped to pieces years ago.

LAVINIA: Aunt Heathcote gave it to us – it was a Christmas present.

HARRIET: Papa forbade us to play it.

EMILY (*placing it on the table and winding it*): He can't forbid us now!

EDWARD (*reprovingly*): Emily!

EMILY: Shh! Be still – listen—

They all listen – no sound comes from the musical box.

JASPER: It's old and tired, it's forgotten how to play.

RICHARD: No, no – there was a little catch – I'm sure there was—

EMILY: Make it play, Richard – please try—

RICHARD tinkers with it and it strikes one note. They all sing 'Let's play a tune on the music box'. They stop singing and the music box tinkles out a tinny little melody.

RICHARD: There!

EMILY (*clasping her hands ecstatically*): Oh, how sweet – how sweet!

HARRIET: The red schoolroom curtains – I can suddenly see them – blowing out in the draught—

RICHARD: The hard pink sugar on the edge of the cake – I can suddenly taste it.

JASPER: Your hand in mine, Jane, when you were brought over to tea by your governess – I can suddenly feel it.

JANE (*taking his hand*): Oh, darling—

EMILY: Again, again – make it play again – I want to remember, too—

RICHARD tinkers with it again. It plays the same sticky little melody.
EMILY begins to sing – they all join in – little snatches of melody come back to them out of their childhood.

HARRIET: There was another tune as well – I remember distinctly – it played another tune—

RICHARD: We mustn't ask too much of it.

JASPER: Try the little catch again.

HARRIET: It was a waltz.

JANE (*looking at JASPER*): Of course it was – a waltz – don't you recall it, my dear love? We danced to it years later – at a ball – just before we were married – it was this – it was this—

She starts to sing – RICHARD *is still at work on the music box – suddenly it begins to play again – the tune that* JANE *is singing.*

EMILY: It's remembered – oh, how clever of it!

RICHARD: Hush, Emily – that was their love song—

JASPER *and* JANE *sing to each other the love song of their youth. The others join in, humming very softly, as they dance together. At the end of it* JANE *sinks to the floor in a deep curtsy,* JASPER *bows over her, taking her hand.*

JASPER: I love you, my heart.

JANE: 'Till death us do part—'

He raises her to her feet and takes her in his arms. LAVINIA *sinks on to the sofa once more in tears.*

RICHARD: Oh, Lavvy!

LAVINIA: Don't mock me – these are true tears.

JASPER: Not sad ones though, I beg of you—

LAVINIA: Mama died when we were little, Papa died four days ago, but life isn't dead, is it – is it?

JASPER: Never, as long as it's gay, as long as it's happy.

EMILY: Poor Papa – poor dear Papa!

LAVINIA: To hell with Papa!

HARRIET: Lavinia!

RICHARD: Lavinia!

EMILY: Oh, Lavvy, how can you!

JASPER: Bravo, Lavvy!

LAVINIA: I mean it – give me some more Madeira, Charles.

CHARLES: Good heavens!

LAVINIA: I hated Papa, so did you, Jasper, and Harriet and Richard and Emily—

EMILY: Oh, Lavvy – don't – don't—

LAVINIA: He was cruel to Mama, he was unkind to us, he was profligate and pompous and worse still, he was mean—

CHARLES (*handing her some wine*): Here, my dear – drink this.

LAVINIA (*taking it*): Certainly I will— (*She raises her glass.*) Now I will propose a toast – To Papa – and to the truth, too – Papa and the truth together – for the first time.

JASPER: I do hope you will not regret this in the morning, Lavinia.

HARRIET: Don't you think you had better retire to bed?

EMILY: I feel frightened.

LAVINIA: This may be wicked. I expect it is – I expect I shall be punished for it – but I don't care. You escaped – all of you – you found husbands and wives and lives of your own – but I had to stay here – with him – For years he has scarcely spoken to me – I've counted the linen – I've added up the bills – I've managed the house – years ago I said good-bye to someone I loved because my miserable unkind conscience told me that it was my duty. I've sat here in this house week after week, month after month, year after year, while he insulted me and glowered at me and betrayed our name with common village loves. The will – the happy will which was read to us to-day was made ten years ago – you realise that, do you not?

JASPER: Lavinia – what in heaven's name––

LAVINIA: What you do not realise is that he made another – a week before he died––

HARRIET: What are you saying?

RICHARD: Lavinia – are you mad?

EMILY (*wailing*): Oh, Lavvy!

LAVINIA: None of us were even mentioned in it. Five thousand pounds was left to Mrs. Wynant. Six thousand pounds to Rose Dalton. Three thousand pounds to Mrs. Waterbury – I can only gather that she was less satisfactory than the others – and the rest to a fund for the erection of a new church containing a memorial of himself in black marble!

JASPER: Lavinia – are you sure of this?

LAVINIA: Quite sure. Burrows witnessed it.

JASPER: And would it be trespassing too far on your indiscretion to ask what became of it?

LAVINIA: Seven and a half minutes after Papa breathed his last, Burrows and I burnt it.

JASPER: Ring the bell, Richard.

RICHARD: Very well. (*He goes to the bell and pulls it.*)

EMILY: I think, Edward dear, another sip of wine would be pardonable in the circumstances.

HARRIET: I agree.

JANE: Black marble – how very nasty.

RICHARD: Black clay would have been more appropriate.

They all pour themselves out a little more Madeira.

EMILY: Poor Mrs. Waterbury.

JANE: Think of the humiliation she has been spared.

HARRIET: I wonder where Rose Dalton is now?

JASPER: In Scotland, I believe – she married a Baptist.

EDWARD: Do you suppose Mrs. Wynant suspects?

JASPER: Suspects what, Edward?

EDWARD: About the – er – about your father – about what Lavinia has just told us?

LAVINIA: I observed an expensive diamond brooch fastening her cloak in church to-day. That, I think, should be a sufficient reward for services rendered.

JASPER: How hard you are, Lavinia.

JANE: And how right.

BURROWS *enters.*

BURROWS: You rang, Mr. Jasper?

JASPER: Yes, Burrows.

RICHARD: We wish to ask you a question, Burrows.

BURROWS: Much better, thank you, Master Richard. A little herb tea soothes all disharmony.

JASPER: A question, Burrows.

BURROWS: Very well, Mr. Jasper.

JASPER: Miss Lavinia gives me to understand that you witnessed my late father's last Will and Testament.

BURROWS (*cupping his ear with his hand*): I beg your pardon, sir?

JASPER: Did you or did you not witness my late father's last Will and Testament?

BURROWS: My affliction is increasing bad, Mr. Jasper, I shall never be able to hear that particular question.

LAVINIA (*softly*): Thank you, Burrows.

BURROWS: Not at all, Miss Lavinia.

RICHARD: Some Madeira, Burrows?

He holds up the decanter.

BURROWS: I should be honoured, Master Richard.

RICHARD (*pouring him some*): Here, then.

BURROWS (*accepting it*): At your service always.

JASPER: Thank you, Burrows.

BURROWS (*catching sight of the musical box*): Have I your permission for a moment.

JASPER: Certainly – what is it?

BURROWS: There should be a little tune, a little tune from the years that are dead – allow me—

He starts the musical box. It plays the same gay little melody that it played before. He stands beside it, bending down to hear it more clearly, then he stands up with his head nodding to the tune and raises his glass.

BURROWS: I drink to you all – (*Then to* JASPER *and* JANE.) And to you, sir, and ma'am – this house was happy when there were children in it—

He drinks. EMILY *and* JANE *and* HARRIET *start to sing. All the others join in. The tune becomes gayer and swifter until they are all hand in hand and dancing round* BURROWS *as—*

THE CURTAIN FALLS

STAR CHAMBER

A Light Comedy in One Act

from

TO-NIGHT AT 8.30

Characters

XENIA JAMES
JOHNNY BOLTON
HESTER MORE
JULIAN BREED
DAME ROSE MAITLAND
VIOLET VIBART
MAURICE SEARLE
ELISE BRODIE
J. M. FARMER
JIMMIE HORLICK
PRESS PHOTOGRAPHER

———

The action of the play passes on the stage of a West End theatre.

TIME: The Present.

The action of the play passes on the bare stage of a West End theatre in London.

The time is about twelve noon.

When the curtain rises JIMMIE HORLICK, *the stage-manager of the theatre, is arranging chairs round a long table. The stage is dim as there is only one working light on.*

J. M. FARMER *enters from the left. He is an amiable-looking man somewhere between thirty and forty. He wears a mackintosh, a bowler hat and glasses, and he carries a brief-case bulging with papers.*

MR. FARMER: Good morning.

JIMMIE: Good morning.

MR. FARMER: I'm Mr. Farmer.

JIMMIE (*shaking hands*): Pleased to meet you.

MR. FARMER: Mr. Bolton not here yet?

JIMMIE: No, nobody's here yet – it's only just twelve.

MR. FARMER: It's a bit dark, isn't it?

JIMMIE: I'll put a couple of battens on and you can have the floats up if you like.

MR. FARMER: Thanks.

JIMMIE *goes to the prompt corner and switches on more light.*

JIMMIE: That better?

MR. FARMER (*taking off his mackintosh*): That's fine. (*He surveys the table.*) Looks nice and businesslike.

JIMMIE: That's the table out of the party scene. Mr. Bolton does a buck and wing on it.

MR. FARMER: How's the show going?

JIMMIE: Wonderful. We dropped off a bit before Christmas, but we're back again now.

MR. FARMER: Are you Mr. Bolton's stage-manager?

JIMMIE: Yes.

MR. FARMER: How is he to work with?

JIMMIE: He's all right as long as you laugh at his gags.

MR. FARMER: I haven't seen him on the stage for years, not since he was at the Gaiety.

JIMMIE: He's still doing the same stuff.

> HESTER MORE *comes on to the stage. She is wearing tweeds, a turtle-neck jumper and a felt hat. A lot of fuzzy hair escapes from under the hat. Her manner is vague to the point of lunacy and she carries a small brown-paper parcel.*

HESTER: These are my shoes.

MR. FARMER: Good morning.

HESTER: My feet got sopping wet so I had to buy a new pair, these are the wet ones – don't they look silly?

MR. FARMER: You're the first to arrive, except me.

HESTER: Who are you?

MR. FARMER: I'm Mr. Farmer, the Secretary of the Fund.

HESTER: Oh, I see.

> *There is a pause.*

MR. FARMER: Nasty out, isn't it?

HESTER: I should have been here earlier still, only I went to the Lyceum, but there wasn't anybody there.

MR. FARMER: Oh.

> *There is another pause.*

This is Mr. Horlick, Mr. Bolton's stage-manager.

HESTER (*shaking hands*): How lovely! Would you mind putting my hat somewhere? (*She takes it off and gives it to him.*)

JIMMIE: Certainly.

HESTER: I think hats are maddening, they get so wet and stupid.

MR. FARMER (*anxious to please*): Yes, I suppose they do really.

HESTER: I can never rehearse in a hat – I feel I want to shake and shake and shake my head until it flies through the air like a moon.

MR. FARMER: Yes, that puts you off, I expect.

HESTER: Nothing puts me off really once I start, because I shut off absolutely everything, but the getting to the shutting-off stage is sheer misery – you have to mean so much yourself before you can begin to make the play mean whatever it ought to mean – you see what I mean?

MR. FARMER (*lost*): Oh, yes – of course.

HESTER: Well, oughtn't we to do something?

MR. FARMER: I'm afraid we can't do much until the rest of the committee arrive.

HESTER: I love committee meetings – there's something sort of ponderous about them – they give me a feeling of complete inevitability, don't they you?

MR. FARMER: Yes, I suppose they do – in a way.

HESTER: Do you like being a Secretary?

MR. FARMER: Yes, very much.

HESTER: Does it give you a thrilling sense of power? I've often wondered what it would be like to be terrifically powerful. Who are you actually secretary to?

MR. FARMER: To the Fund.

HESTER: I always thought one had to be secretary to a person not a thing. Have you a portfolio?

MR. FARMER: A what?

HESTER: Portfolio – Of course, I see a portfolio as black and battered and made of watered silk – a sort of Victorian hold-all filled with Grandmother's sketches – You haven't got a safety-pin, have you?

MR. FARMER: I'm afraid I haven't.

HESTER: It doesn't matter in the least bit really, but this skirt actually belongs to my sister – I live with her when I'm rehearsing.

MR. FARMER: Are you starting a new play soon?

HESTER: Yes, but I'm deeply angry about it – it's a translation by Cedric Gibbons – they always make me do plays like that when all I ever want really is to be gay! Has anybody got a cigarette?

MR. FARMER (offering her his case): Here. I'm afraid they're only Gold Flake.

HESTER: I worship Gold Flake because they have lovely pictures of fish, and I worship fish, too – aren't I a fool?

MR. FARMER (laughing deprecatingly): Not at all – I quite agree – Fish can be very interesting – some fish, that is—

HESTER: I naturally didn't mean ordinary dull ones, like cod and those mad-looking flat things – I meant splendid, thrilling fish like you see in aquariums – brilliantly coloured – silver and gold flake – Oh dear!

She goes off into gales of laughter.

JOHNNY BOLTON *comes briskly on to the stage. He is a star comedian of middle age, but perennial youthfulness. He is wearing plus-fours, a camel-hair coat, a check cap and a very bright scarf.*

JOHNNY: Hallo! hallo! hallo! – sorry to be late – good morning, old man! How are you, Miss More? – We seem to be the early birds—

HESTER (*weakly*): Birds and fish – Oh dear, oh dear—

JOHNNY (*puzzled*): Pardon?

MR. FARMER: It's nothing, Mr. Bolton – we were just talking about fish when you came in, that's all—

JOHNNY: We haven't met for ages, have we, Miss More? – I remember you as a little kiddie in *Peter Pan.* You've done great things since then!

HESTER: Everybody's been very kind – I can't think why.

JOHNNY: What's your new play?

HESTER: *Hurrah, We Die!*

JOHNNY: My God!

HESTER: It's more an investigation than a play really.

JOHNNY: What of?

HESTER: Oh, impulses and urges and foolish rowdiness.

JOHNNY: Oh, I see.

VIOLET VIBART *and* JULIAN BREED *come on to the stage.* VIOLET VIBART *is an elderly actress of considerable reputation.* JULIAN BREED *is known beyond a shadow of doubt to be the leading young actor of London. He has a beautiful speaking voice, and a manner that is only artistic in moments of stress. His clothes are casual and he moves with a certain modest authority.*

JULIAN: I'm terribly sorry to be late, but it was entirely Violet's fault really – hallo, Johnny – good morning, Hester darling—

HESTER: Julian – I'm going mad—

JULIAN: I've known that for a long time, dear—

VIOLET: It wasn't my fault at all – Julian promised to pick me up and then he said he hadn't and I had to telephone – Where's Xenia?

JOHNNY: Not here yet – what's the betting she'll be last? Any odds?

VIOLET: I do think dear Xenia, as President, ought to be here on time, don't you? – it's awfully naughty of her.

HESTER: I've been here for hours and hours and hours talking to Mr. Thing.

JULIAN: Who's missing?

MR. FARMER (consulting a list): Apart from our President, Miss James, there's Miss Brodie, Mr. Searle and Dame Rose Maitland—

VIOLET: Rosie will turn up all right, she's been on committees ever since I can remember—

JULIAN (laughing): Oh, Violet, you're superb!

VIOLET: Well, it's perfectly true, and after all she's not rehearsing now, is she?

MR. FARMER: I understand that Mr. Searle is doing a film at the moment.

JULIAN: Maurice is always doing a film – I'm furious with him.

VIOLET: You really can't blame him; after all, if he can't get quite the parts he wants in the theatre—

JULIAN: They wanted him to do a season at the Old Vic and he refused.

VIOLET: Oh, that was naughty of him—

JULIAN: And I myself offered him Petrovitch in The Inspector from Tobolsk.

VIOLET: I suppose you were playing Ivan?

JULIAN: Of course, but after all, Ivan dies in the second act.

VIOLET: Yes, and the play dies with him.

JOHNNY: This is all too highbrow for me, I shall have to go into me number in a minute—

HESTER: It must be heavenly to act with music all the time; I don't mean weird pipings, I mean jolly jiggerty-jig music—

JOHNNY: Come and work with me, Miss More – I'll teach you how to tap-dance – it would be a sensation – Miss Hester More – from Shakespeare to Schwartz—

HESTER: Who's Schwartz?

JOHNNY: The little chappie that wrote the show I'm doing here now – he's a wizard – all I have to do is to go to him and say:

'Bill, I want a couple of new gags for the second act' – most authors would say, 'Give me a few days, I got to go home and think.' Not so Bill Schwartz aren't I right, Jimmie? Out comes an envelope from his pocket – 'How's this, old boy?' he says – and there you are – a couple of sure-fire laughs; for instance, you know when I come on in the wheelbarrow just before the bathing number? well, it's old stuff, I know, they've seen it for years – but still I had to do something – I get out and do a pratt-fall – it's a laugh, of course, but you need something more there – I thought to myself, this is not so hot, so I go to Bill. 'Look here, old man,' I say – 'it's all very well relying on me to hold the show together, but after all, even I can't go on making bricks without straw till Kingdom Come; you've got to give me a laugh line that's going to knock 'em for a loop.' Well, I come down to the theatre that night, feeling a bit mad, you know, after all, it isn't as if I had another star to help me to carry the show; Maisie's all right, very pretty and all that, but it's a weak voice and she's got *no sense of comedy whatsoever*, she's got to have everything built up round her – Well, I come down to the theatre that night—

MAURICE SEARLE *comes hurriedly on to the stage. He is an exceedingly handsome, virile young man, but his looks are somewhat marred by the fact that, for the purposes of the film he is at present working on, he has had to grow his hair almost down to his shoulders.*

MAURICE (*loudly*): Don't look at me, anybody! I'm doing a film!

VIOLET: Oh, Maurice, is it *worth* it?

MAURICE (*taking off his coat*): I'm a sight – I'm ashamed to go out in the street—

HESTER: I think you look marvellous – I always said you had a period face—

JULIAN: There are periods and periods—

MAURICE: Don't be a cad, old boy – one's got to live—

VIOLET: It really is rather a shock, Maurice dear.

HESTER: You're mad, Violet – it's lovely – it suits his bone structure—

JULIAN: Why don't you go the whole hog, Maurice, and wear armour?

MAURICE: Shut up, you old fool, Julian, I didn't come here to be laughed at, I came to a committee meeting.

VIOLET (*with a look at* JOHNNY): Anyhow, you came in the *nick* of time!

HESTER: I long to do a film but nobody will let me.

MAURICE: Nonsense, Hester, they'd be damn glad to get you.

HESTER: No, they all say I'm *too* hideous.

JULIAN: I think that for us to do films is sheer money-grubbing anyhow, the theatre is our place and in the theatre we should stay.

VIOLET: If we can, Julian dear.

JOHNNY: I had a scenario sent me the other day – one of the funniest situations I've ever read – an absolute foolproof part for me—

JULIAN (*sotto-voce to* VIOLET): It would have to be.

JOHNNY: Pardon?

JULIAN: Nothing, I was only wondering whether we ought to get on with the meeting even without the President.

JOHNNY: —The situation's this, see – a Russian Grand Duke – exiled, you understand, during the Revolution – sold all his jewellery, hasn't got a bob and has to take a job as a salesman in a ladies' corset shop – there's a set-up for comedy if ever I saw one – and he meets this girl, see—

JULIAN: Which girl?

JOHNNY: A girl he met in Paris when he was on his uppers, and he doesn't know that she was one of the Imperial Ballet dancers who's also been exiled – that's to give Gracie Golden a chance to use her dancing – they've got her under contract, you see, and they've got to do something with her – so along they come to me – Ben Oelrichs came himself, as a matter of fact – 'Look here, old man,' he says, 'we're in a bit of a jam at Elstree – it's up to you to help us out – here's a part in a million for you and all you have to do is to write your own ticket.' 'All very fine,' I say, 'but I've got to have Bill Schwartz on that set every minute of the day to think out gags for me' – I've been in this profession long enough to know that it's no use trying to make people laugh if you haven't got the material there to do it with – so I call up Bill: 'Look here, old boy,' I say, 'you've got to stand by the old firm—'

At the beginning of this speech everyone has been reluctantly attentive, but by now they have drifted into individual conversations with each other, snatches of which are occasionally audible, such as:

MAURICE: I implored them to let me have a wig, but they said that it would always show in close-ups—

VIOLET: I don't see that it really matters as long as you are not seen about *too* much—

JULIAN: I've always thought him the unfunniest comedian in the world on the stage, but his dreariness off it amounts to genius—

HESTER: Shhh! he'll hear you—

JULIAN: That egomania is pathological—

HESTER: I think he's rather sweet, really, like a sort of rubber horse—

JOHNNY, by this time, is reduced to MR. FARMER, *whom he pins down mercilessly.*

JOHNNY: —'Okay!' he says. 'How about this for a start?' – and I give you my word he coughed up three of the funniest gags I've ever heard. For instance – two men are sitting in a cab shelter, see? As a matter of fact it needn't really be a cab shelter, it could be a bar or a café, or even a seat in the park – anyway, they're sitting there and a girl goes by – she stops a minute, looks at them and then walks on. 'See that bit of skirt?' says one—

At this moment DAME ROSE MAITLAND *advances majestically on to the stage. She is imposingly dressed and slightly autocratic in manner. She is followed by* ELISE BRODIE *who is pretty but not particularly distinguished. She is obviously the type of star who plays leading parts adequately and whose home life is well known to be irreproachable.*

DAME ROSE (*advancing*): Violet! I thought you were dead!

VIOLET (*as they kiss*): I really don't see why, dear—

DAME ROSE (*continuing her greetings*): —Hester – you look charming – Julian – darling boy – (*She kisses him.*) Mr. Bolton – it was generous and dear of you to lend us this stage for the meeting— (*She turns to* MAURICE.) —My God!

MAURICE: Don't look at me, Dame Rosie – I'm doing a film—

DAME ROSE: Cela va sans dire!

JULIAN: She met Rejane, you know.

HESTER: Hallo, Elise.

ELISE (*kissing her*): I had a dreadful time with John this morning, that's why I'm so late – he refused to go to school – and Patricia's had a rash for a whole week—

DAME ROSE: Mr. Farmer, I'm delighted to see you – I hope you have everything in order— (*She looks at* JIMMIE HORLICK.) Who is this?

JOHNNY (*bounding forward*): Jimmie Horlick, my stage-manager – son of the great Robert Horlick, you remember him, Dame Rose, I'm sure—

DAME ROSE (*taking both* JIMMIE's *hands*): I should have known you anywhere! Your father was my friend, and when I say friend I mean friend. Well, well, well, let's get to business.

MR. FARMER: I am afraid our President, Miss James, is not here yet.

DAME ROSE: That doesn't matter in the least, we will proceed without her.

VIOLET: Don't you think that would be a little ultra vires, Rosie dear?

DAME ROSE: Ultra fiddlesticks! – we can't wait about all day. Kindly tell us where you want us to sit, Mr. Farmer.

ELISE (*to* JULIAN): —I was just telling Hester – if it was an ordinary rash I shouldn't worry, but it looks very angry to me and it's all over her poor little tummy—

DAME ROSE: Whose poor little tummy?

ELISE: Patricia's—

DAME ROSE: Who is Patricia?

ELISE: My child, Dame Rosie, my youngest child.

DAME ROSE: Poor little thing! Where do you want us to sit, Mr. Farmer?

HESTER: If I had children I should let them run wild in the woods all the year round.

VIOLET (*patronisingly*): Dear Hester—

HESTER (*with spirit*): Naked.

DAME ROSE: What did you say, my dear?

HESTER: Just naked.

DAME ROSE: Mr. Farmer, you had better take the foot of the table. Julian, darling boy, come and sit next to me – Mr. Bolton, will you be on my right—?

VIOLET: Surely our President should take the chair—?

DAME ROSE: My dear Violet, in the absence of the President it is my privilege, as Vice-President, to take the chair.

VIOLET: I am also a Vice-President.

DAME ROSE: That's beside the point – will everyone kindly be seated?

HESTER: I believe I'm a Vice-President, too, in a sort of way.

DAME ROSE (*with polite firmness*): I think if you consult the constitution of the Fund, my dear, you will find that you are merely a Trustee.

HESTER: All right, I'll be a Trustee then, I don't mind a bit.

JULIAN (*to* MAURICE): I'm going to do the whole production in different coloured tweed—

MAURICE: Are you using rostrums?

JULIAN: Yes – each scene will be played on different levels – the designs are marvellous—

JOHNNY: Don't use a revolve, that's all I can say; we had one in *Oh For To-night* and it held us up all the way through the show – I remember one matinee day I came on to do that cod soldier number with Dickie Black – you remember it came just at the opening of the last act – well, I come in to the theatre and start making up when Bob Fry comes flying into the room – he was my stage-manager then – 'Look here, old boy,' he says, 'we're up the spout, the bloody revolve's gone wonky—'

DAME ROSE (*sternly*): Mr. Bolton!

JOHNNY: Pardon?

DAME ROSE: I think we should really concentrate on the business that we are gathered together to discuss—

HESTER: Gathered together sounds awfully sweet, doesn't it? Almost religious—

DAME ROSE (*in ringing tones*): Mr. Farmer – I have much pleasure in declaring this meeting open.

> *At this moment* XENIA JAMES *comes on to the stage. She is pretty, over-made-up, only slightly over-dressed and bursting with charm.*

She is leading, or being led by a very large dog indeed, probably a Great Dane.

XENIA: My God! the traffic! – It took me over twenty-five minutes to get from Hertford Street to Antoine's and hours and hours to get from there to here and now I've kept you all waiting and you'll think I'm absolutely frightful – Oh, dear! – there are moments in life when I quite definitely wish I were dead – Darling Dame Rosie, please forgive me— (*She kisses her.*) —Violet – you are an angel to come— (*She kisses her.*) — Elise! I thought you were divine the other night; I couldn't come round to see you because I was with a party, but your second act wrecked me utterly, the mascara streamed down my face and Ronnie said I looked exactly like a zebra – Hester! you look perfectly lovely, have you just come up from the country? – how I wish I had hair like yours rushing away like that, mine has to be actually tortured to make it look like anything at all, I swear it does – Antoine hates me, he groans whenever I go into the shop, and whenever he groans Atherton growls and it's all too horrible – Julian darling, I've got a message for you from Marjorie but I'll give it to you afterwards – hold Atherton a minute – he's frightfully good – Maurice, darling, for God's sake don't sit where I can see you or I shall giggle and spoil everything – Hallo, Johnny, it was most awfully sweet of you to let us have this theatre for the meeting, I haven't seen your show yet because I've been away, but I'm coming next week I swear, we start rehearsing on Monday – I'm nearly frantic – Bobbie's in the country and can't be found and the last act's unplayable, positively unplayable, and you know what Bobbie is, he won't rewrite a word unless you hit him on the head – I promise you all here and now that I shall never do another play of his as long as I live – Mr. Farmer – where do I sit?

MR. FARMER: You take the chair, Miss James.

XENIA: It sounds awfully important, doesn't it? – I'm sure I ought to have a hammer – excuse me, Dame Rosie darling – Give me Atherton, Julian, he'll sit as quiet as a mouse – won't you, my angel? – he worships me, this dog, it's fantastic, it really is – Atherton Blake gave him to me just two weeks before he died, you know, and it was the most extraordinary thing, I felt that there was somehow a part of that Atherton in this Atherton, d'you know what I mean? – it was as though – Oh, I don't know, but anyhow from that moment onwards he's never left me—

DAME ROSE: Declare the meeting open, my dear, and let's get to business.

XENIA: Lie down, Atherton, who's a good dog? Come on – give Dame Rosie a paw – paw, Atherton – give paw— (*In sterner tones.*) Atherton, give Dame Rosie a paw at once and don't be a damn fool – all right, don't then, I'll talk to you about this later —(*To everybody.*) He's quite human, you know – we have the most awful rows – I sometimes think he's the only person in the whole wide world who really understands me – only the other night— ·

DAME ROSE: Xenia! we're wasting time – declare the meeting open.

XENIA: Darling Dame Rosie, I adore you – it's wide open as far as I'm concerned – Mr. Farmer – what do I say?

MR. FARMER: Just say 'I declare the meeting open.'

XENIA: I declare the meeting open – there now! (*She smiles radiantly.*) Lie down, Atherton, and don't be silly, it's no use pretending *you've* never been on a stage before – why, you're an old pro, aren't you, my darling? – he was with me in *Lady's Laughter*, you know—

JOHNNY: I don't trust animals on the stage, I learnt my lesson years ago in *Queen For A Day*; we had two horses in that and a flock of geese and what they didn't do was nobody's business—

VIOLET: I once played a whole scene with a parrot—

JULIAN: How lovely for you, darling—

Everybody laughs.

HESTER: I'd like to play a play with nothing but animals – think how heavenly it would be if only you could get them to moo and bark and neigh and do everything on cue—

JOHNNY: Try and stop 'em, that's all I say – just try and stop 'em—

DAME ROSE: Really, Mr. Bolton, you're disgraceful, you really are!— (*She breaks into laughter.*)

XENIA: Now we really must concentrate – I do see that – we really must – Mr. Farmer – will you begin, please?

MR. FARMER (*rising*): Certainly.

XENIA: First of all, before you start I should just like to say one thing and that is that I think we ought all to propose a vote of thanks to dear Mr. Farmer, not only for coming here today, but for all the wonderful work he has done for Garrick Haven.

Everybody mutters: 'Hear! hear!'

Thank you, Mr. Farmer. (*She smiles bewitchingly at him.*)

MR. FARMER (*deprecatingly*): I assure you I've done nothing, nothing at all—

JOHNNY: You can't get away with that, old boy, you've done wonders – the place wouldn't be standing if it hadn't been for you—

HESTER (*very loudly*): Hear! hear!

DAME ROSE: Hester! You made me jump.

MR. FARMER: Mr. President, ladies and gentlemen – as you all know, Garrick Haven was originally a private house and when the Garrick Haven Fund for a home for destitute actresses was established in the year nineteen hundred and two—

DAME ROSE: Yes, yes, yes, that was the year I went to His Majesty's.

MR. FARMER: —the executive committee of that time selected this fine old Georgian house on the outskirts of Ham Common—

XENIA: It's the sweetest house I've ever seen, you know, I went there last year—

MR. FARMER: —At that time the inmates numbered eleven, exclusive of the personnel which was comprised of Mrs. Ellsworth, matron—

VIOLET: Dear old Fanny – do you remember her, Rosie?

DAME ROSE: Drank like a fish.

MR. FARMER (*continuing*): —Dr. Harris, resident physician, and Mr. and Mrs. Grief, housekeeper and general handyman respectively. Mr. Horace Bevell was Honorary Secretary, the position that I have the privilege of holding at the present moment—

HESTER: Hear! hear!

JULIAN: Be quiet, darling—

HESTER (*in a loud whisper*): I love him – he's got a round, dear face—

JOHNNY: What happened to old Horace?

VIOLET: He died.

JOHNNY: Well, well, now I never knew that – he was a great pal of my dad's, you know, I remember being taken to see him when I was a kid at the old Rivoli, or rather Johnson's Music Hall as it was then – What a comedian! Whew! There wasn't any trick he didn't know – for instance, I remember one gag he cracked to this day – he came on dressed as a fireman and—

XENIA (*tapping the table, sweetly but firmly*): Johnny – order, please – Mr. Farmer wants to talk to us.

JOHNNY: Sorry! Exit Johnny Bolton, the man who made Kitchener laugh!

Everybody titters.

DAME ROSE: Continue, Mr. Farmer.

MR. FARMER (*clearing his throat*): In those days the total capital of the Fund amounted to just seventeen hundred pounds. In the year 1935 our assets were fifty-eight thousand pounds exclusive of certain slightly speculative investments with which I will not trouble you now—

HESTER: I think we ought to hear everything, *don't* you?

VIOLET: Isn't it wonderful—?

MR. FARMER: I need hardly tell you that, apart from a few outside subscriptions, this splendid financial security has been achieved entirely by the efforts of the Theatrical Profession at the annual Garrick Haven Fun Fayre.

XENIA: It's very gratifying, isn't it? I ran the roundabouts last year and I swear I've never enjoyed anything so much in my life.

VIOLET: Herrick's let me down dreadfully over my Tea Tent, Mr. Farmer – they sent me no sugar at all, and no spoons!

JULIAN: That made it all right then, didn't it, darling?

ELISE: I've been meaning to write to you for ages, Mr. Farmer, about my Lucky Dip—

DAME ROSE: Never mind about your Lucky Dip now, my dear—

ELISE: But I think Mr. Farmer ought to know. There were a lot of tin-tacks among the sawdust and some horrid sticky stuff as well—

JOHNNY: We did fine with our Hula-Hula Cabaret, but the tent was on the small side you know, old boy, on the small side—

XENIA: Darling Johnny, we must concentrate, we really must – Order – order! (*She raps on the table with her vanity-case.*) —oh, dear, I've broken the glass – seven years' bad luck—

JULIAN: Next year, Mr. Farmer, I should be very much obliged if you would put the Children's Opera at the *other* end of the grounds – Elizabeth and I could hardly hear ourselves speak – it's a little trying to have to do the Balcony scene with some beastly child banging a drum five yards away from you—

MAURICE: You didn't have to do the Balcony scene!

VIOLET: Any anyhow, dear Elizabeth's voice is louder than any drum!

JULIAN (*with a false laugh*): Oh, Violet, you're superb!

The conversation now becomes simultaneous.

MAURICE: My Roulette started off all right but the wheel kept sticking and I was down seventeen pounds by the end of the afternoon—

XENIA: Perhaps it doesn't count if it's only cracked—

ELISE: —it wasn't exactly jam and it wasn't exactly treacle, and we couldn't think what it was – but one old lady got it all over her gloves and made an awful scene—

VIOLET: They were waiting four deep in a long, long queue stretching right down as far as the Tombola, and there I was with only Jane and poor old Laura to help me and you know what a featherbrain she is, I sent her rushing off down the King's Road with an enormous basket—

JULIAN: —it wasn't my idea to do excerpts from Shakespeare, anyhow, but the public demand it – what I should really like to do next year is something jolly—

DAME ROSE: I should like to state here and now, Mr. Farmer, that the mismanagement over my Ice Creams was nothing short of disgraceful – It's all very well to buy them in blocks, but they don't stay in blocks unless you have an ice-box to put them in – I should have thought that would have been obvious to the meanest intelligence – it's a positive insult to the public to charge them two-and-six for a cardboard saucer of lukewarm custard with lumps in it—

ELISE: Robert – that's my husband, you know – brought both the children along – 'For God's sake don't let them put their hands in that,' I said, 'they might catch almost *anything*—'

MAURICE: Fourteen came up twenty-two times running and so consequently we were absolutely cleaned out before five o'clock—

XENIA: Order please, everybody – Oh, dear! – we *ought* to get on with the meeting—

JOHNNY (*loudly*): Order, there – Order!

XENIA: Thank you, Johnny dear—

JOHNNY (*jumping to his feet*): Excuse my butting in but as a subscriber of many years' standing I should just like to say that as far as I am concerned, and I am sure as far as everyone here to-day is concerned, I should like to say that any work we any of us do for this particular charity is willing work and, what's more, glad work! These dear old souls – our own sisters in the profession – have, most of them, been faithful servants of the public for many long years – and for us to feel – all of us, that is, in the world of the theatre—

JULIAN (*sarcastically*): Tinsel world of the theatre—

JOHNNY: Pardon?

VIOLET: Hush, Julian.

DAME ROSE: You're perfectly right, Mr. Bolton, and we're all in complete agreement with you – please proceed, Mr. Farmer.

MR. FARMER: We now come to the purpose of this meeting. As you all know, no structural alterations, in fact no alterations of any kind, can be made in Garrick Haven without the approval and consent of the full Executive Committee. I have, therefore, acting on a letter received from our President, Miss James, on the twenty-fourth of November 1935, in reply to a letter of mine of the third of October of the same year – a proposal to put before you for the building of a new wing, and

I have with me the various builders' and plumbers' estimates which, with your consent, I will now read.

XENIA: Atherton! You smell awful – I've been wondering what it was for hours, and it's you! – What have you been doing, you naughty bad dog—?

DAME ROSE: Really, Xenia – it was a mistake to have brought him at all—

XENIA: Would somebody be really sweet and take him out or something? – I really can't bear it another minute— (To Atherton.) You're a filthy old pig, that's what you are, and Mother's livid with you—

JOHNNY: He'd be all right in the property-room, wouldn't he?

XENIA: I hope so.

JOHNNY: Jimmie – take Miss James's dog into the property-room.

JIMMIE. Does he bite?

XENIA: Bite! He wouldn't bite a child!

ELISE: I should just hope not.

XENIA: Go on, Atherton – go with the nice gentleman – here – take him by the lead—

    JIMMIE gingerly takes Atherton's lead.

JIMMIE (weakly): Come on, old fellow.

XENIA (as he is led away): He breaks my heart every time I look at him, you know – those great mournful eyes – I swear he's the only real friend I have in the world – he's sensitive to every mood I have – when I'm sad he comes and puts his paw on my knee and when I'm gay he romps with me—

JULIAN: In those circumstances I should be permanently sad.

XENIA: It's all very fine to laugh, Julian, but that dog is definitely part of my life—

DAME ROSE: I still maintain that it was a mistake to bring him to a committee meeting.

XENIA: Dear Dame Rosie, he's my dog and I am the President!

DAME ROSE: Please proceed, Mr. Farmer.

MR. FARMER (clearing his throat): Before we deal with the estimates I feel that it is my duty to read you a round-robin letter signed by all the inmates of Garrick Haven with the exception of old Mrs. Baker—

ELISE: I wonder what her stage name was?

MR. FARMER: Joy Collins, I believe—

VIOLET: Good Heavens! I remember being taken to see her when I was a little tiny child—

DAME ROSE: Never mind that now, Violet – to our muttons, to our muttons.

MR. FARMER: She has, I believe, the reputation of being rather a rebellious spirit in the Home and refused to sign unless all her own personal complaints were included in the document; as these comprised several closely written sheets of foolscap, it was considered advisable—

XENIA: What ingratitude! It's really quite horrifying, isn't it? (*She laughs merrily.*)

MR. FARMER: At all events here is the letter – I read it without prejudice—

HESTER: That's absolutely sweet of you, and quite typical.

MR. FARMER: 'Dear Mr. Farmer, we the undersigned would be very glad if you would read the following letter to the Committee. We are very over-crowded in Garrick Haven and although we are very happy and contented here on the whole, we the undersigned feel that another bathroom and another indoor lavatory, as we only have one of each at the moment, would be not only more comfortable but really necessary, as the inside one is very inadequate and the outside one is rather a long way away and in the winter months very cold. We would be very glad if the Committee would look into this. We are – yours very sincerely – Mary Spink – Laura Richmond – Gloria Denton—', etc., etc.

XENIA: Poor angels – something must be done at once.

> JIMMIE HORLICK *returns, having deposited Atherton in the property-room.*

MR. FARMER: Their complaint, being perfectly reasonable—

VIOLET: Although a little high-handed in tone, don't you think?

MR. FARMER: I communicated with Miss James and have here the following estimates—

XENIA (*to* JIMMIE): Is he all right?

JIMMIE: Good as gold – he dropped off to sleep.

XENIA: We must all be very quiet.

MR. FARMER (*reading*): 'A report from Messrs. Belling, Sons and

Hapgood, embodying a summarised estimate for the proposed new wing to be added to the west elevation of Garrick Haven, Ham Common, on an approved design by Mr. Henry Struthers, F.R.I.B.A., the building to be of red-faced brickwork to harmonise with the Georgian exterior of the main building—'

HESTER: Red-faced brick sounds so embarrassed somehow, doesn't it?

DAME ROSE: Shh, Hester!

MR. FARMER: '—and to comprise a separate entrance, entrance hall 10 feet 8 inches by 16 feet 2 inches, recreation-room 43 feet by 28 feet 5 inches with raised platform-stage at far end.'

XENIA: How lovely for them, they'll be able to give little plays at Christmas, won't they?

JOHNNY: It wouldn't be a bad idea if we all went down once a month and gave a show for them – I mean – as far as I'm concerned – I'm sure my little company would be only too pleased—

MAURICE: Is the stage to have adequate lighting equipment?

JULIAN: I wonder we don't give them a revolve and they could all ride round and round on it all day.

DAME ROSE: Don't be flippant, Julian. C'est une chose sérieuse!

MR. FARMER: '—Staircase 4 feet 6 inches wide to upper floor, which will consist of landing, corridor 47 feet by 4 feet on to which will give bedrooms (5 on each side) of approximately 10 feet square each, and leading to 2 bathrooms, 2 lavatories and a washing and drying room, fittings for which are embodied by Messrs. Joyce and Spence in their accompanying estimate for all interior and exterior plumbing and sanitary work and fitments—'

XENIA (*in response to a whisper from* JULIAN, *goes off into gales of laughter*): —Julian – how *can* you! – you are dreadful—!

MR. FARMER (*reading more quickly*): '—The structural work to be carried out in best quality English brick, rendered in Portland cement and sand, 1 part to 4, reinforced against weather by the addition of 'Pudlo'—'

MAURICE: Good God, what's Pudlo?

JULIAN: Shut up, Maurice.

MR. FARMER: '—the roof to be of red hung tiles, with gutters and damp-course of good quality lead – The specification includes cavity walls, metal window-frames and woodblock flooring to all rooms, hardwood interior woodwork, 3 coats white lead paint gloss finish and electric wiring, light and power points throughout. The plans may be inspected at Mr. Struthers's office, 6 Sedgwick Road, Richmond, between 10 a.m. and 4 p.m. on any day except Saturday. The estimated cost, including additional estimate from Messrs. Joyce and Spence, to be three thousand and eighty-two pounds, seventeen shillings and fourpence.'

XENIA: It all sounds absolutely perfect, Mr. Farmer – Do you think I ought to go and look at the plans?

DAME ROSE: You wouldn't understand them if you did, my dear.

XENIA: Darling Dame Rosie, as a matter of fact you're quite wrong – house-building happens to be one of my things, you know – my own house in Essex I did entirely by myself – every single brick—

MAURICE: I might drop off and cast an eye on them on my way back from the studio one night—

JULIAN (*rising to his feet*): Forgive me for interrupting, but there is just one thing I should like to suggest – I am perfectly sure the actual structural work would obviously be adequately carried out by any reputable firm, but what I want to make a plea for is the look of the thing from the *inside* – for instance, I have always found that the interiors of charity institutions are terribly austere and sort of cold – couldn't we appoint someone like Rex Whistler or Oliver Messel to do a sort of pageant of theatrical history all round the walls of the dormitory? – and if they could leave a few spaces in the painting I have a lot of old play bills that Mother left me in her will, which would look marvellous, and after all, it would be something for the poor old girls to look at—

JOHNNY (*springing to his feet*): —Better still, what about some of those old-time melodrama posters in colour? – you know – *The Fatal Wedding* and *The Girl from the Jam Factory* – I mean to say, it would make the dear old souls laugh their heads off – I mean—

DAME ROSE: Just a moment, Mr. Bolton – Have we all agreed to pass the estimate read to us by Mr. Farmer—?

XENIA (*in ringing tones*): Unconditionally – Passed unconditionally!

VIOLET: You don't think, perhaps, that three thousand and eighty-two pounds, seventeen shillings and fourpence is a shade expensive?

XENIA: Certainly not – if anything, I should say it was dirt cheap. Why, doing up that flat I had in Portland Place cost me more than that and all I had put in was two bathrooms and a telephone extension.

MR. FARMER: I take it that the estimate is passed?

XENIA (*gloriously*): Unanimously, Mr. Farmer.

JULIAN (*to* HESTER): You could start with the old barn-storming days and gradually work up to the Old Vic—

HESTER (*with spirit*): You're wrong, Julian – you're wrong – it would distract them – their lives are nearly over, they want peace, peace, peace. Gentle greys and broken white—

DAME ROSE: Well, when I'm on my last legs I certainly shan't want to look at pictures of the Old Vic!

XENIA: Mr. Farmer – Mr. Farmer – please let's get on – I have a lunch at one and a fitting at two – Silence, everybody, silence! Oh, dear!

MR. FARMER: Well, I have here the estimate from Messrs. Joyce and Spence—

ELISE: It's awfully sad, isn't it, when you analyse it? Those poor old darlings – I wish we could do more than we do—

HESTER: We ought to do much more – much much much more – Who knows but that some of us may be there one day – looking back at the past with mournful eyes—

JULIAN: Like Atherton.

XENIA: Oh, I wonder if he's all right? – Mr. Horlick, would you be an angel and just tiptoe in and have a look at him? – No, I think I'd better do it myself – go on with the estimate, Mr. Farmer, I shan't be a moment—

She creeps off in the direction of the property-room.

MR. FARMER (*reading, very hurriedly*): 'For work to be carried out at Garrick Haven, comprising removing of existing independent boiler in main building, supplying and fixing new no. 3 size

Hearts of Oak improved domestic boiler, connecting same with existing system in main building. To supplying new 60-gallon tank connecting up with 6 radiators in new wing and 4 in main building, to 220 feet lead piping, flow and return pipes, wiped soldered joints and branch joints for circulating, connecting from boiler to existing and new bathrooms and washroom with 213 feet $1\frac{1}{2}$-inch lead piping and testing—'

XENIA *comes tiptoeing back.*

XENIA: He's fast asleep and giving little jumps; I expect he's dreaming of some lovely wood filled with bunny rabbits – How's the estimate going?

MR. FARMER: '—To supplying and fitting 2 porcelain enamelled baths, chromium taps and fitments in new bathrooms—'

XENIA: Doesn't it sound luxurious? The old sweets will feel like the Queen of Sheba—

MR. FARMER: '—To supplying and erecting new cold water 60-gallon storage tank on the roof of north elevation new building, flanged edging and connecting to 2 new lavatories—'

XENIA: Darling Mr. Farmer, couldn't you cut it short now? – I'm sure it's all perfectly in order and I really have to fly—

JOHNNY (*rising*): Before this meeting breaks up, I should just like to say—

MR. FARMER: I fear that it would be out of order for you to pass the estimate unread—

JULIAN (*rising*): I'm afraid I must go, anyhow, Mr. Farmer – I have a very important appointment—

A PRESS PHOTOGRAPHER *comes on to the stage.*

PHOTOGRAPHER: Excuse me—?

XENIA: My goodness, just in time! – Go on reading, Mr. Farmer, and we'll all be listening—

MR. FARMER: But, Mr. President, ladies and gentlemen—

XENIA: Please, Mr. Farmer – I can't stay more than another minute—

JOHNNY: We ought to be signing a resolution, you know, give the picture a bit of action—

MR. FARMER *reluctantly continues to read the estimate while* XENIA *and* JOHNNY *arrange a group for the* PHOTOGRAPHER; *the following dialogue takes place during the reading.*

MAURICE: Has anybody got a pen?

JULIAN: Here—

XENIA: We haven't got any paper – where's some paper?

DAME ROSE: Never again! Never again as long as I live will I come to a meeting like this – it's outrageous – nothing has been settled at all – talk talk talk – nobody does anything but talk – where do you want me to stand?

XENIA: Here, dear, by me—

VIOLET: I can't see what we're all being photographed for – surely it's rather waste of time—?

MAURICE: Let me get behind you, Julian – I can't be taken like this—

MR. FARMER (*reading dully*): '—To supplying and fixing in same good quality pedestal fitments, improved modern one gallon flush cisterns connected soil pipes and main outdoor drainage. To complete in accordance with the plans approved by Mr. Henry Struthers, F.R.I.B.A., and the local council surveyors, which plans may be seen at Messrs. Joyce and Spence's office, West Acton Green, between 10 a.m. and 4 p.m. on any day except Saturday, will cost two thousand, one hundred and four pounds, thirteen shillings and eightpence.'

> By this time the group has been satisfactorily posed and the PHOTOGRAPHER takes the picture.

XENIA (*charmingly, to the* PHOTOGRAPHER): Thank you *so* much.

VIOLET: Is that all, Mr. Farmer?

MR. FARMER: Well, there are one or two little matters—

JOHNNY: I should just like to say one thing—

JULIAN: Well, before you say it I really must go – Good-bye, Xenia dear – good-bye, Dame Rosie – Good-bye, everybody – Mr. Farmer, if you're interested in my idea for decorating the dormitory, just let me know—

MAURICE: Hold on a minute, can you give me a lift?

JULIAN: Yes – only I can't wait.

MAURICE: Good-bye – good-bye, everybody—

> He and JULIAN dash out, followed by the PHOTOGRAPHER.

MR. FARMER: Am I to take it that you all pass the estimate?

XENIA: Dear Mr. Farmer, *of course* we do – there was never any question of it – Now I really must go – Do you want me to declare the meeting closed or anything?

MR. FARMER: There are just one or two little formalities—

JOHNNY: I just want to say one thing—

XENIA: Be quiet a minute, Johnny – I want to say just a few words – will you all sit down for a minute?

DAME ROSE: Look here, Xenia – I really do think—

XENIA (*firmly*): Please, Dame Rosie—

HESTER (*loudly*): Silence for the President! Oooh! Was that the right thing to say?

XENIA (*in ringing tones*): What I want to say to you all is this: first, how proud and honoured I am to have been elected the President of this wonderful charity. We have all known what it is to be poor and needy and a day may come when we may all know poverty again – therefore – I beg you all – together with me, put your shoulders to the wheel and give, give, give all you can – Garrick Haven must live – Garrick Haven must be flourishing long after we are dust and ashes, long after our names are but echoes from a forgotten tune – It is only a small thing really – but for us of the Theatre it is a part of our life's blood. You do see what I mean, don't you? I mean, here we are, all of us, on the top of the ladder of success, but who can tell when that ladder may not crash to the ground leaving us bruised and broken and oh! so terribly tired?

JOHNNY (*loudly*): Hear! hear!

XENIA: Thank you, Johnny – Now then – I am willing to lead off with a cheque for a hundred pounds and all I beg of you is to give just as much as you can afford, if not a little more! Mr. Farmer, how much do we need?

MR. FARMER: Nothing at all, Miss James; although, naturally, any contributions to the Fund would be gratefully accepted.

XENIA (*undaunted*): Well, whenever you're in trouble – whenever you are in need, remember we all are here, ready and eager to help. Thank you, Mr. Farmer, for everything you have done in the past and for everything you will do in the future— (*She glances at her wrist-watch.*) My God, it's nearly half-past – Good-bye – good-bye – darlings – good-bye—

She rushes off the stage.

JOHNNY (*rising*): May I take this opportunity of saying, Mr. Farmer, that I heartily endorse everything that our President has said – We have known each other for many years, Xenia and I, and you can take it from me that girl has a heart of pure gold – many a time in the past I have known her give all she had to help some poor soul who has fallen by the way—

> ELISE *and* HESTER, *after blowing a few kisses, leave at the beginning of this speech.* VIOLET *and* DAME ROSE *gather up their bags and furs.*

I know I can say with truth and conviction that all of us here to-day are working for one motive and one motive alone, that is the upholding of and the carrying on of this splendid work – I myself have no fish to fry – and I am sure that you, Dame Rosie, have no fish to fry—

DAME ROSE: I certainly have not.

JOHNNY: In fact, we are one and all animated by one desire – that is—

DAME ROSE: Good-bye, Mr. Bolton – I hope we shall meet again soon. Come Violet—

VIOLET: Good-bye, Mr. Bolton.

DAME ROSE: Good-bye, Mr. Farmer. You have been most kind.

MR. FARMER: Good-bye, Dame Rose.

VIOLET: Good-bye, Mr. Farmer – Good-bye, Mr. Bolton.

JOHNNY (*discouraged*): Oh – good-bye.

> DAME ROSE *and* VIOLET *sweep off the stage.*

MR. FARMER (*gathering up his papers*): Well, Mr. Bolton—

JOHNNY: Feel like a spot of lunch?

MR. FARMER: It's very kind of you.

JOHNNY: Come over to the club – I've got a few ideas I'd like to discuss with you—

MR. FARMER: Thanks very much—

JOHNNY: Lights, Jimmie.

JIMMIE: Yes, Mr. Bolton.

JOHNNY (*as he and* MR. FARMER *go off*): I was supposed to meet Bill Schwartz at one o'clock, he'll give me the raspberry all right for keeping him waiting – he doesn't give a damn for anybody – only the other night, I come into the theatre see, rather early for once – I wasn't feeling too good as a matter of fact – I open my dressing-room door—

By this time they have gone. JIMMIE *switches off the lights, leaving only one working light on, and goes off the stage, too.*

When the door has closed behind him, Atherton is heard howling dismally in the property-room as

THE CURTAIN FALLS